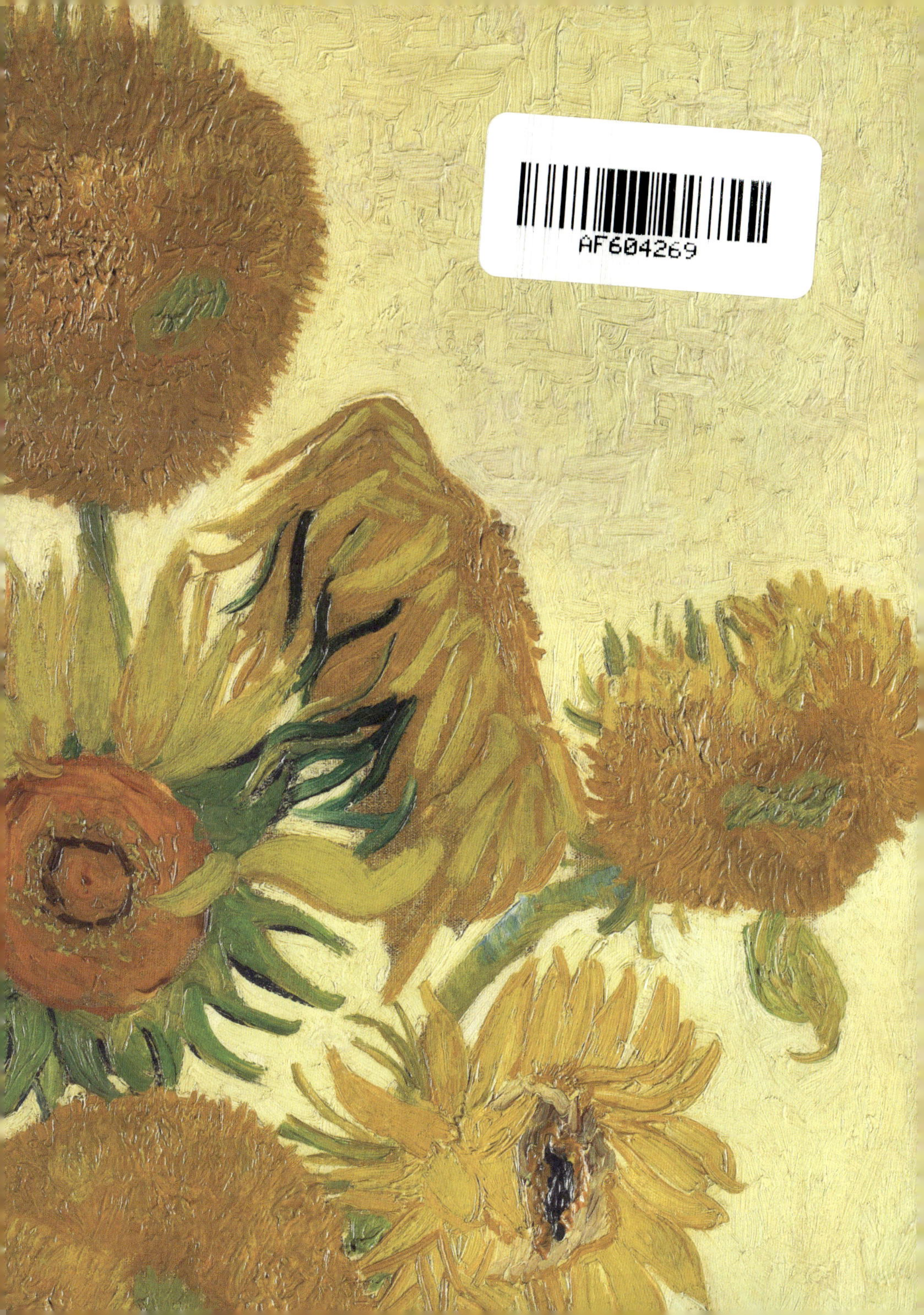

The Works

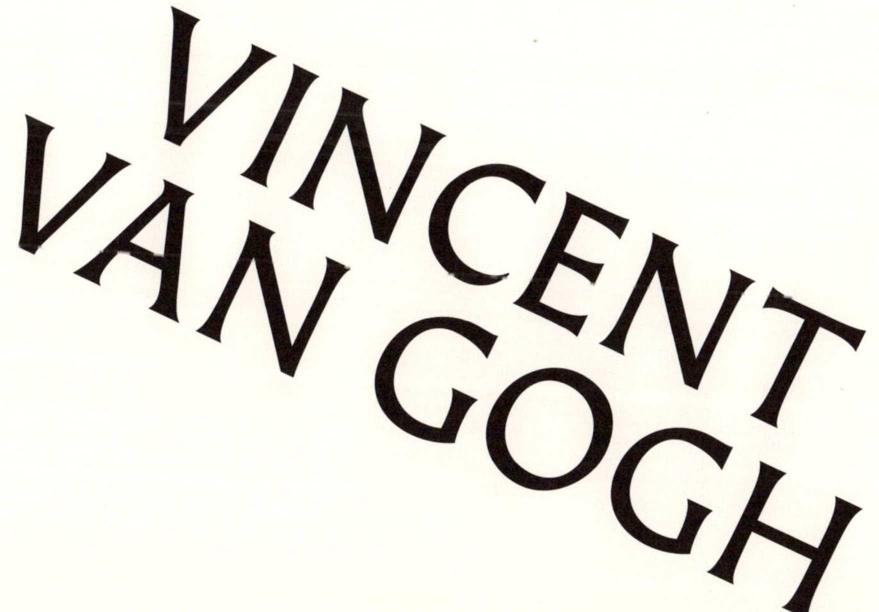

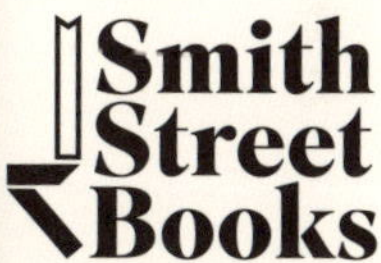

The essential masterpieces
by Sally Grant

Introduction

Vincent Willem van Gogh was born on 30 March 1853 in the village of Zundert in North Brabant, a province in the southern Netherlands. He undertook several career paths before, at age twenty-seven, deciding to become a painter. Van Gogh embarked on this with passionate intensity for ten years, producing over 2,000 artworks. But, after several breakdowns, Van Gogh took his own life in July 1890.

What is astonishing is that during this sole decade the largely self-taught artist created some of the most arresting, and most famous, images in art. While his early Dutch paintings are full of dark, earthy tones, a move to Paris introduced him to Impressionist colour and light. Van Gogh, however, was to innovate his own expressive use of colour, which was fully realised after he moved to the south of France. Flattened planes of pure, bright colour were joined by equally suggestive, animated brushwork in the works made during the last two years of his life.

A key artist of Post-Impressionism, Van Gogh created landscapes, still lifes and portraits that attest to a love of the natural world and an empathy for humanity that still resonate powerfully over 130 years since their creation.

Throughout this book are quotations from Van Gogh's letters, which are often as expressive as his paintings. The numbers in brackets after quotes, reproduced with permission, correspond to the letters as found on vangoghletters.org.

Bleaching Ground at Scheveningen

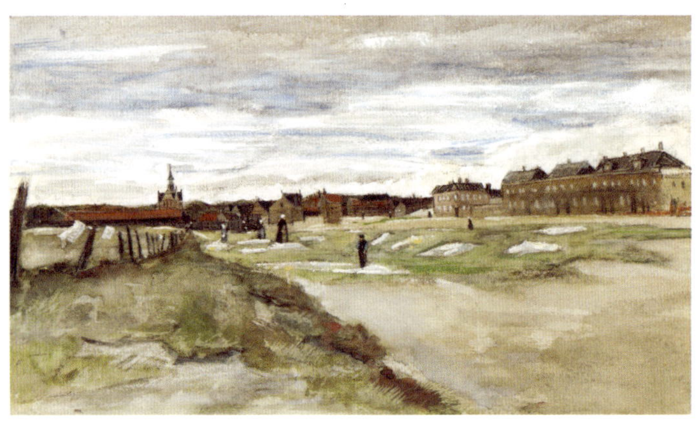

Watercolour
heightened with
white gouache
54 cm × 31.8 cm
(21¼ in × 12½ in)

July 1882
The Hague

Vincent van Gogh left school at the age of sixteen, but it was not until he was twenty-seven years old that he decided to become an artist. After employment at an art dealers, as a teacher and assistant minister, in a bookstore, and as a preacher, Van Gogh found his true calling. He began copying the works of earlier artists and, when he moved to Brussels in 1880, received guidance from the Dutch painters Willem Roelofs and Anthon van Rappard. On returning home to the Netherlands, Van Gogh took his first painting lessons under the tutelage of the well-known Hague School artist, and his cousin by marriage, Anton Mauve.

At the end of 1881, after quarrelling with his parents, Van Gogh moved to The Hague. There, strongly influenced by the French Barbizon School, Mauve and his fellow Hague School artists were painting plein-air landscapes and scenes of everyday life in subtle, earthy tones. The watercolour *Bleaching Ground at Scheveningen* is one of Van Gogh's early achievements, its wash of brushstrokes – highlighted with white gouache – conjures an expansive landscape brought to life by the depiction of several small figures and the white sheets fluttering in the breeze.

Bleaching Ground at Scheveningen

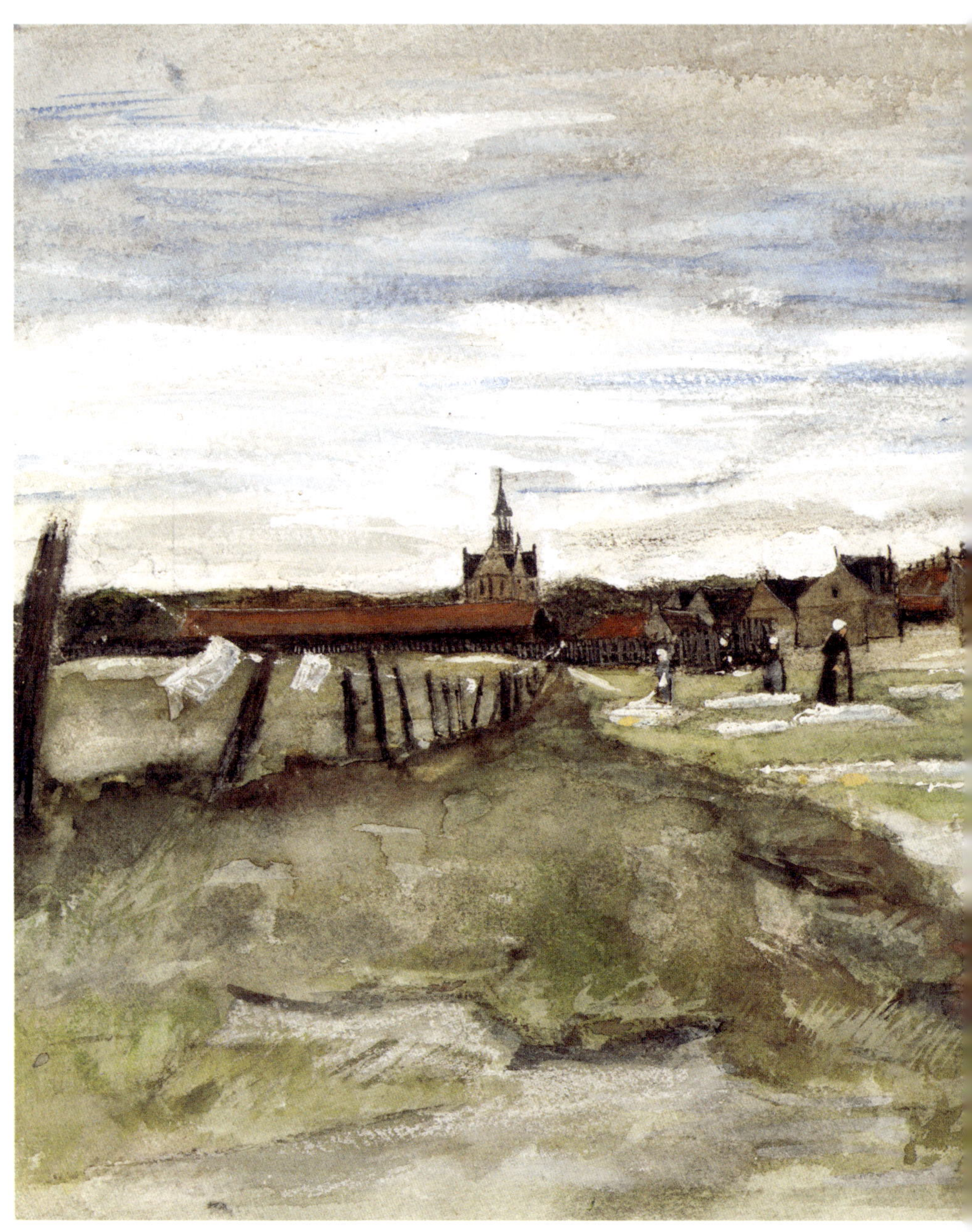

July 1882
The Hague

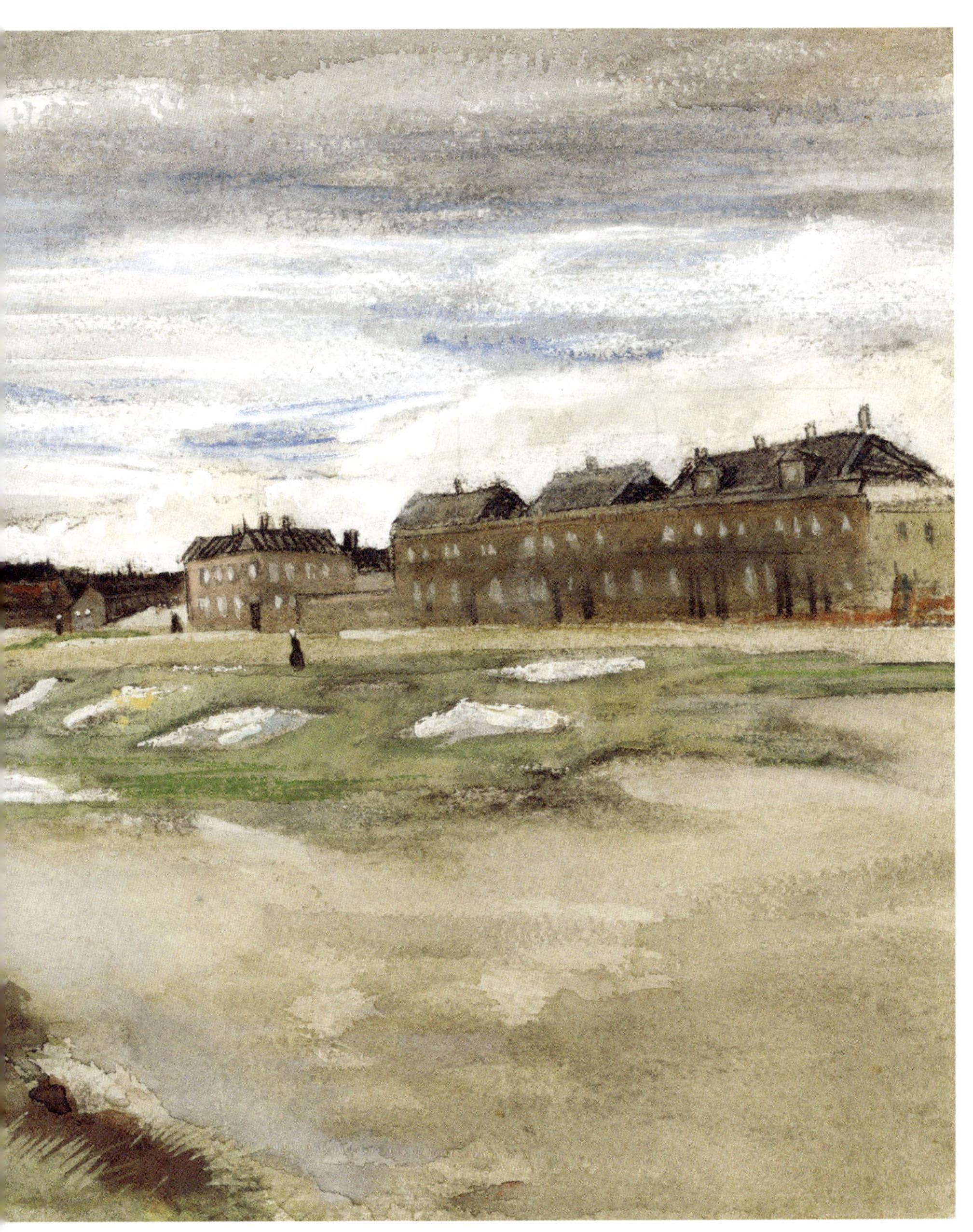

Beach at Scheveningen in Stormy Weather

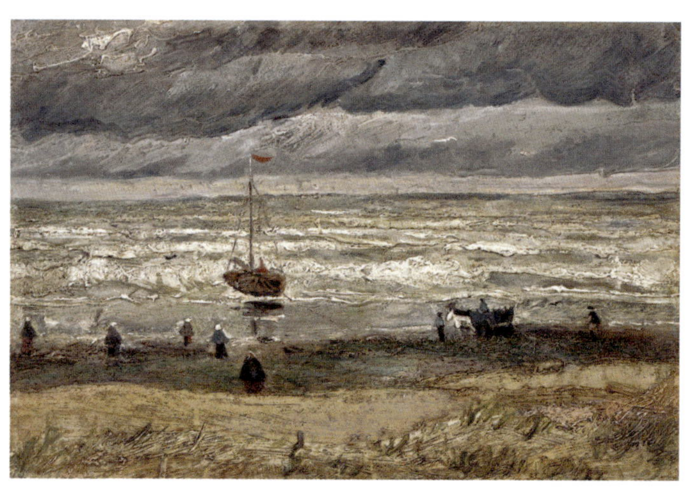

8

Oil on canvas
34.5 cm × 51 cm
(13⅝ in × 20⅛ in)

August 1882
The Hague

In 1882, while living in The Hague, Van Gogh visited the nearby coastal village of Scheveningen (see also *Bleaching Ground at Scheveningen* on page 4). In late August, Vincent wrote to his brother Theo:

'All this week we've had gales, storms and rain here, and I've been to Scheveningen many times to see it. And came back with two small seascapes. There's already a lot of sand in the one, but with the second … I had to scrape everything off twice because of the thick layer of sand completely covering it.' (259)

Of *Beach at Scheveningen in Stormy Weather*, the seascape with 'already a lot of sand' – and one of Van Gogh's earliest oil paintings – he wrote further:

'The sea was the colour of dirty dishwater. At that spot there was a fishing-boat, the last in the row, and several dark figures. There's something infinite about painting – I can't quite explain – but especially for expressing a mood, it's a joy.' (259)

Beach at Scheveningen in Stormy Weather

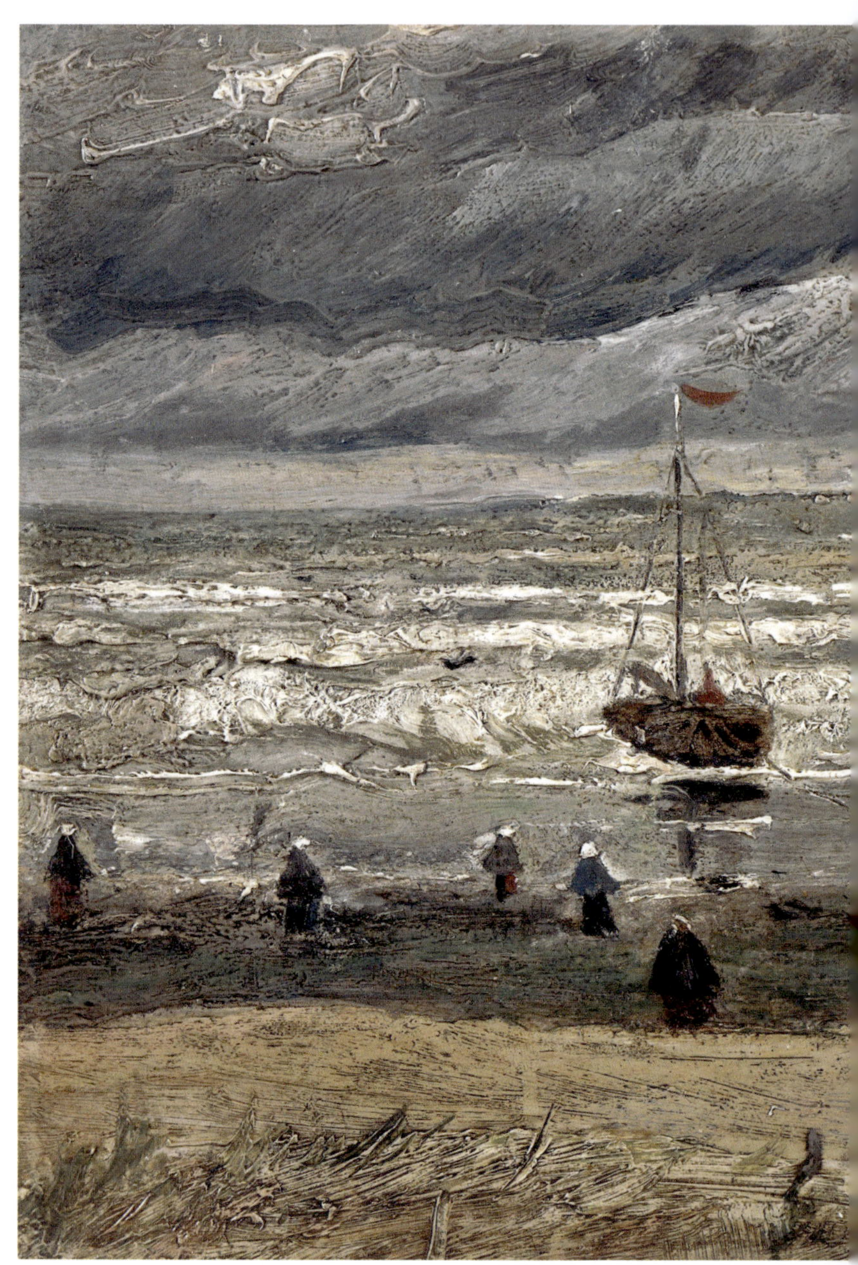

August 1882
The Hague

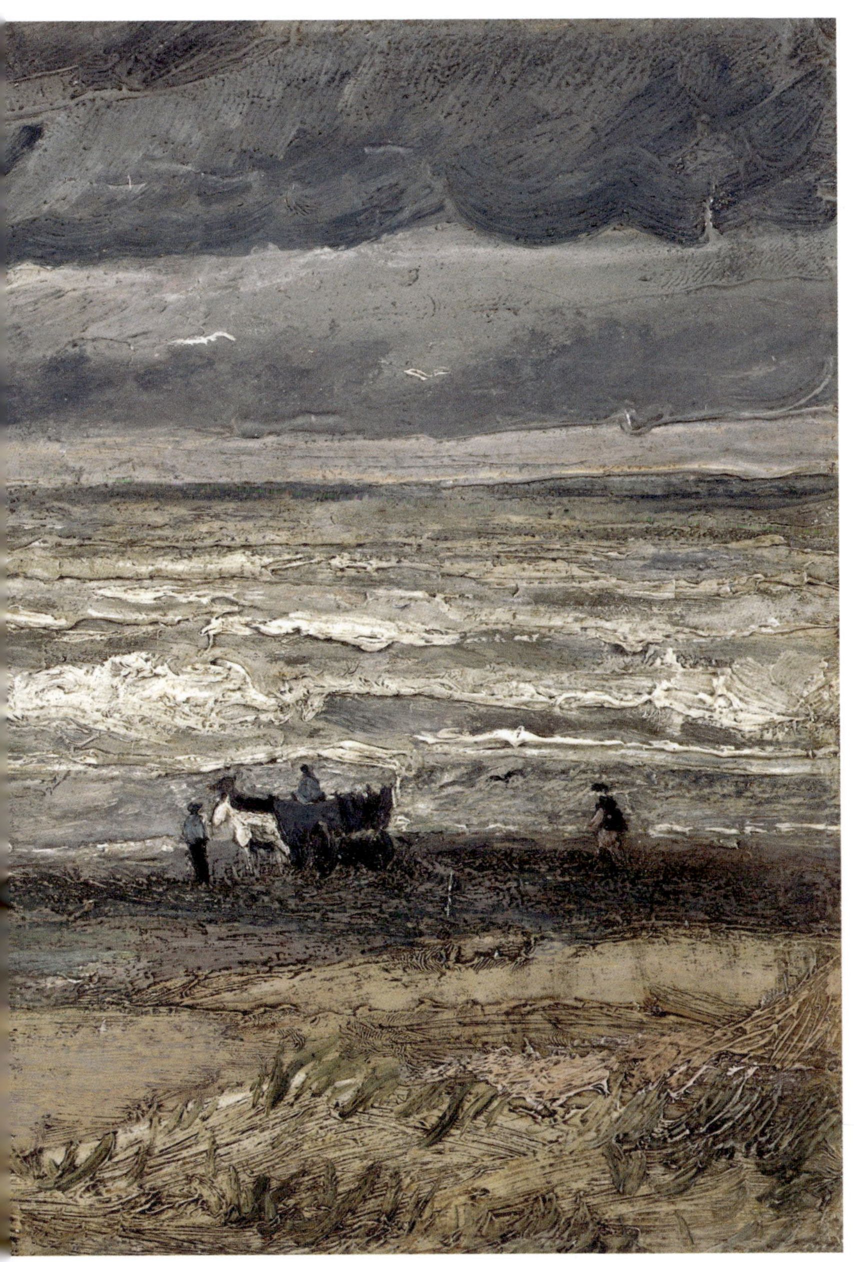

Congregation Leaving the Reformed Church in Nuenen

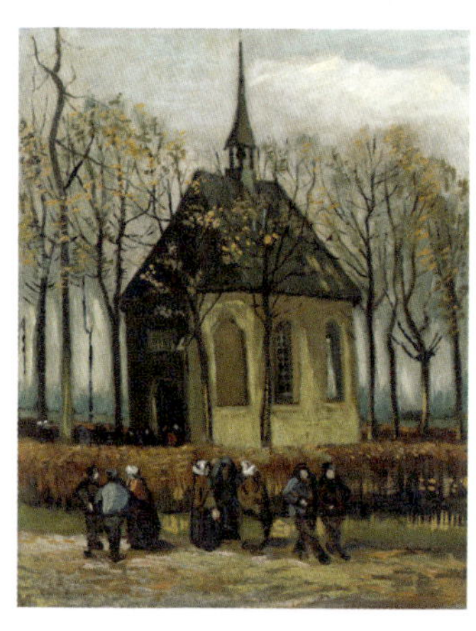

Oil on canvas
41.5 cm × 32.2 cm
(16⅜ in × 12⅝ in)

January-February 1884
Nuenen

Van Gogh's relationship with his parents was frequently tense. His father was a Protestant minister, and though Vincent had been fervently religious for a time, he began to have spiritual doubts. When he refused to go to church at Christmas in 1881, his father asked him to leave their home in Etten. Van Gogh moved to The Hague, but it did not help family relationships when he began living with a model, Sien Hoornik, and her young daughter. The unwed Hoornik, who had worked as a prostitute, was also pregnant.

By September 1883, however, Van Gogh and Hoornik's relationship had broken down and he left The Hague and moved to Drenthe in the Netherlands' north-east. While the rural landscape deeply affected Van Gogh, he was also incredibly lonely. He returned home to his parents, who were now living in Nuenen, that December.

Congregation Leaving the Reformed Church in Nuenen depicts parishioners outside the church where Theodorus van Gogh had been pastor since 1882. It is one of several works that capture life in the agrarian community (see also *The Parsonage Garden at Nuenen* on page 16).

Congregation Leaving the Reformed Church in Nuenen

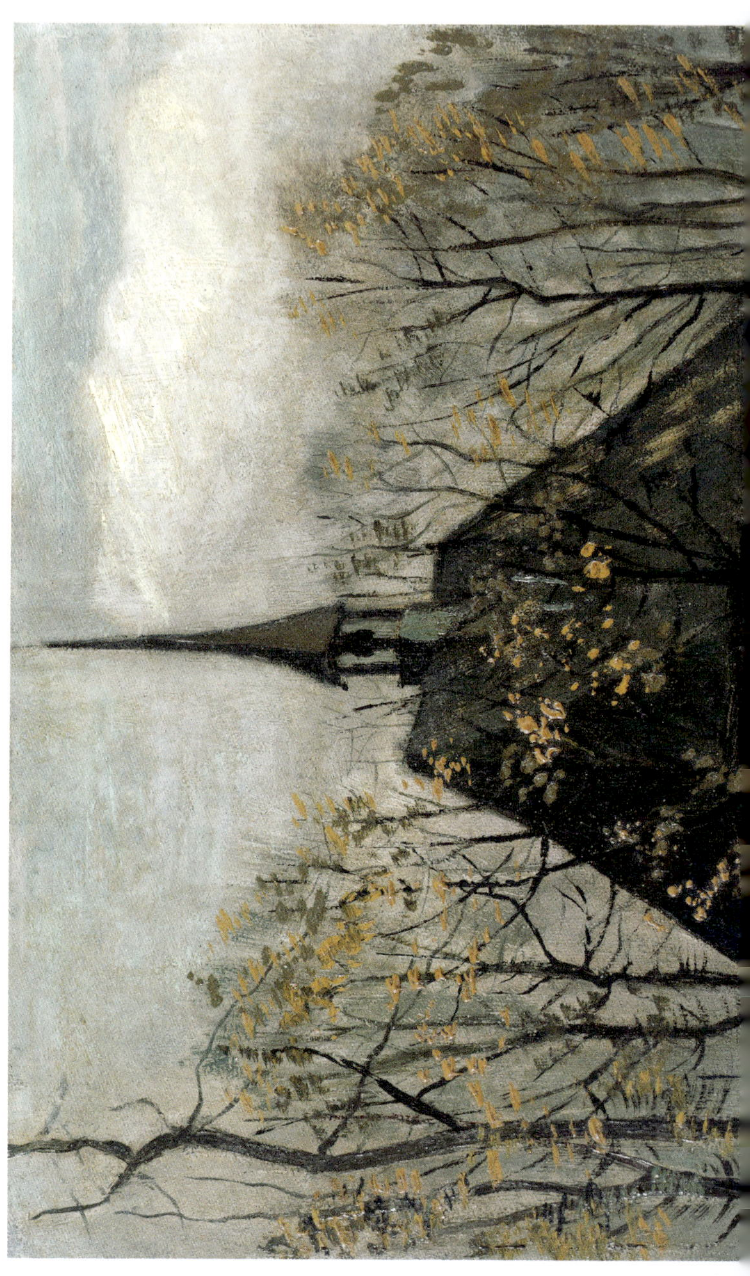

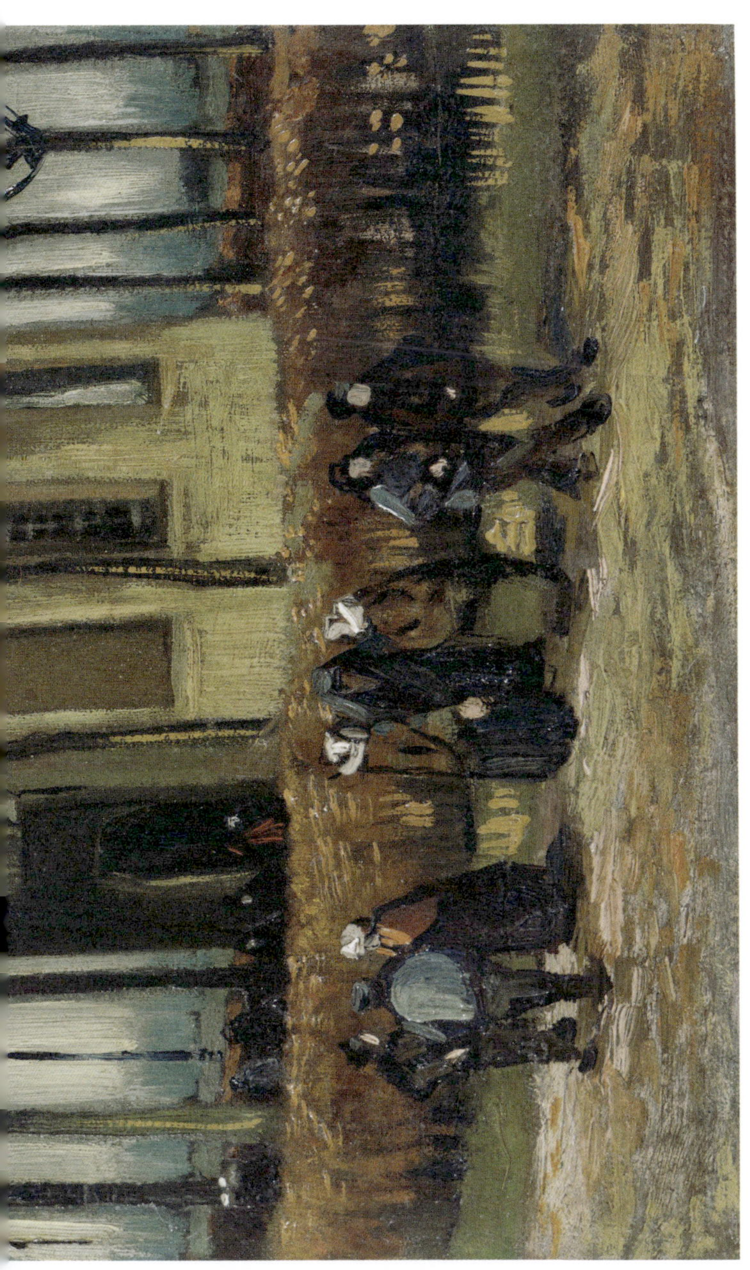

The Parsonage Garden at Nuenen

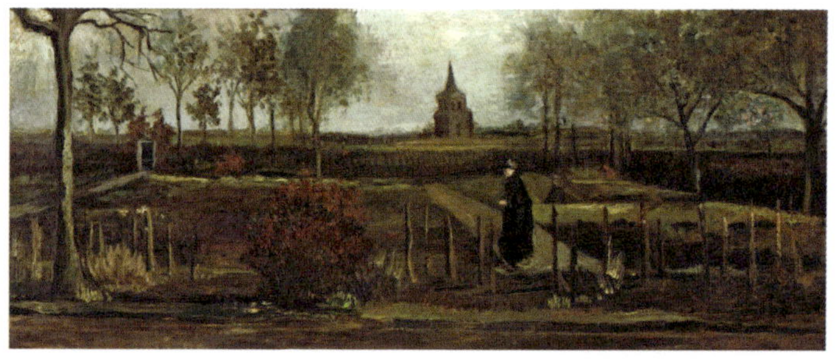

Oil on canvas
25 cm × 57 cm
(9⅞ in × 22½ in)

Spring 1884
Nuenen

After two years living in The Hague and, briefly, Drenthe, Van Gogh moved to his parents' home in Nuenen (see *Congregation Leaving the Reformed Church in Nuenen* on page 12). Considering his strained relationship with his father, it couldn't have been easy, but the subsequent two years would be defining for Van Gogh's artistic career. In Nuenen he could concentrate on painting and less on financial concerns.

Van Gogh drew and painted several views of the landscape surrounding the family parsonage, including the old church tower, which can be seen in the background of *The Parsonage Garden at Nuenen*. Painted in Van Gogh's early dark palette (how this will change!), the canvas's wide format emphasises the flat, open nature of the Dutch countryside.

Offsetting this horizontality are the vertical forms of trees and fence posts and, most notably, of the woman clad in black and the church tower. Our eye is always drawn back to these two subjects. They would seem to offer a contemplative account of Van Gogh's views on 'how a faith and religion mouldered away', but that 'the life and death of the peasants is and will always be the same' (507).

The Parsonage Garden at Nuenen

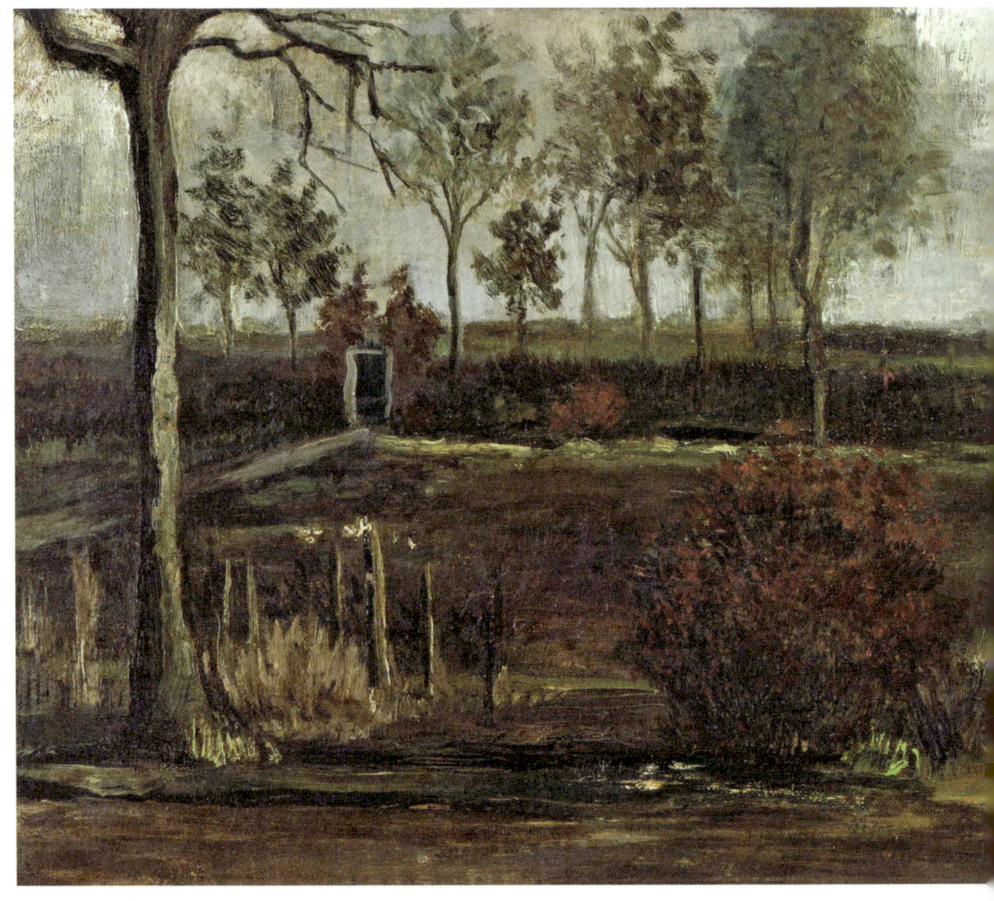

Spring 1884
Nuenen

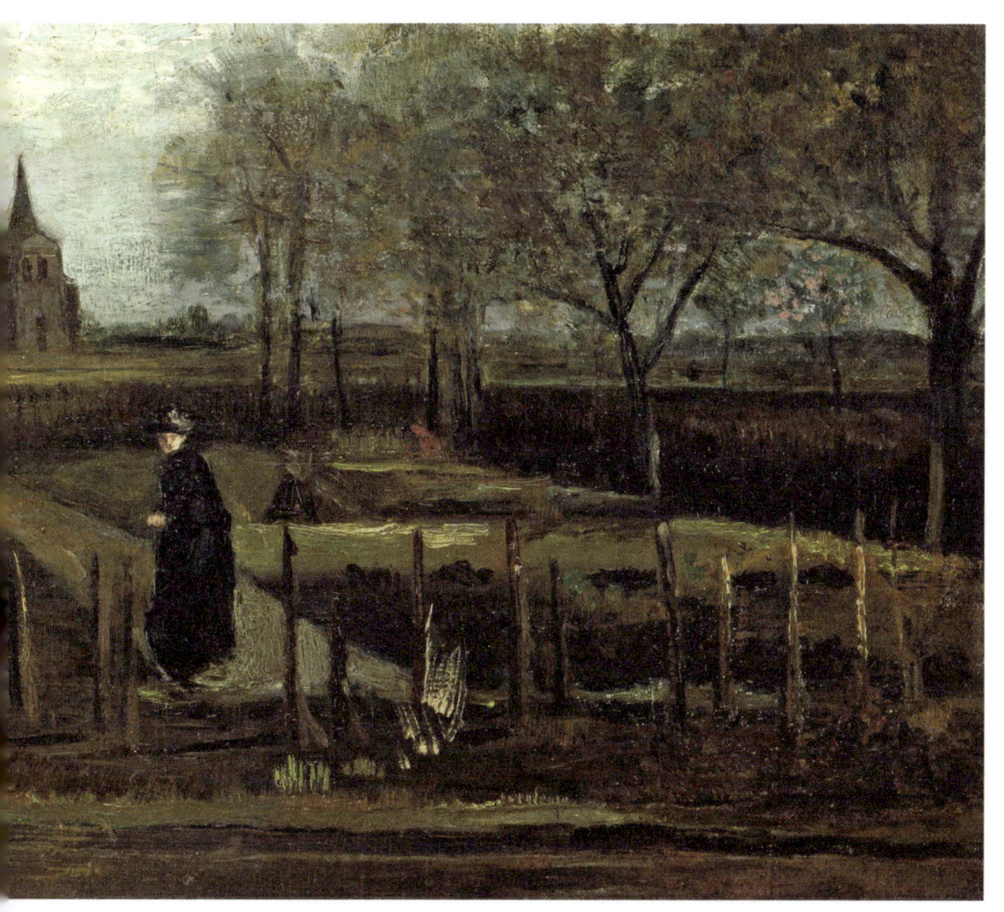

Head of a Peasant Woman

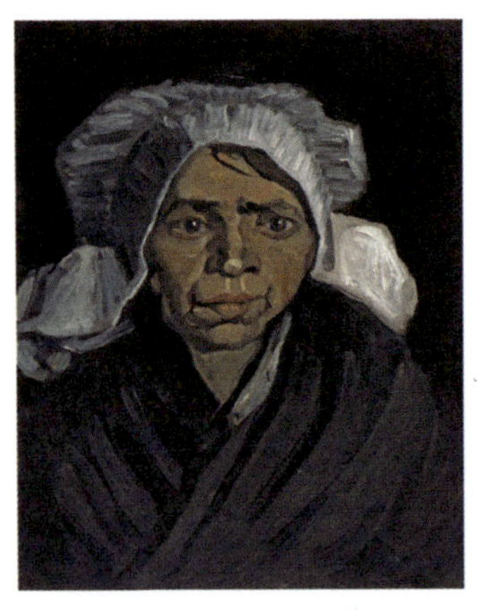

Oil on canvas
43.8 cm × 34.6 cm
(17¼ in × 13⅝ in)

December 1884
Nuenen

In autumn 1884 Van Gogh began painting a series of fifty heads. His models were the country people of Nuenen, where his father was pastor (see *The Parsonage Garden at Nuenen* on page 16). Set against a dark background, the subjects are depicted realistically through freely worked brushstrokes. In the present painting, we can see this in the representation of the woman's white cap, and particularly in the broadly brushed passage on the right. Van Gogh vividly described the representational and formal importance of these white gauze caps, which were traditionally worn by local women, in a letter he wrote to Anton Kerssemakers, a wealthy tanner he'd begun teaching to paint:

'Anyway, I'm working with almighty pleasure these days, for I would much rather paint figures than anything else. Then – the heads of these women here with the white caps – it's difficult – but it's so eternally beautiful. It's precisely the chiaroscuro – the white and the part of the face in shadow, that has such a fine tone.' (478)

These 1884–1885 head studies would be integral to Van Gogh's first masterpiece, *The Potato Eaters* (page 24).

Head of a Peasant Woman

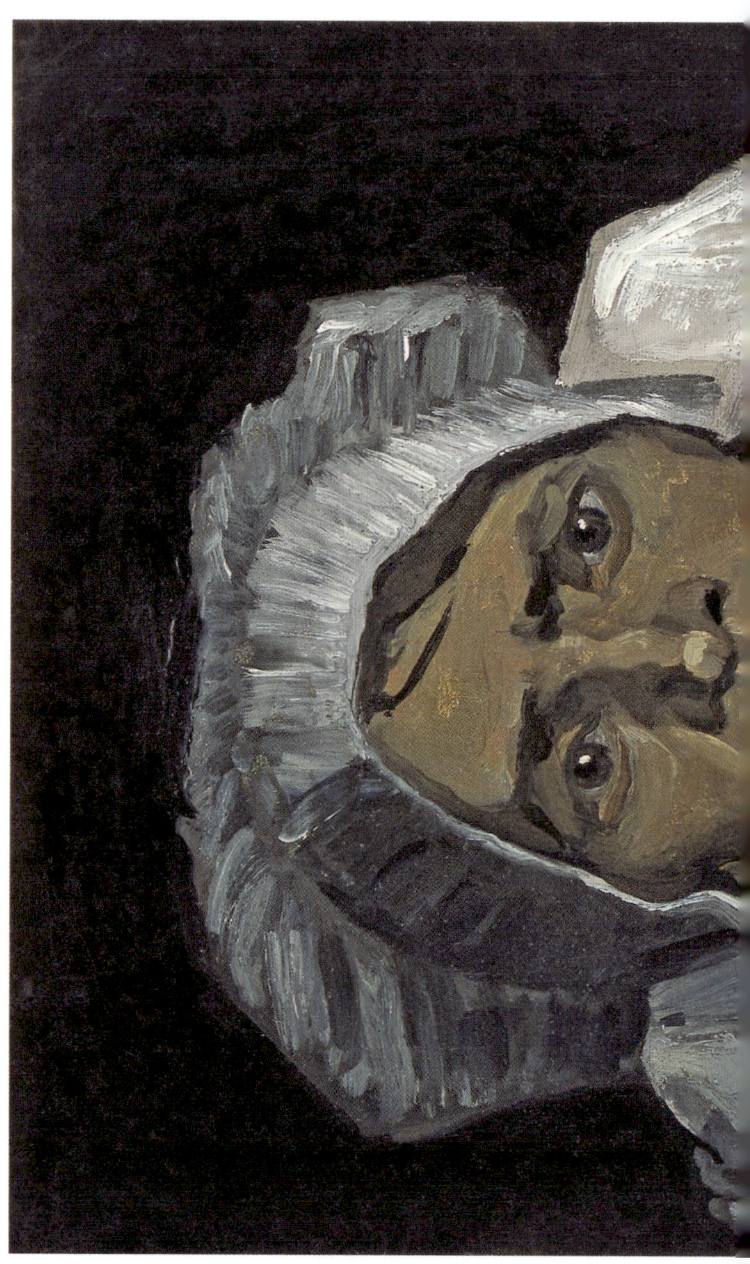

December 1884
Nuenen

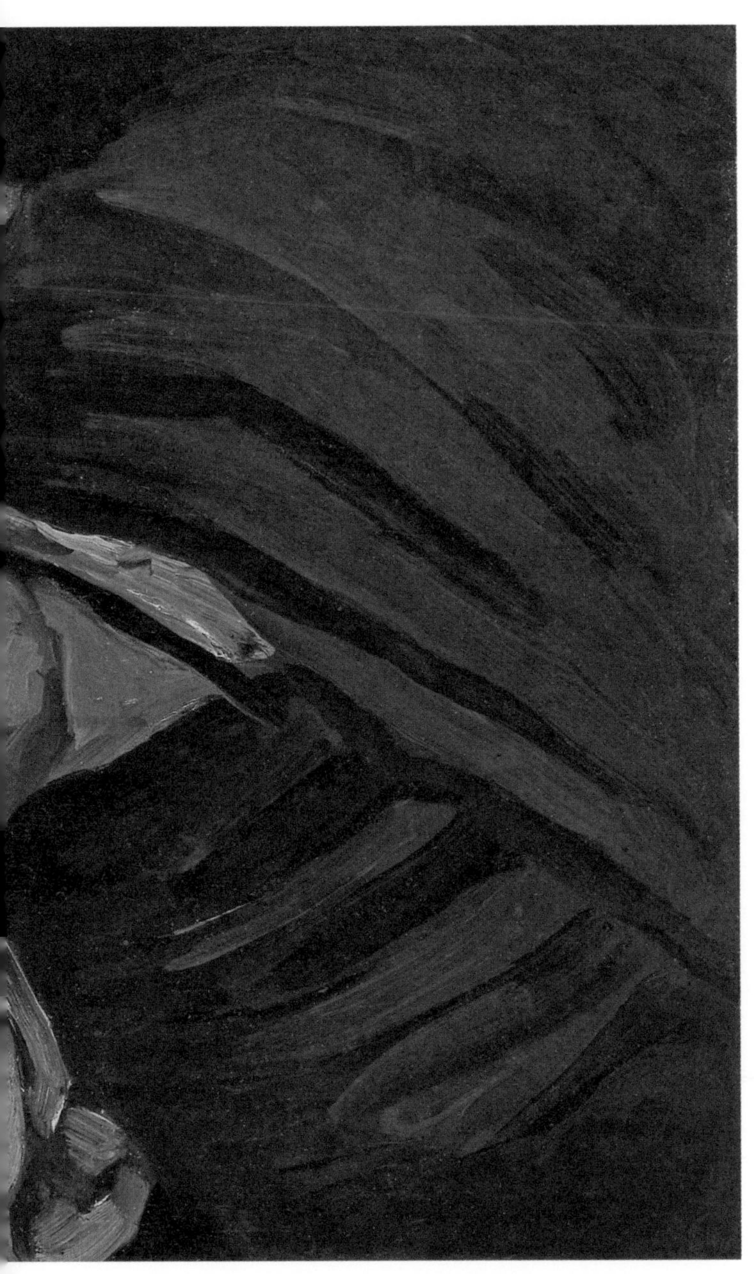

The Potato Eaters

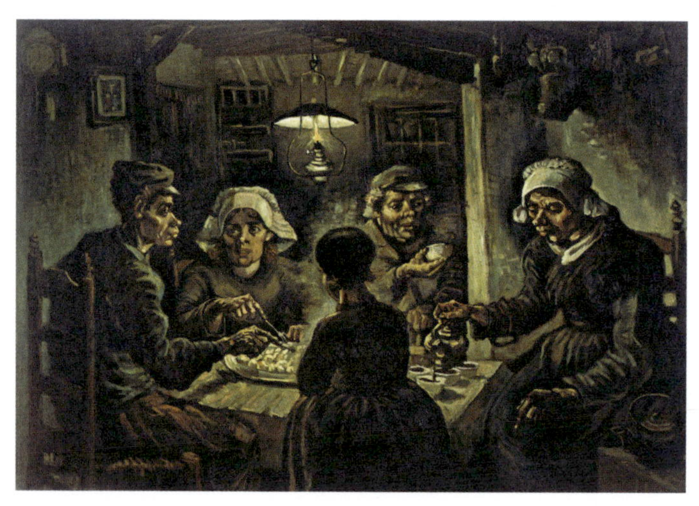

Oil on canvas
82 cm × 114 cm
(32¼ in × 44⅞ in)

April-May 1885
Nuenen

The many studies of hands and heads that Van Gogh made in winter 1884–85 (see *Head of a Peasant Woman* on page 20) ultimately led to his first truly great work, *The Potato Eaters*.

The large oil painting depicts five people in a rustic cottage gathered together for a meal of potatoes and coffee. Van Gogh was particular about the canvas's dark, grey tones, going so far as to repaint the figures' flesh: 'The colour they're painted now *is something like the colour of a really dusty potato, unpeeled of course*. While I was doing it I thought again about what has so rightly been said of Millet's peasants – "*His peasants seem to have been painted with the soil they sow*".' (499)

To bring the truth of peasant life to the canvas necessitated an earthiness that Van Gogh knew his critics would not understand. But, by comparing *The Potato Eaters* to a carefully woven fabric, he clarified his intent: 'I've had the threads of this fabric in my hands the whole winter long, and searched for the definitive pattern – and if it's now a fabric that has a rough and coarse look, nevertheless the threads were chosen with care' (497).

The Potato Eaters

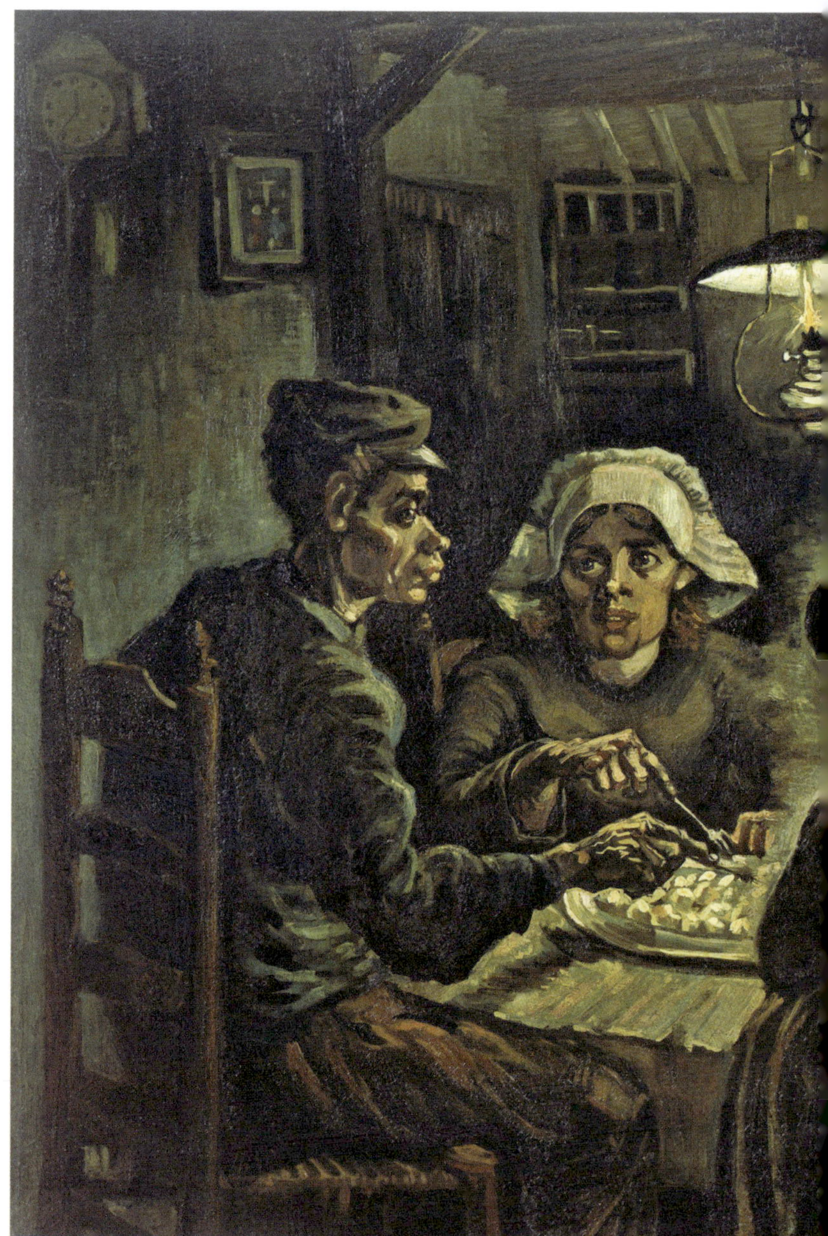

April-May 1885
Nuenen

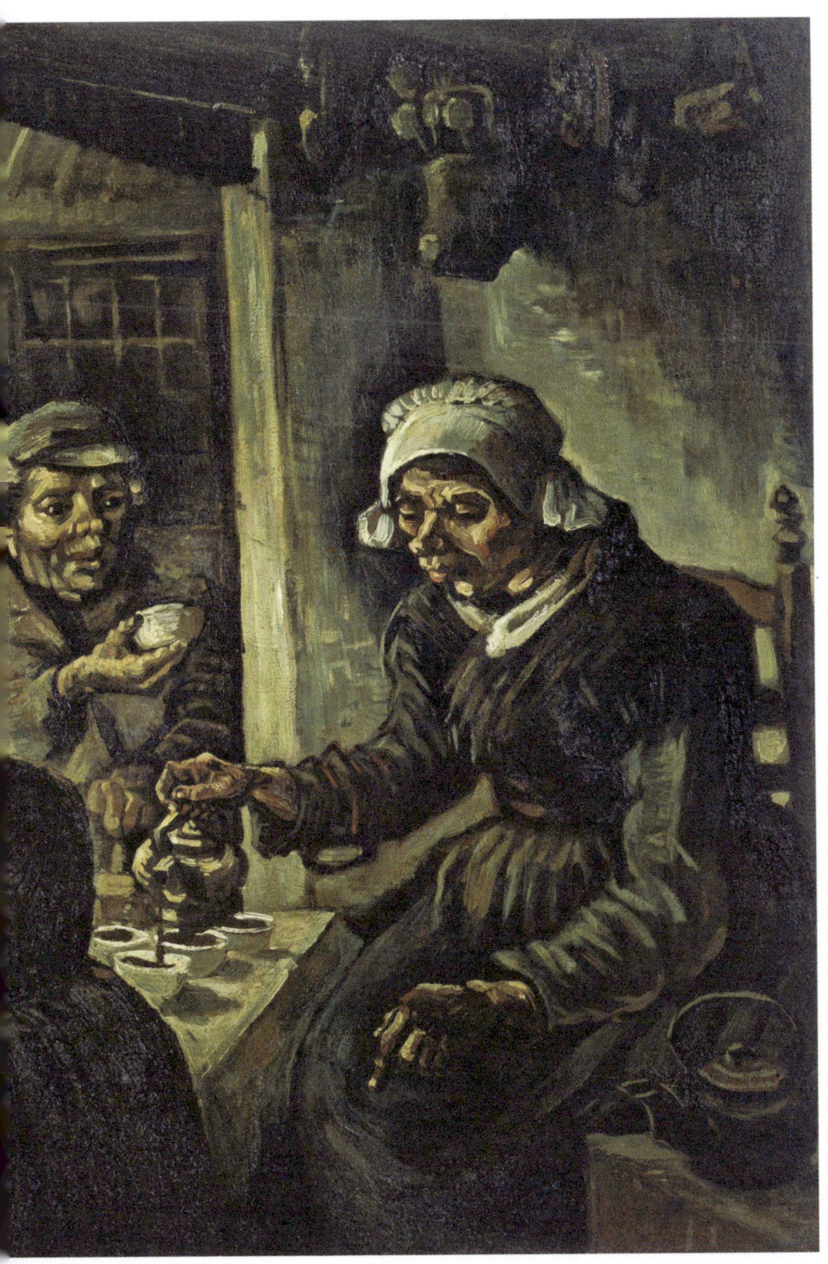

A Peasant Woman Digging in Front of Her Cottage

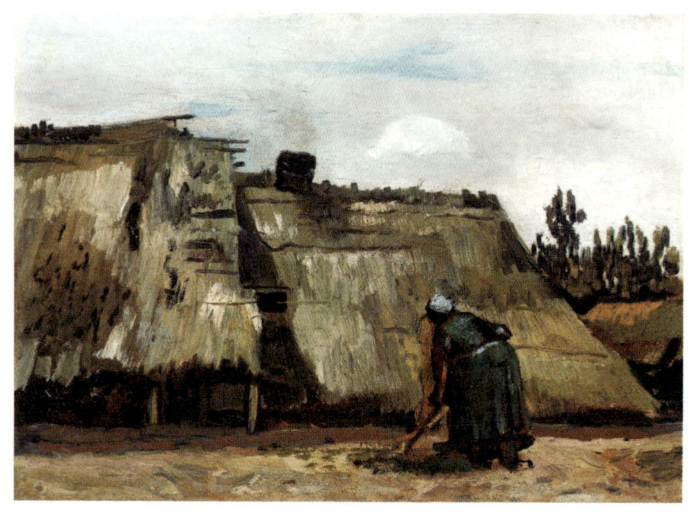

Oil on canvas
31.3 cm × 42 cm
(12⅜ in × 16½ in)

June-July 1885
Nuenen

As 'a painter of peasant life' (489), Van Gogh sought to bring the truth of that life to the canvas. In this quest, he was profoundly influenced by the French painter Jean-François Millet, whose works Van Gogh copied in his early training as an artist. For Van Gogh, modern art was to be found in 'showing the FIGURE OF THE PEASANT IN ACTION', of which Millet was 'the eternal master' (515).

After completing the statement piece *The Potato Eaters* (page 24), Van Gogh made a series of studies of cottages in the Nuenen countryside. But these rustic dwellings are not simply picturesque; Van Gogh saw an essential honesty in the peasant's life in the countryside, and their homes were a facet of that existence, so much so that he described them as '"*people's nests*", which remind me so much of the nests of wrens' (507).

This nest-like quality is particularly apparent in this painting. The low-hanging roofs of the cottages are roughly painted in earth tones, forming a pattern of thick vertical brushstrokes interlaced with horizontal markings. Here, the woman's dark green dress stands out, her tie to the land indicated by the mirrored green patch on the ground.

A Peasant Woman Digging in Front of Her Cottage

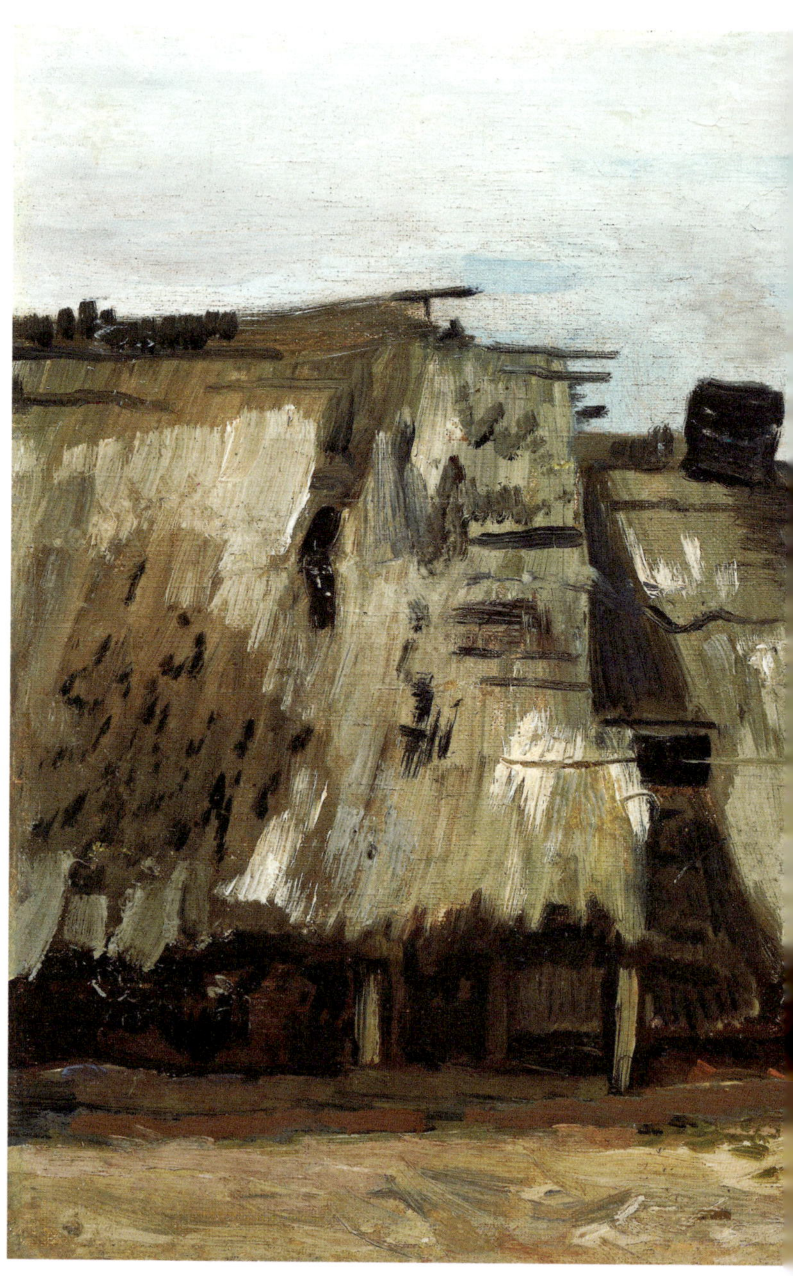

June-July 1885
Nuenen

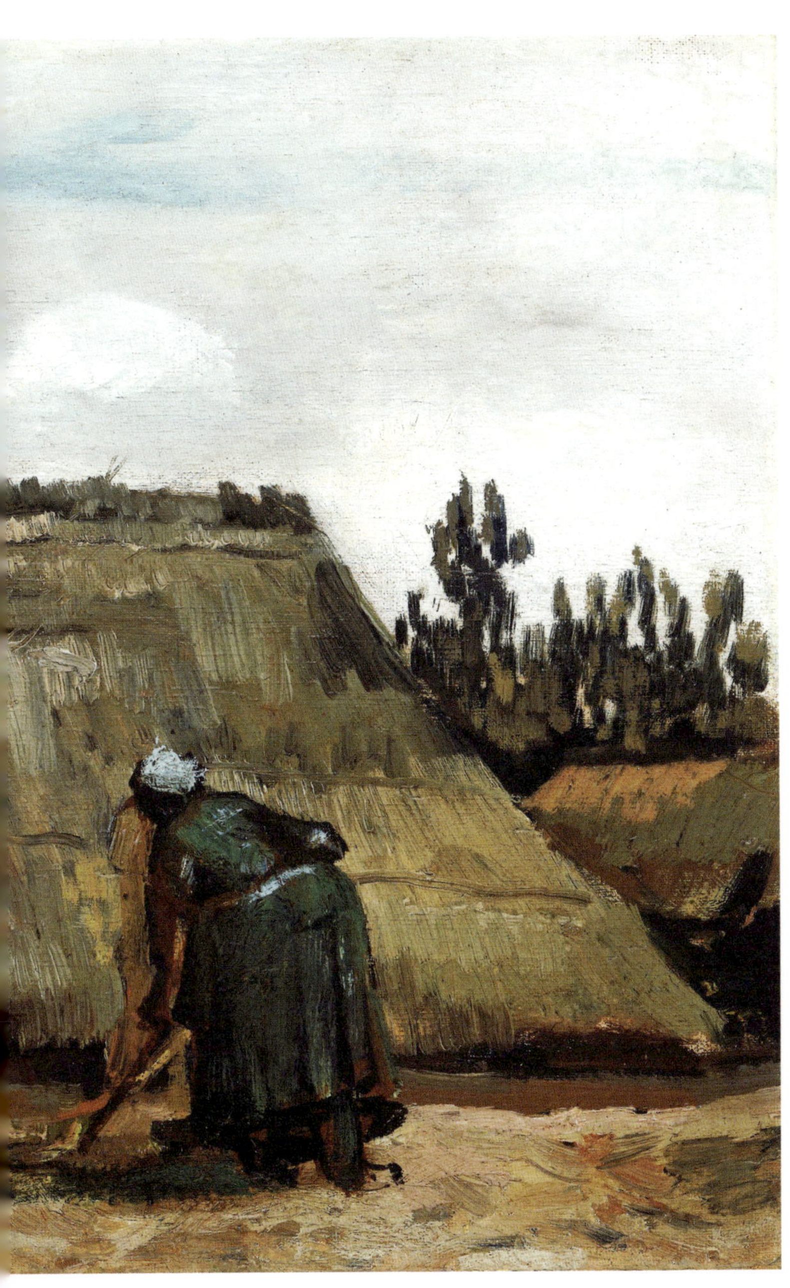

Head of a Skeleton with a Burning Cigarette

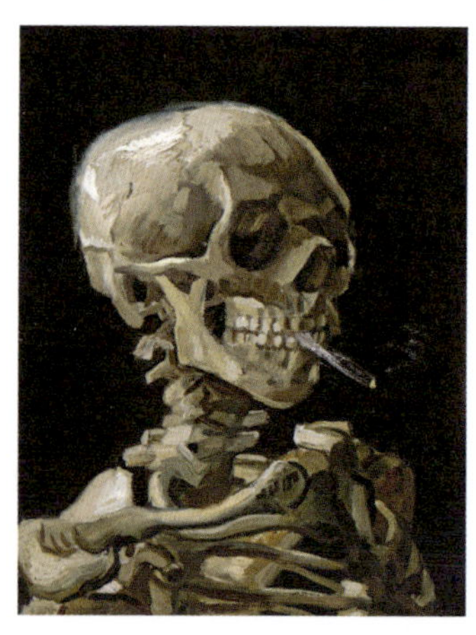

Oil on canvas
32.3 cm × 24.8 cm
(12¾ in × 9¾ in)

January-February 1886
Antwerp

Van Gogh's father died suddenly of heart disease in March 1885, and while his mother was able to stay at the parsonage in Nuenen for another year (see *The Parsonage Garden at Nuenen* on page 16), Van Gogh began living in his studio that May. In November 1885, he moved to Antwerp.

During what would be a three-month stay, Van Gogh was able to view paintings by Peter Paul Rubens, the rich colouring and dynamic brushwork of which made 'a strong impression' (547). We will see how these aspects influenced Van Gogh's later works. He made studies of heads and of city views, and by enrolling in the Antwerp Academy, he could also work from the nude model. It was likely while at the academy that Van Gogh created the small oil painting *Head of a Skeleton with a Burning Cigarette*.

Drawing plaster casts and skeletons was part of the artistic curriculum. It would seem that Van Gogh's extra step of *painting* a skeleton's torso – and placing a cigarette between its teeth – was a satirical poke at the academy's conservativism. It is certainly a lively rendition of the model.

Head of a Skeleton with
a Burning Cigarette

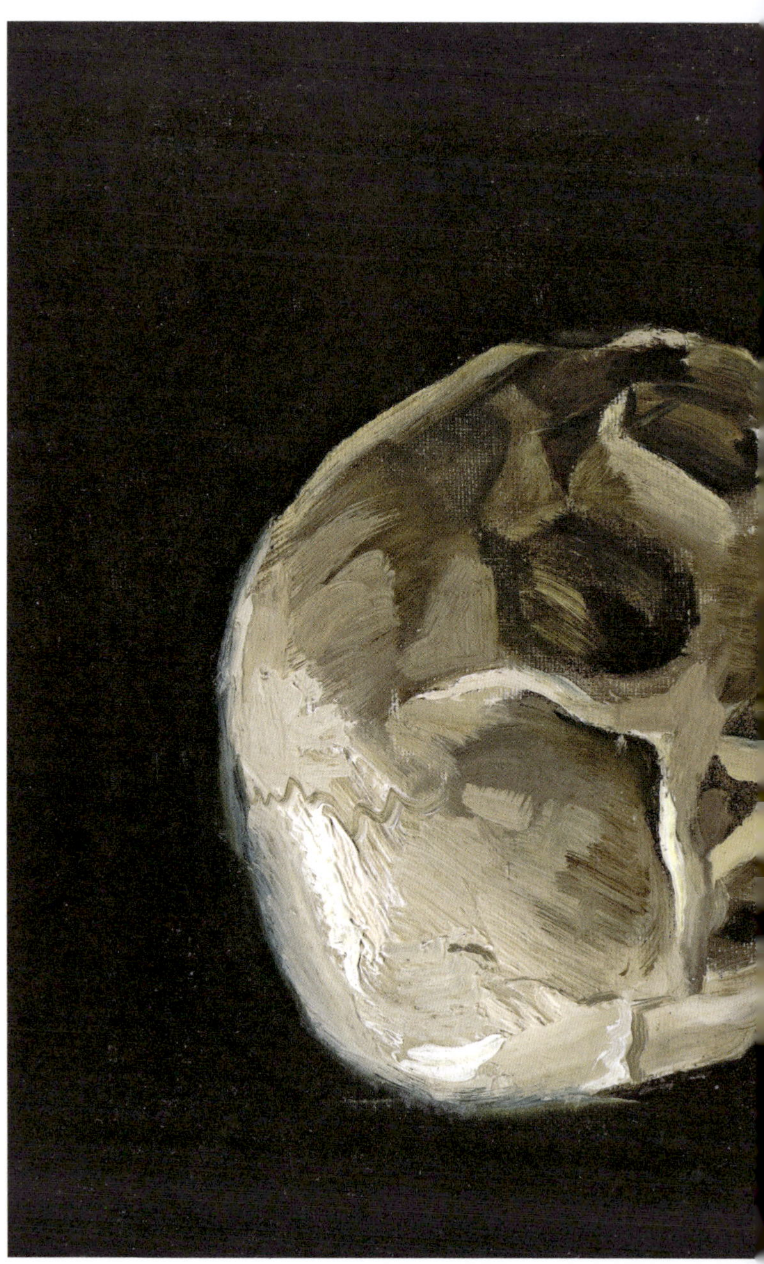

January-February 1886
Antwerp

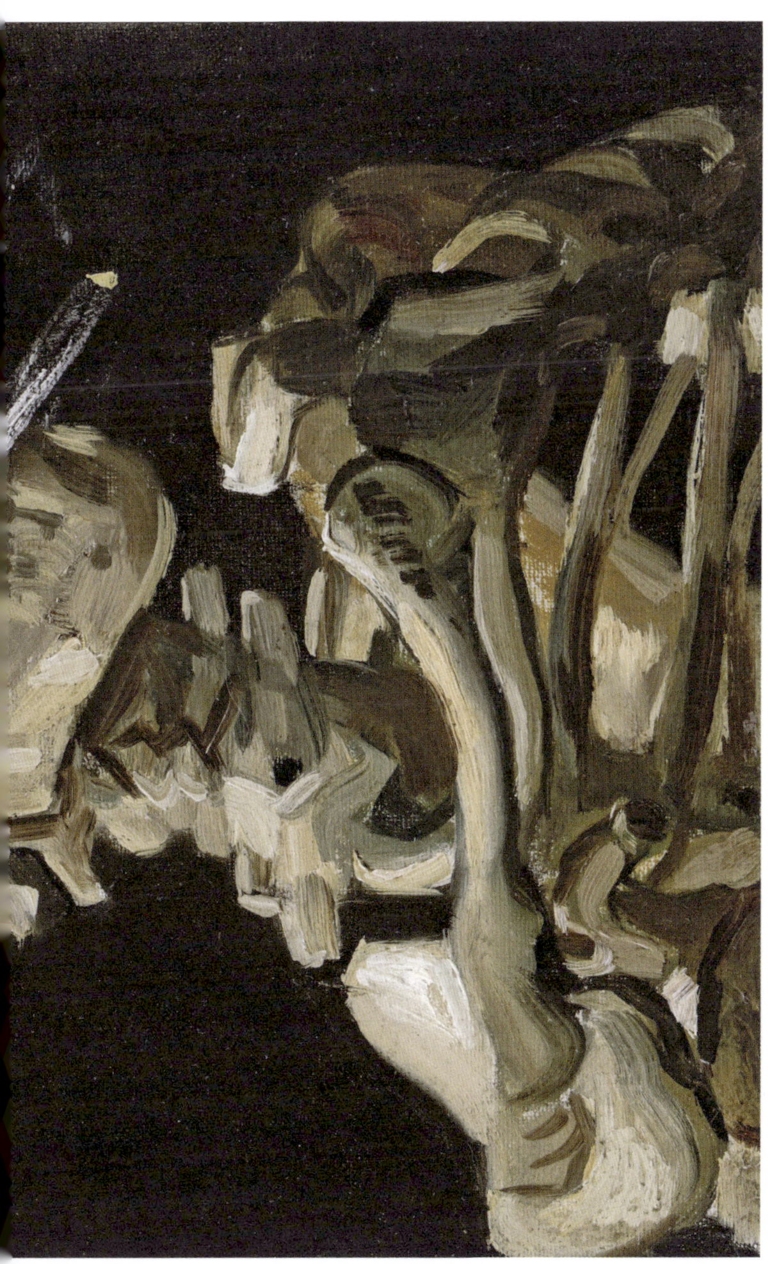

Terrace in the Luxembourg Garden

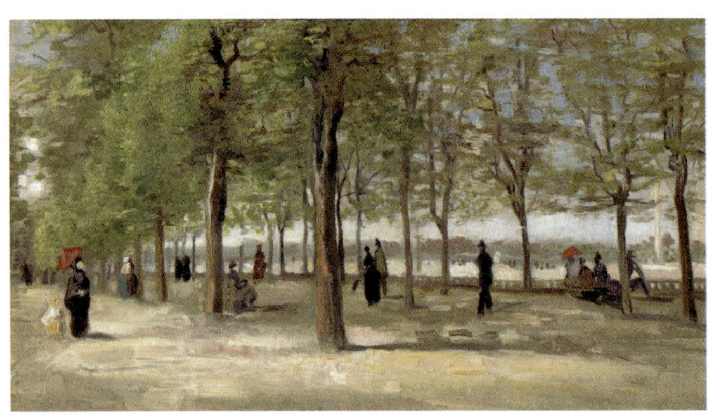

Oil on canvas
27 cm × 46 cm
(10⅝ in × 18⅛ in)

Spring 1886
Paris

'My dear Theo, Don't be cross with me that I've come all of a sudden. I've thought about it so much and I think we'll save time this way. Will be at the Louvre from midday, or earlier if you like. A reply, please, to let me know when you could come to the Salle Carrée.' (567)

And so, on or around 28 February 1886, Vincent van Gogh announced his arrival in Paris to his brother Theo. While they'd previously discussed Vincent's relocation from Antwerp, he ultimately decided just to turn up. The two brothers then lived together in Theo's apartment on the Rue de Laval, before moving to Montmartre in the summer.

Terrace in the Luxembourg Garden reveals the city as a new visual stimulus for Van Gogh and his close study of French Impressionism. The park setting and the strolling public are sketchily painted in strokes of varying colours. We can see this especially in the rendering of the woman and child on the left, where the adult's face is a creamy dab, and the quickly executed passage of yellow and white is enough to give the 'impression' of a young girl in a summer dress.

Terrace in the Luxembourg Garden

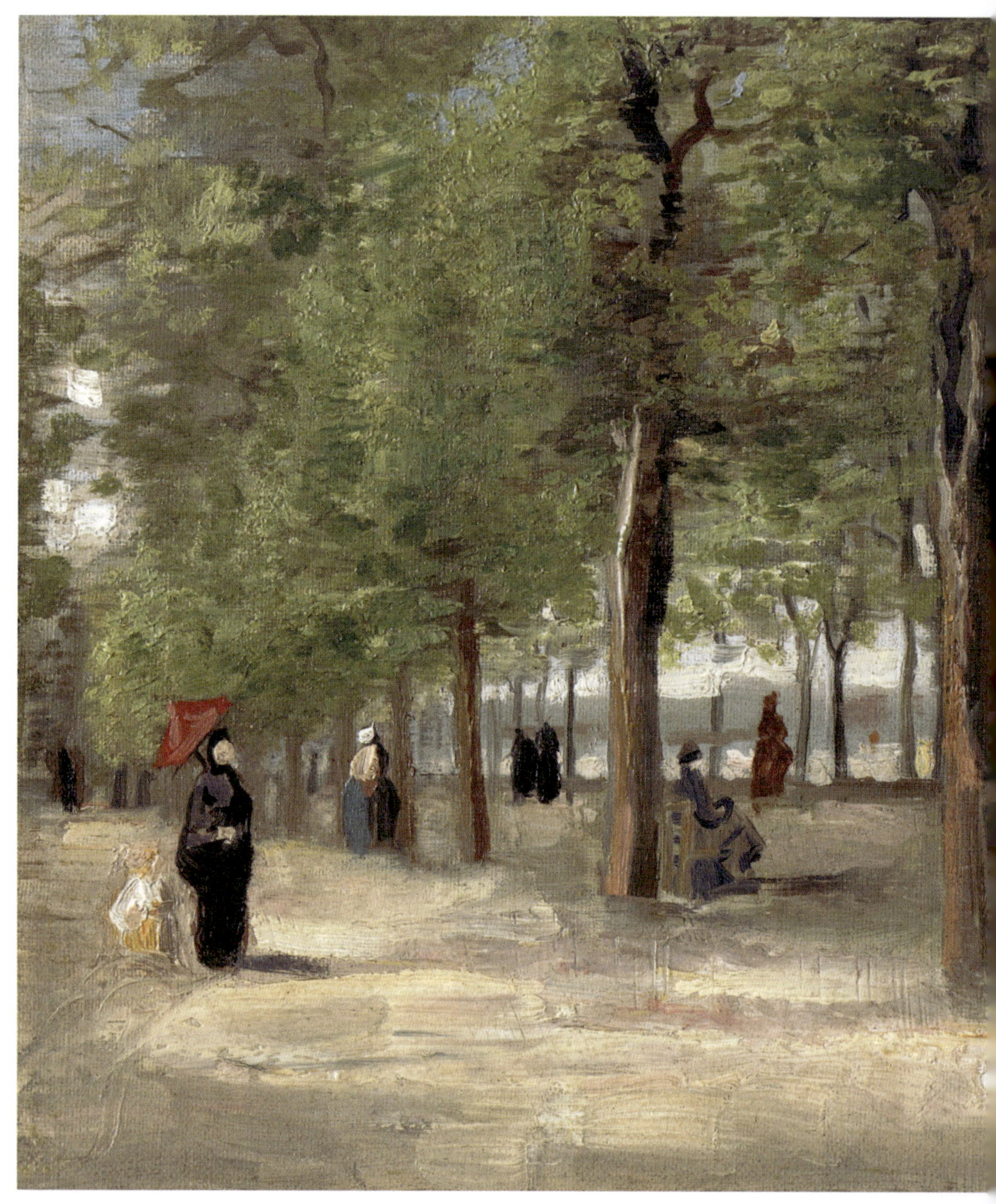

Spring 1886
Paris

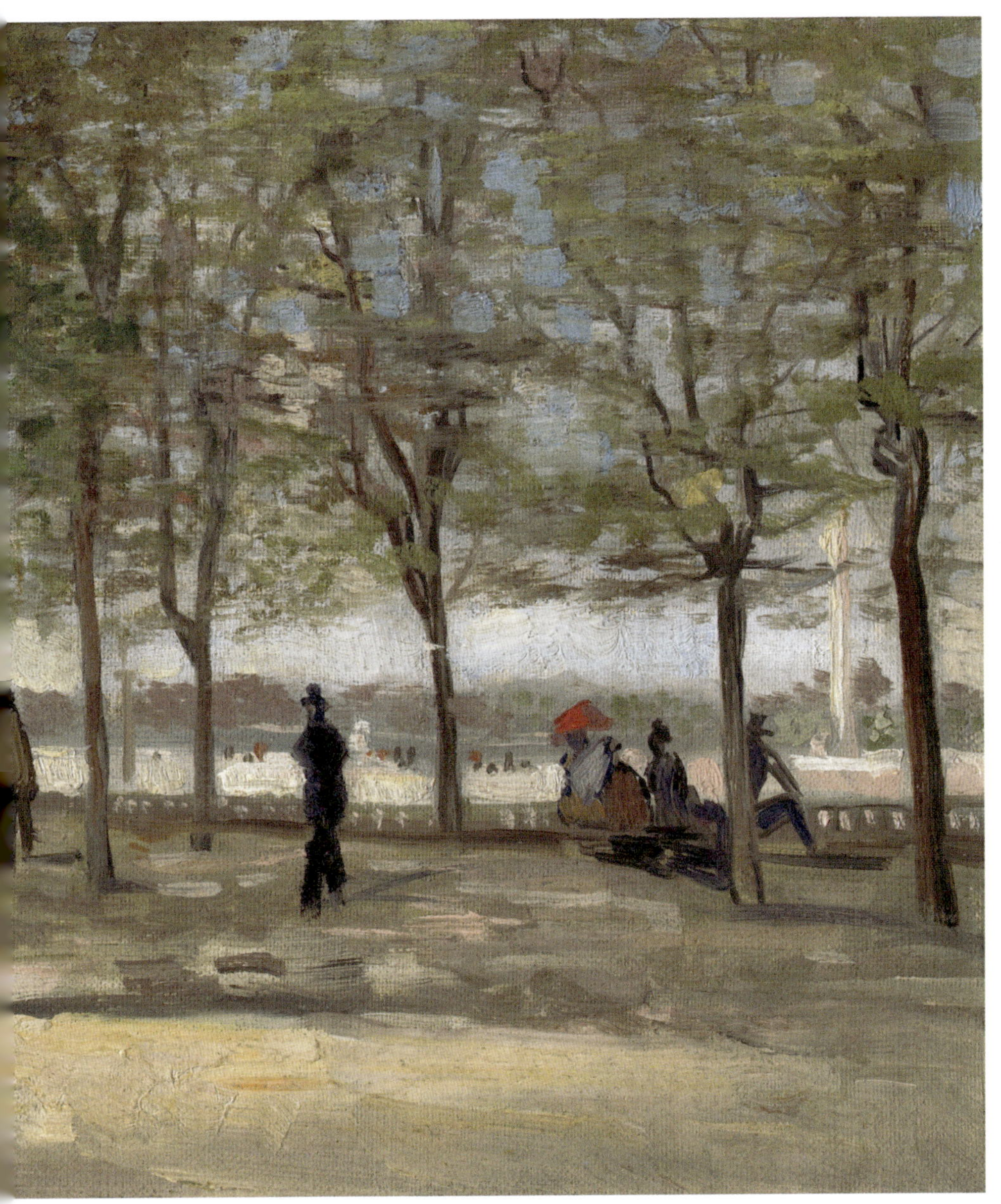

Vase with Poppies

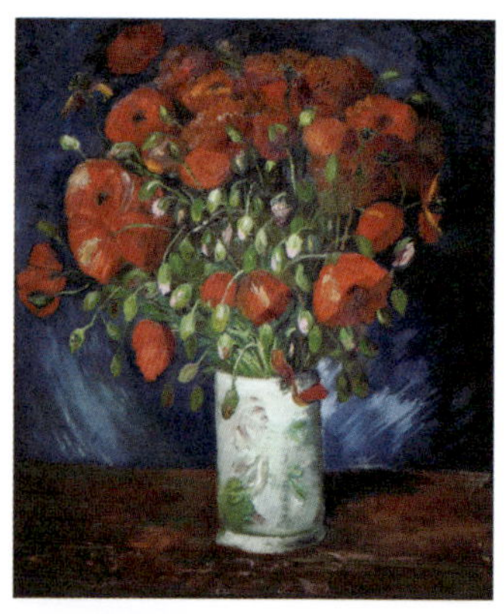

Oil on canvas
56 cm × 46.5 cm
(22 in × 18¼ in)

July-September 1886
Paris

Theo van Gogh worked in Paris at international art dealers Goupil & Cie, where Vincent had also been employed (1869–1876) before he became an artist. Theo was thus immersed in the contemporary art world, and after Vincent joined him in the city the two brothers were of mutual help with artistic contacts. For Vincent, Paris also meant the opportunity to see how the colour theory he'd read about was put into practice by the Impressionists and what it would mean for *him*.

Vase with Poppies is an early indication. In autumn 1886, Van Gogh wrote to the English painter Horace Mann Livens (1862-1936), describing what he'd been working on: 'I have made a series of colour studies in painting simply flowers, red poppies, blue corn flowers and myosotys.' He added that he was 'seeking oppositions of blue with orange, red and green, yellow and violet … trying to render intense COLOUR and not a GREY harmony.' (569)

In *Vase with Poppies*, we can sense Van Gogh's passionate enthusiasm in rendering the vibrant red poppies and their complementary greenery. These Parisian 'colour studies' would be crucial for the development of his artistic style.

Vase with Poppies

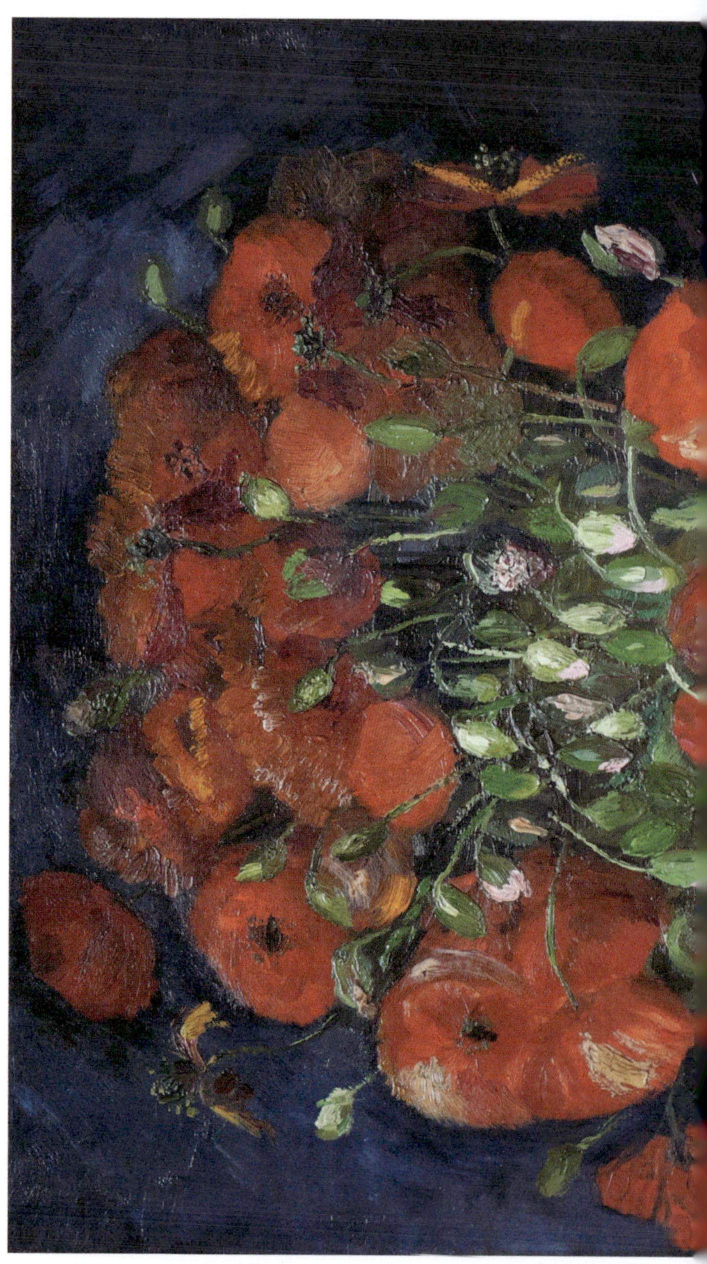

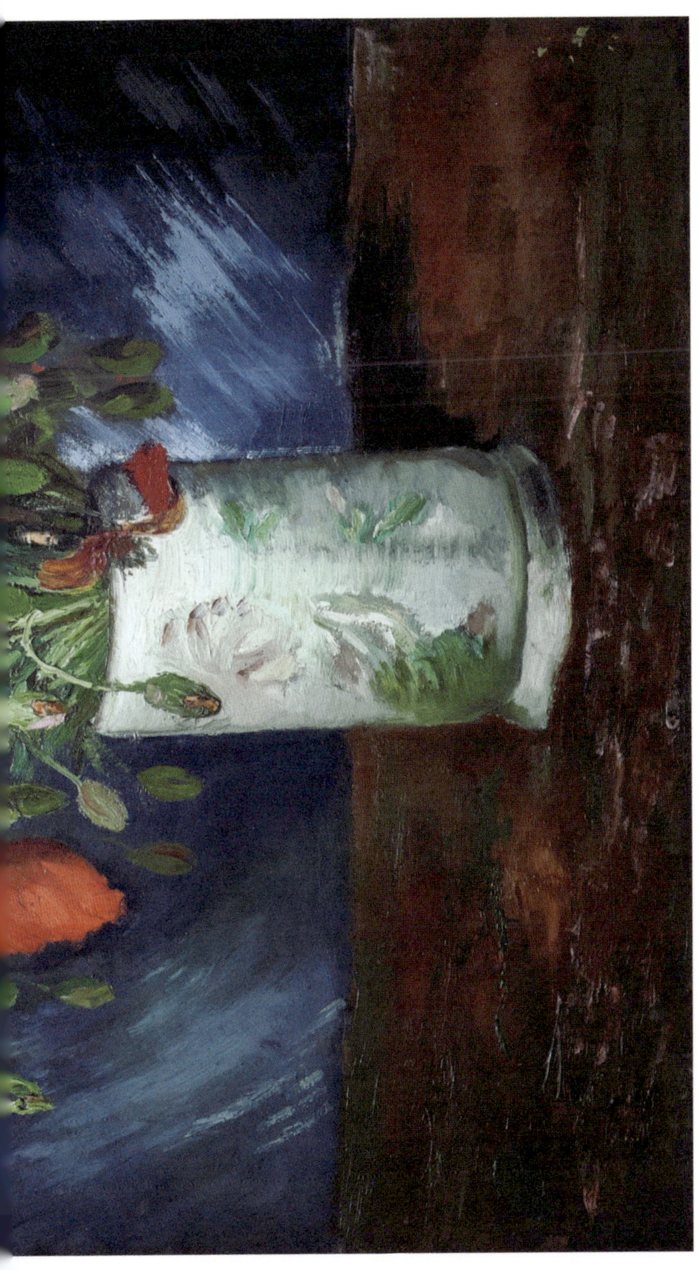

Self-Portrait with Dark Felt Hat at the Easel

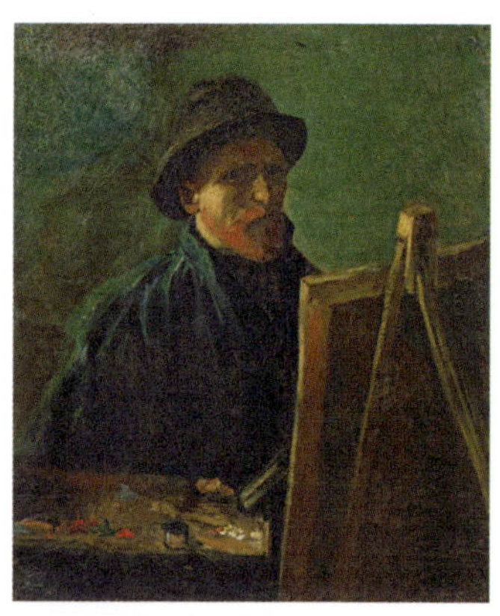

Oil on canvas
46.5 cm × 38.5 cm
(18¼ in × 15⅛ in)

September-
November 1886
Paris

Van Gogh painted more than thirty-five self-portraits, around twenty-five of which were created during his two years in Paris (1886–88). This is one of his earliest. Smoothly painted in the dark palette of his early works, Van Gogh is largely subsumed in shadow. His red beard and the patch of reflected light on his right cheek stand out in a field of greens – the richly glowing background, Van Gogh's dark painter's smock and his even darker hat.

While in Paris, Van Gogh became immersed in the world of the artistic avant-garde. He worked for a while in the studio of Fernand Cormon, where he became friends with painters like Henri de Toulouse-Lautrec and Émile Bernard, and he could view first-hand the work of the Impressionists.

With palette in hand and his easel jutting towards the viewer, Van Gogh presents himself as an artist who is part of this milieu. It is interesting to note the unmixed paint colours on the palette, for they are the same ones used in the flower studies Van Gogh had been working on that summer (see *Vase with Poppies* on page 40).

Self-Portrait with Dark Felt Hat at the Easel

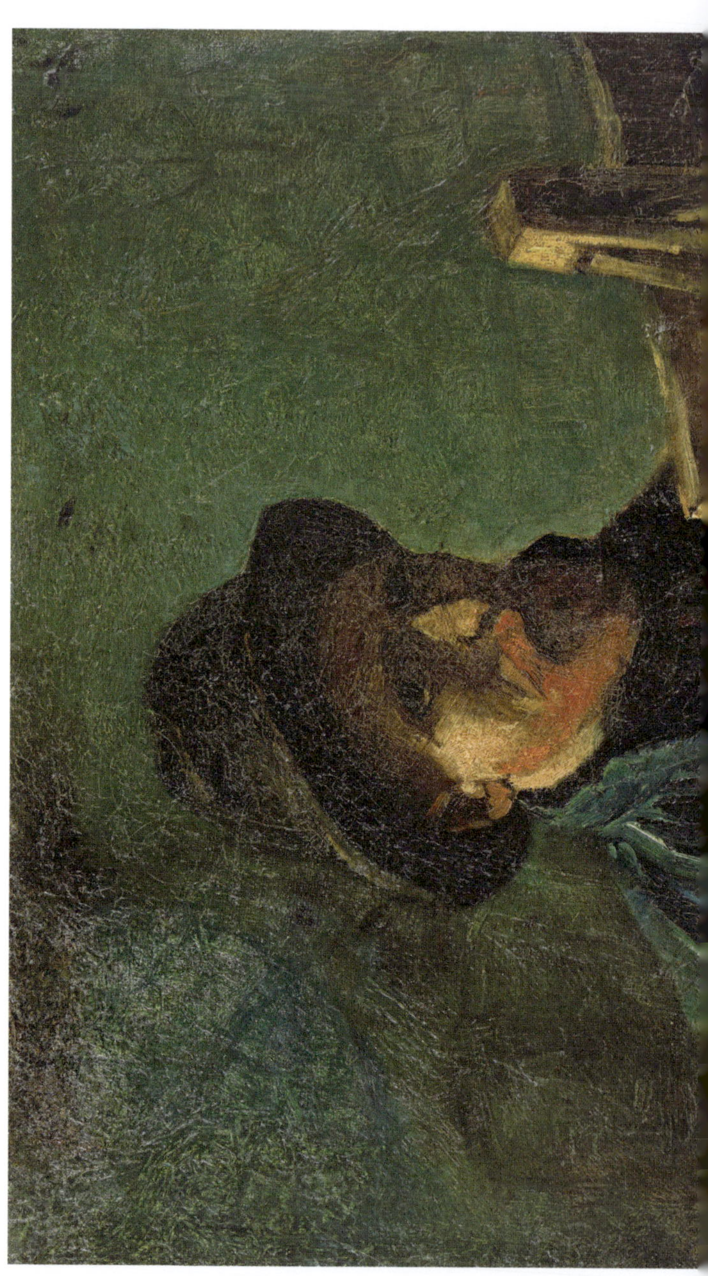

September-November 1886
Paris

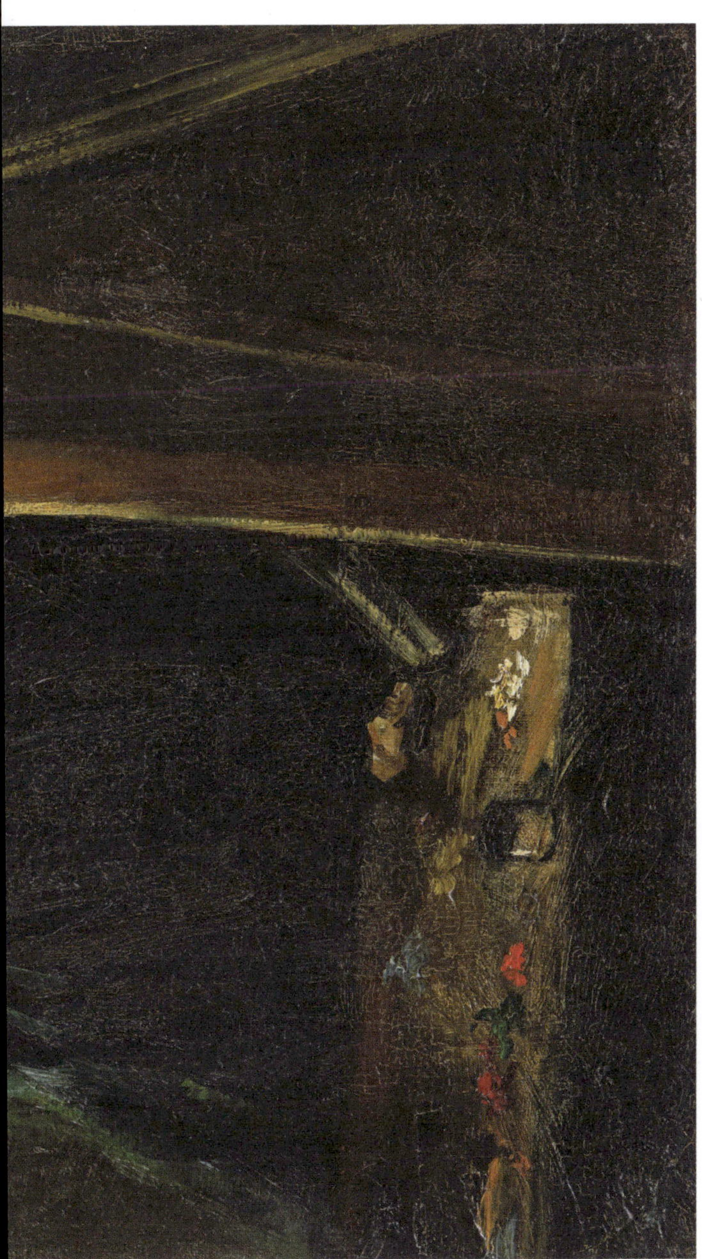

Self-Portrait or Portrait of Theo van Gogh

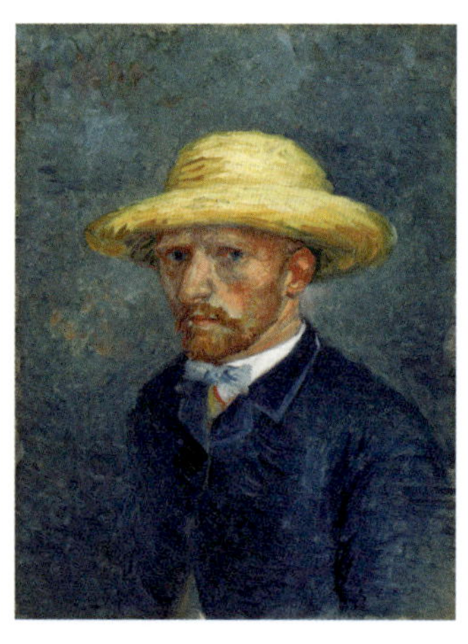

Oil on cardboard
19 cm × 14.1 cm
(7½ in × 5½ in)

Summer 1887
Paris

In 2011 it was suggested that this painting, previously thought to be a self-portrait of Vincent van Gogh, was actually of his younger brother Theo (1857–1891). After further studies, the Van Gogh Museum concluded that the subject couldn't be identified definitively and gave the work this double title.

Whoever the portrait represents, it allows us to shine light on Theo, whose importance in Vincent's life cannot be overstated. Most of Vincent's letters were written to Theo, and it's thanks to him that this extensive correspondence has been preserved. While the brothers' relationship was sometimes strained, they believed in each other wholeheartedly.

Theo supported Vincent financially, and Vincent saw him as a collaborator, as indicated by a letter of April 1888: 'So here's a plan of attack that will cost us some of the best paintings we've made together' (592). On Theo's side, he never doubted his brother's skill, writing presciently: 'I regard the money I give [Vincent] as payment for his work and as such he earns it. Perhaps it will take a long time, but one day it will be valuable.' (n.7, 508)

Self-Portrait or
Portrait of Theo van Gogh

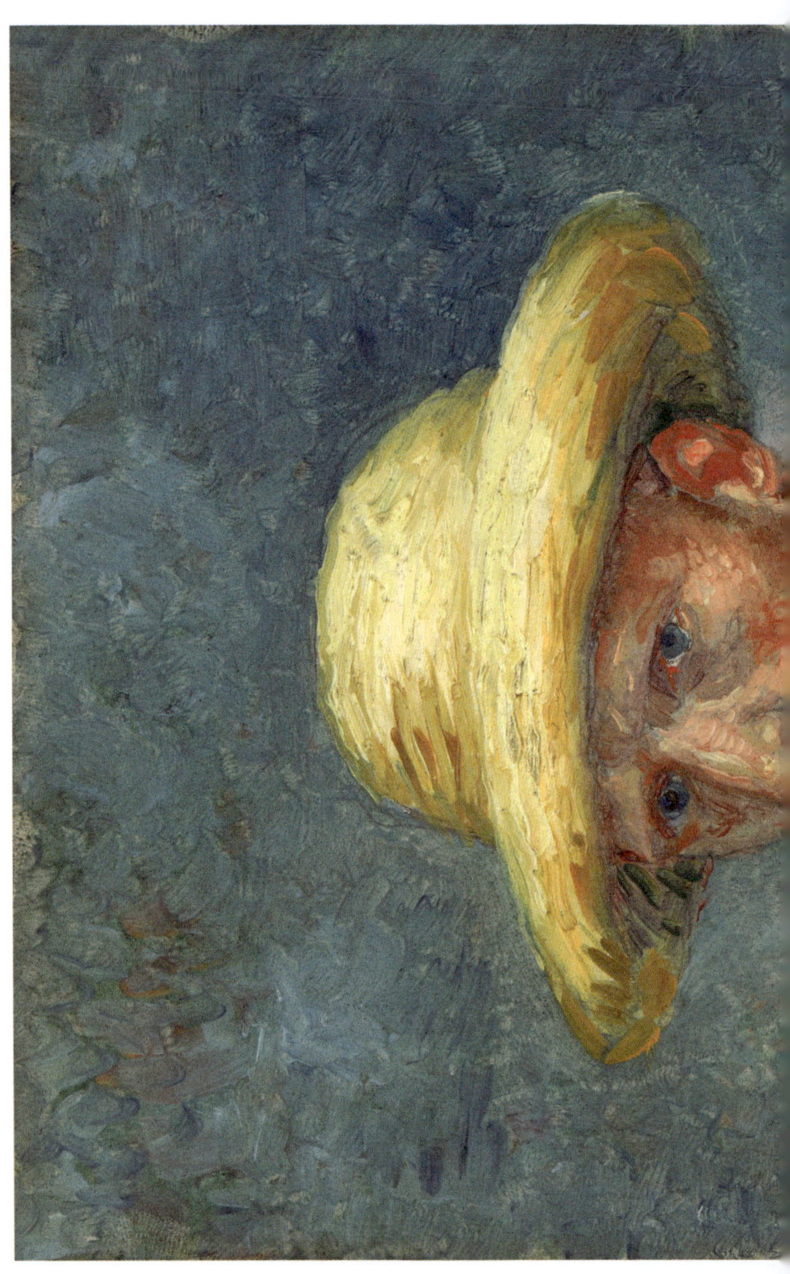

Summer 1887
Paris

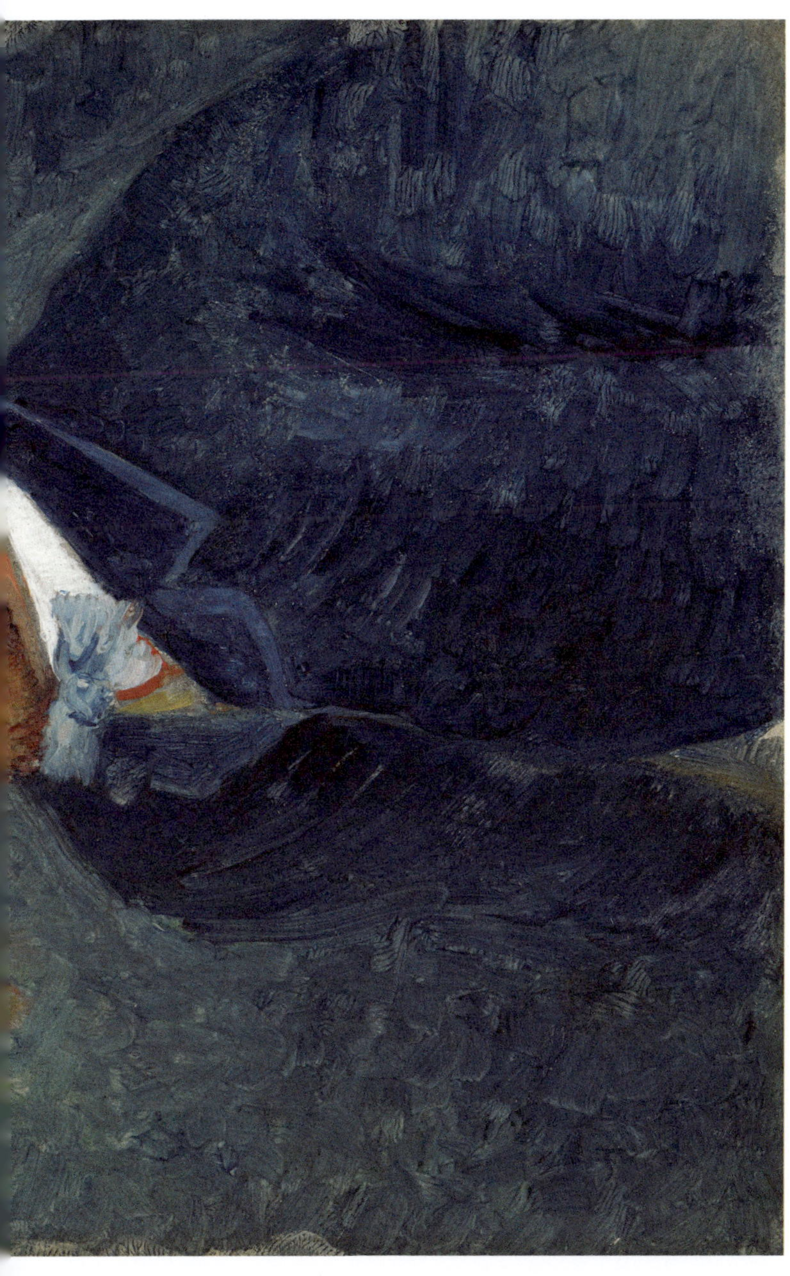

Terrace and Observation Deck at the Moulin de Blute-Fin, Montmartre

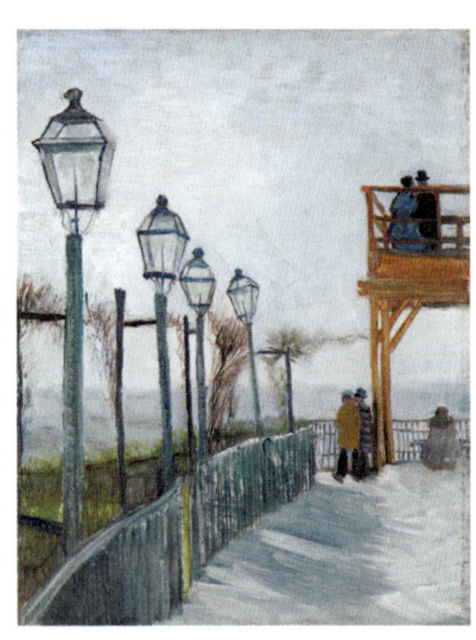

Oil on canvas
43.6 cm × 33 cm
(17⅛ in × 13 in)

Early 1887
Paris

This small oil painting recalls Van Gogh's earlier use of greys (see *Beach at Scheveningen in Stormy Weather* on page 8), but how much lighter and more luminous these shades are now. The sky is washed with white and blue, but look at the terrace's animated paving, with its broad, sweeping strokes!

Around this time, Van Gogh also painted a series of studies of windmills, including the Moulin de Blute-Fin, which was not far from Vincent and Theo's Montmartre apartment. The terrace and observation deck next to this windmill offered panoramic views of the city but, such is the horizontal band of blue-grey mist in this painting, they appear to look out to the sea. The cool, wintry landscape is enlivened by the green grass on the left and by several warm elements – the leafless branches, a sightseer's tawny coat and the architectural structure of the observation deck.

The painting's daring compositional angle is matched in its ingenuity by the depiction of the wavy fence, lively lampposts and terrace paving. As much as the canvas is a great Impressionist work, it is also an early indication of Van Gogh's ability to imbue a subject with expressive life.

Terrace and Observation Deck at the Moulin de Blute-Fin, Montmartre

'Paris is Paris. There is but one Paris and however hard living may be here, and if it became worse and harder even – the French air clears up the brain and does good – a world of good.'

- Vincent van Gogh

Early 1887
Paris

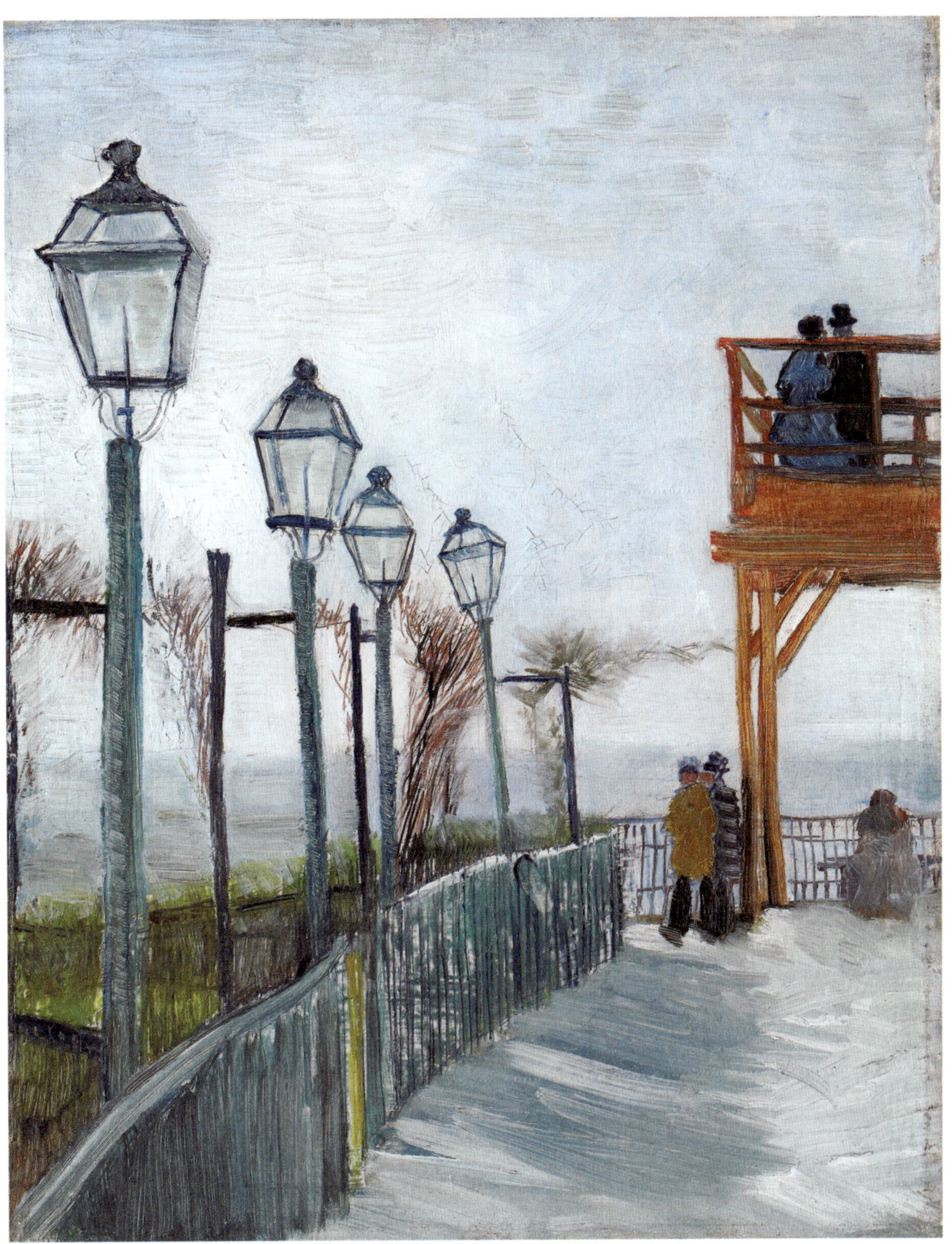

Agostina Segatori Sitting in the Café du Tambourin

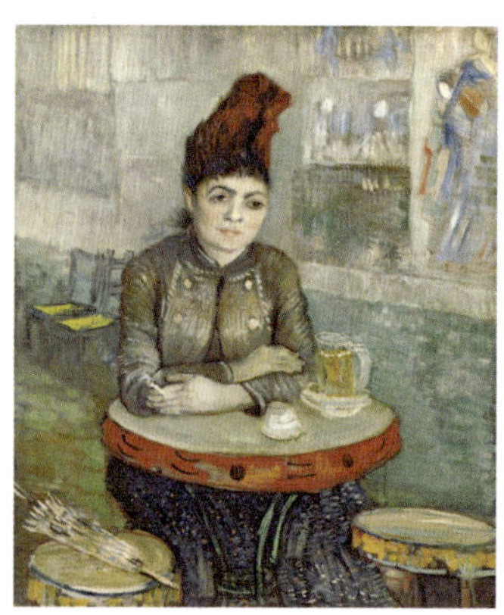

Oil on canvas
55.5 cm × 47 cm
(21⅞ in × 18½ in)

January-March 1887
Paris

Van Gogh didn't have much luck with love. In his late twenties, he fell head-over-heels for his cousin Kee Vos-Stricker, but she rejected him. In The Hague he lived with Sien Hoornik for a time (see *Congregation Leaving the Reformed Church in Nuenen* on page 12), and when he moved back in with his parents in Nuenen, he had a brief but doomed courtship with a neighbour, Margot Begemann.

When Van Gogh moved to Paris, he frequented the popular Montmartre artists' hangout the Café du Tambourin, and he had a love affair with its Italian owner and former artist's model, Agostina Segatori. In this painting from early 1887, Van Gogh depicts Segatori at one of the café's signature 'tambourine' tables, with a cigarette in hand and a beer to the side. The vertical form of her elaborate red headpiece is mirrored by the image on the wall, likely one of the Japanese prints Van Gogh included in an exhibition he organised that spring (see *Japonaiserie: Flowering Plum Tree (after Hiroshige)* on page 64).

After Van Gogh moved to the city of Arles in the south of France, he seems to have resigned himself to living, as he told his friend Bernard, 'like a monk who goes to the brothel once a fortnight' (632).

Agostina Segatori Sitting in the Café du Tambourin

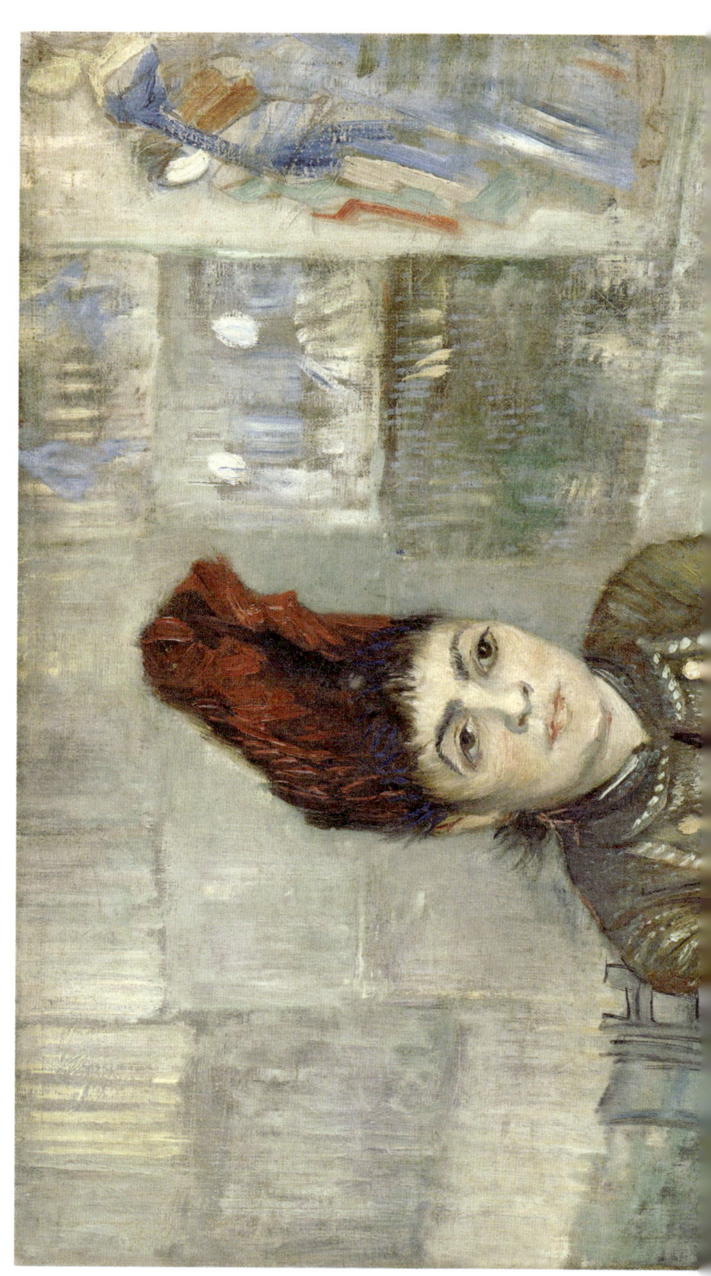

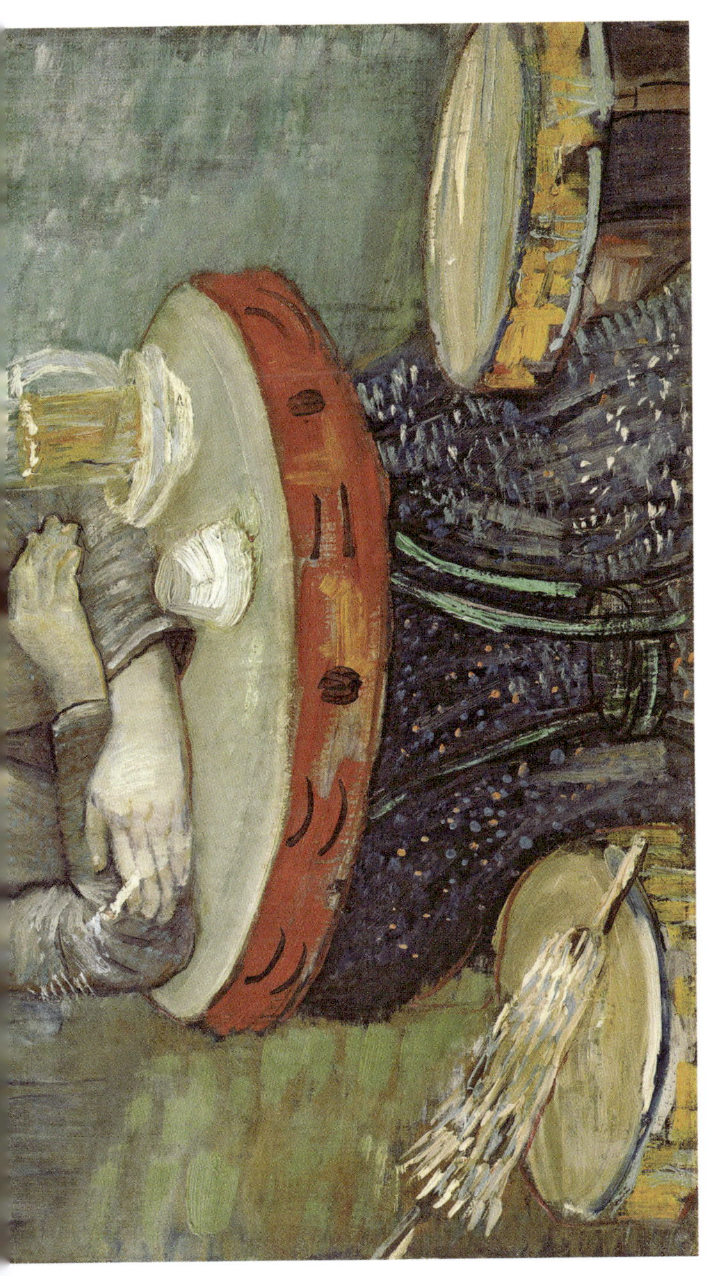

Still Life with Basket of Apples

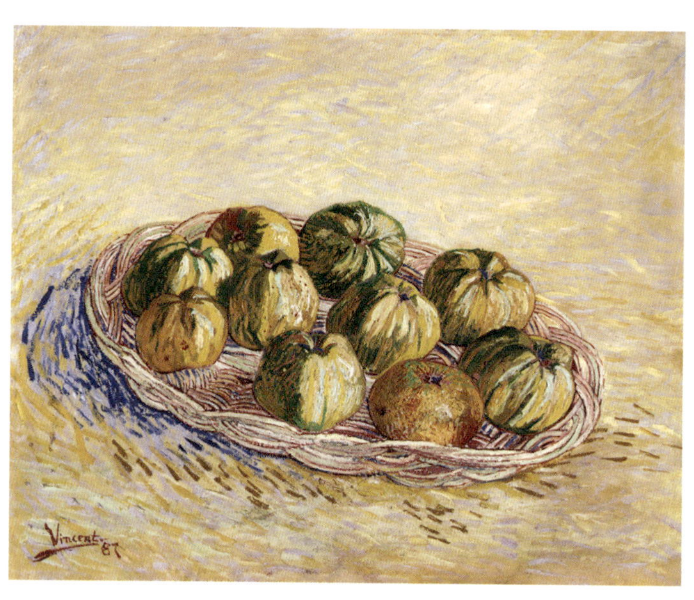

Oil on canvas
46.7 cm × 55.3 cm
(18⅜ in × 21¾ in)

Late 1887
Paris

If we compare *Vase with Poppies* (page 40) with this still life, we see how much Van Gogh's artistic concerns changed over the course of a year. In the earlier composition, painted in summer 1886, there is a sense of spatial depth. This has been largely eliminated here, where the basket of apples is located in a field of repeated brushstrokes. We are presented with a close-up view of the objects accentuated by the basket being tipped forward, a technique reminiscent of Paul Cézanne.

This viewpoint has the effect of focusing our attention on what is represented and, particularly, on *how* and *with what*. The apples are constructed from strokes of yellow, green and red and highlighted with thick patches of white. The fruits' stem and blossom ends are rendered in dabs of burgundy and indigo. These colours are mirrored in the weave of the basket, while the indigo is repeated in the basket's cast shadow, which is also a flurry of paint strokes.

Considering Van Gogh's remarkable ability to draw our attention to the beauty of everyday objects and the creative possibilities of paint, it is no wonder he so prominently signed this canvas 'Vincent 87'.

Still Life with Basket of Apples

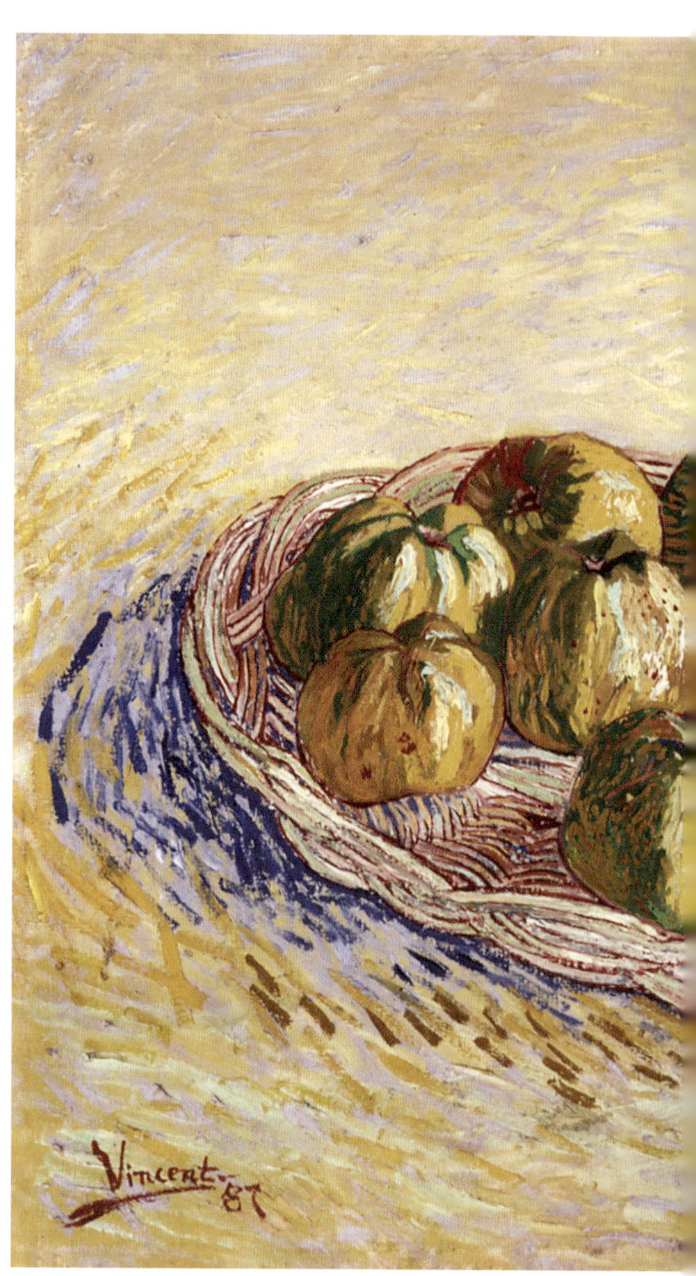

Late 1887
Paris

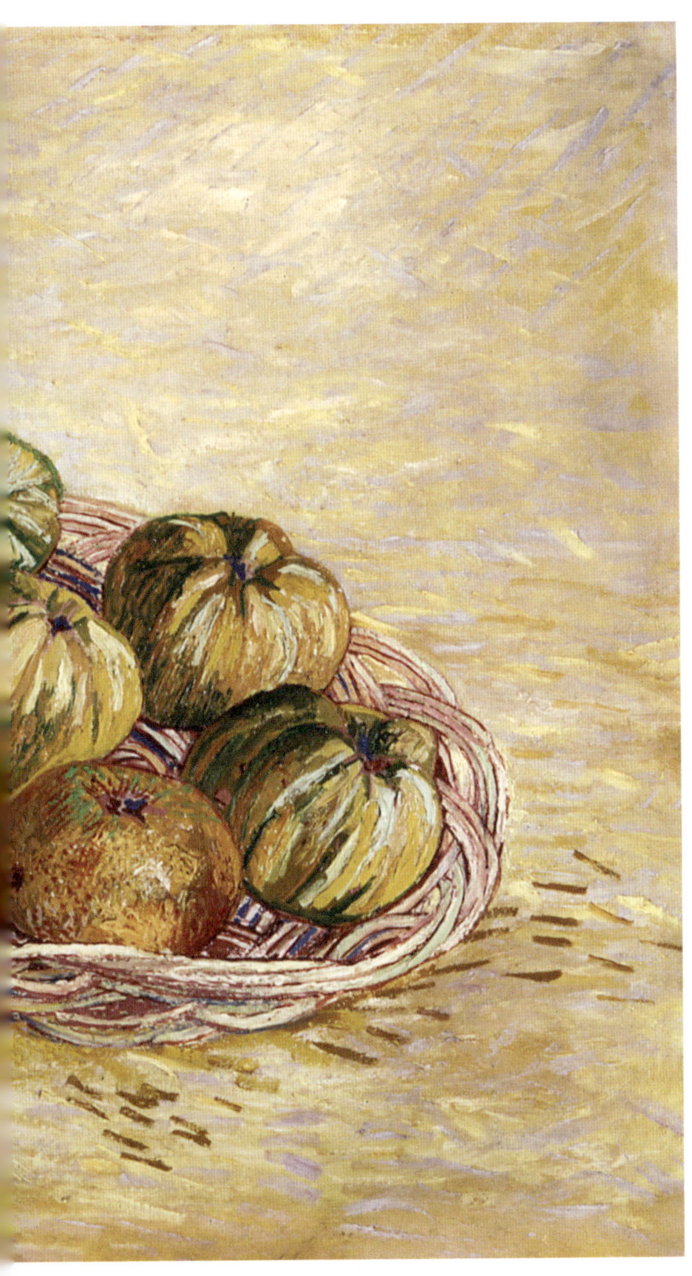

Japonaiserie: Flowering Plum Tree (after Hiroshige)

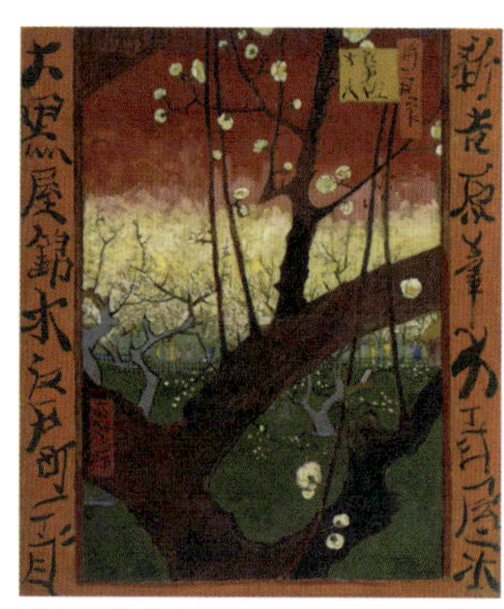

Oil on canvas
55.6 cm × 46.8 cm
(21⅞ in × 18⅜ in)

October-November 1887
Paris

When Van Gogh arrived in Antwerp in November 1885, he wrote to Theo that his studio was 'quite tolerable, mainly because I've pinned a set of Japanese prints on the walls that I find very diverting.' (545) This is the first written reference to Van Gogh's interest in Japanese woodcut prints, but when he got to Paris he found them a significant focus of the art-world vanguard (see *Portrait of Père Tanguy* on page 68).

Van Gogh made trips to the shop of Siegfried Bing, a dealer in Japanese prints, and he began to amass quite a collection (now in Amsterdam's Van Gogh Museum). In March–April 1887, Van Gogh even organised an exhibition of Japanese prints at the Café du Tambourin, a frequent hangout for the city's artists and literati (see *Agostina Segatori Sitting in the Café du Tambourin* on page 56).

This oil painting is one of three copies Van Gogh made of Japanese prints. It's based on Utagawa Hiroshige's *Plum Garden in Kameido* (1857), and Van Gogh was undoubtedly fascinated by Hiroshige's unusual composition and strong colour harmonies, features that influenced his works from then onwards.

Japonaiserie: Flowering Plum Tree (after Hiroshige)

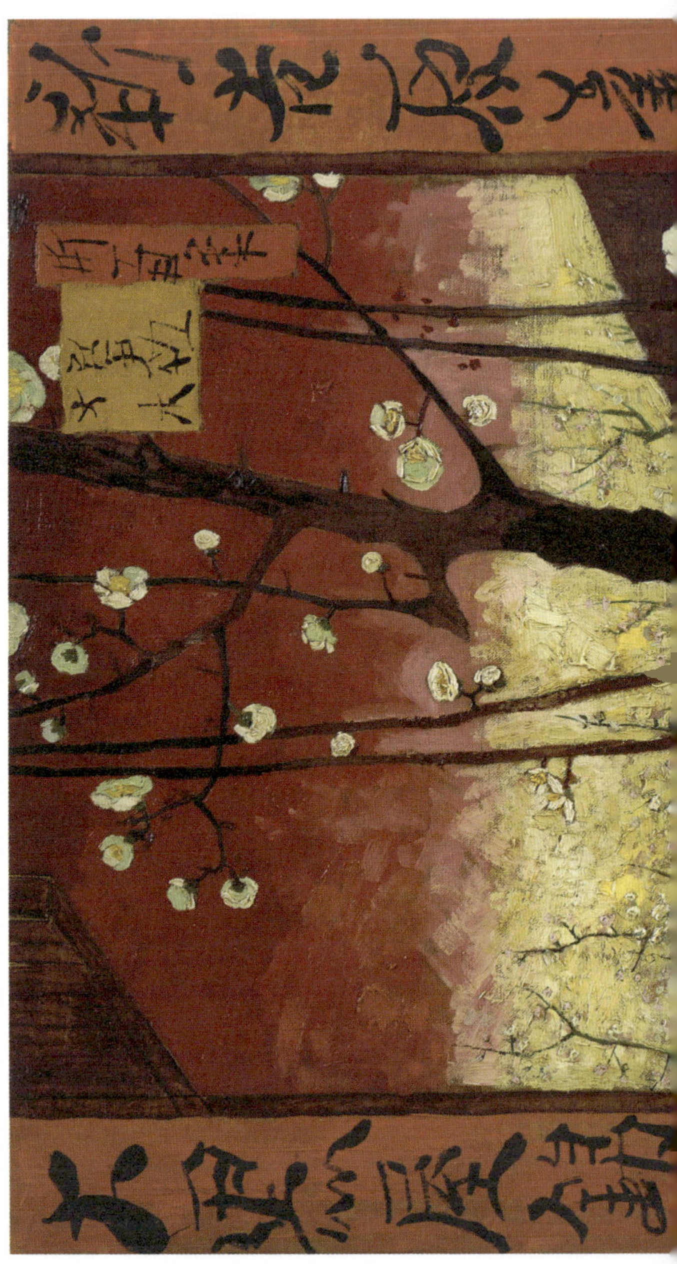

October-November 1887
Paris

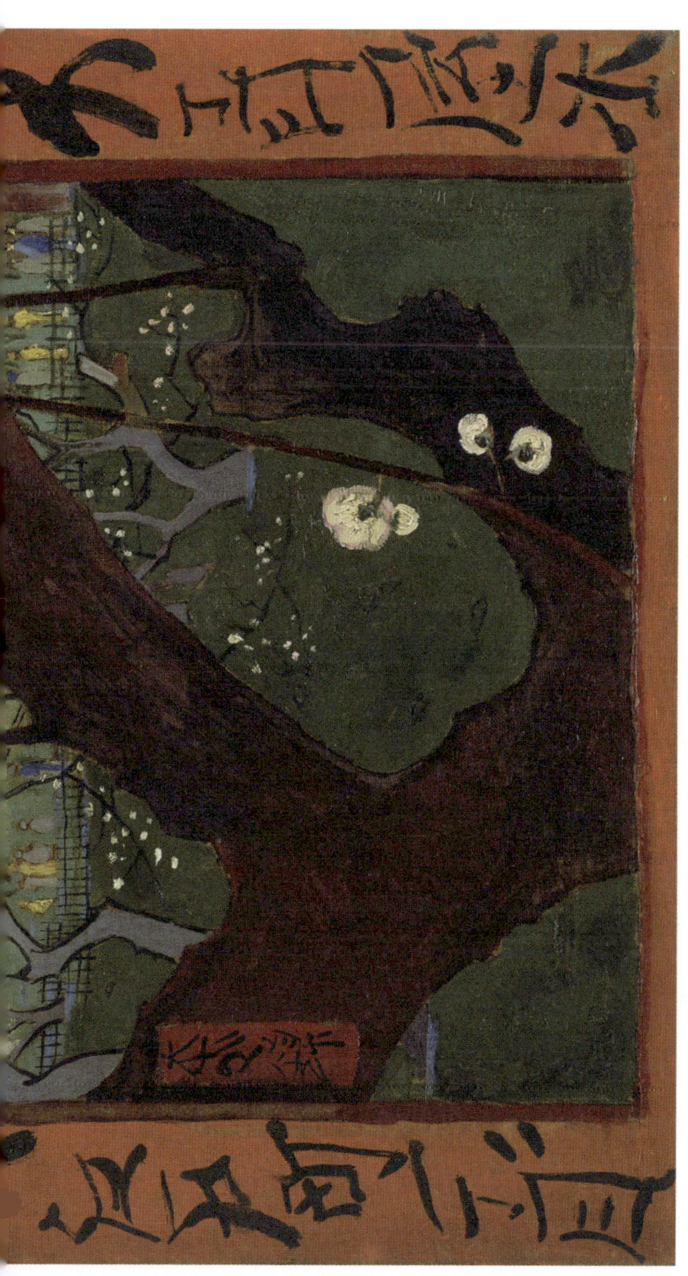

Portrait of Père Tanguy

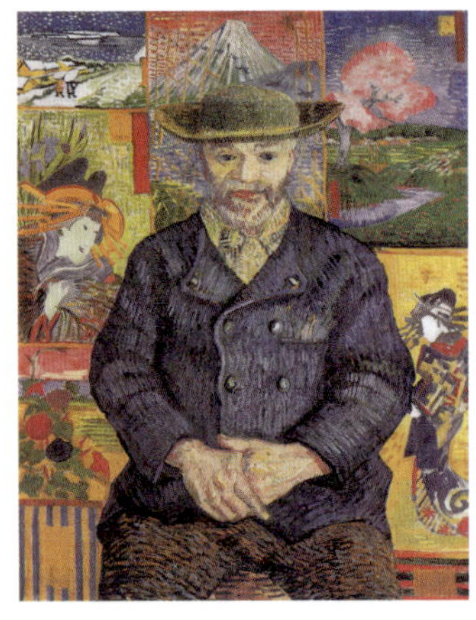

Oil on canvas
92 cm × 75 cm
(36¼ in × 29½ in)

Winter 1887-88
Paris

While in Paris, Van Gogh made three portraits of Julien François Tanguy, whose Montmartre art supply store was a hub for the avant-garde. Such was the esteem held for this great supporter of the painting community, he was affectionately termed 'Père' (Father) Tanguy.

Van Gogh's fondness for his sitter is clear. With his eyes lowered and hands clasped in front of him, Tanguy appears to be lost in his own thoughts. He is represented frontally and in the centre of the composition, surrounded by depictions of Japanese prints, which he and Van Gogh both admired. During this time, Van Gogh also painted three independent oil copies of Japanese woodcut prints (see *Japonaiserie: Flowering Plum Tree (after Hiroshige)* on page 64).

The prints' colour harmonies make a striking pictorial setting and are a foretaste of the bright hues Van Gogh would employ when he moved to Provence a few months later. By contrast, Tanguy wears a deep blue pea coat and earth-toned hat, shirt and trousers. It's as though one of the hard-working countryfolk Van Gogh so greatly empathised with has been transported to an art dealership specialising in Japanese art.

Portrait of Père Tanguy

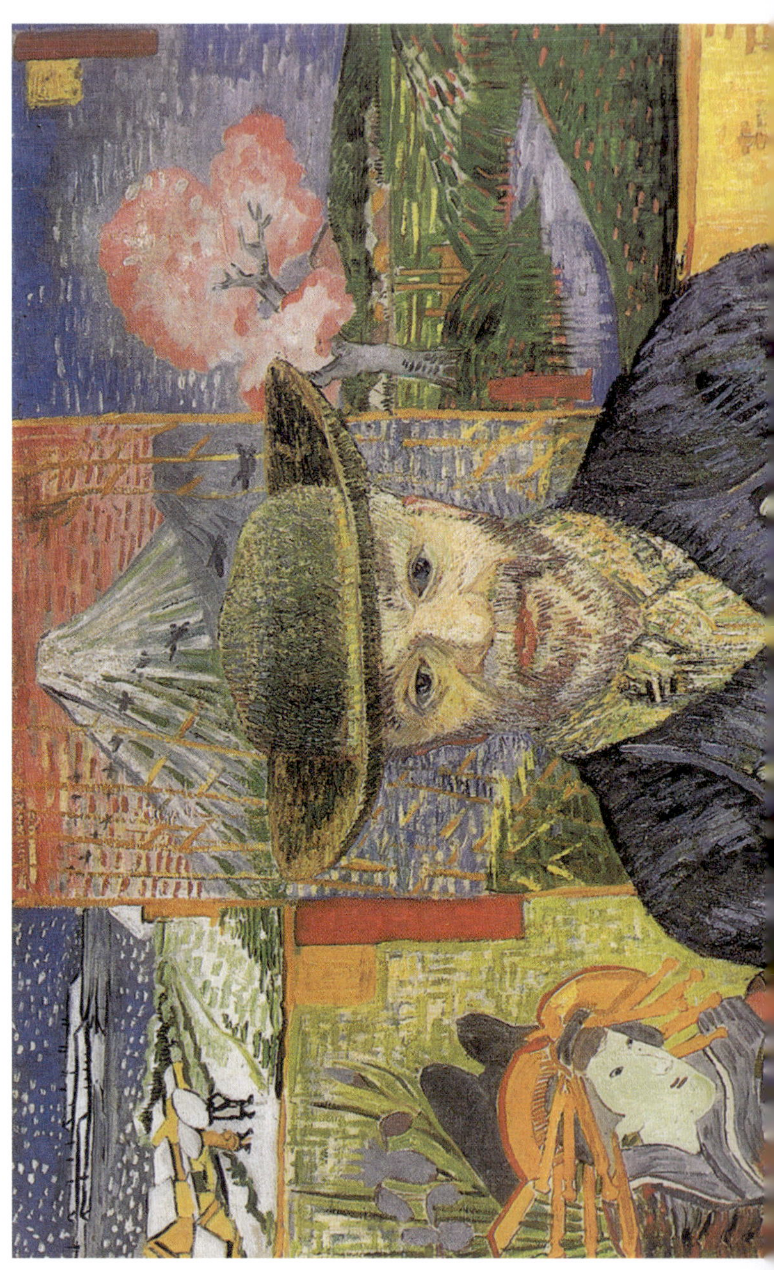

Winter 1887-88
Paris

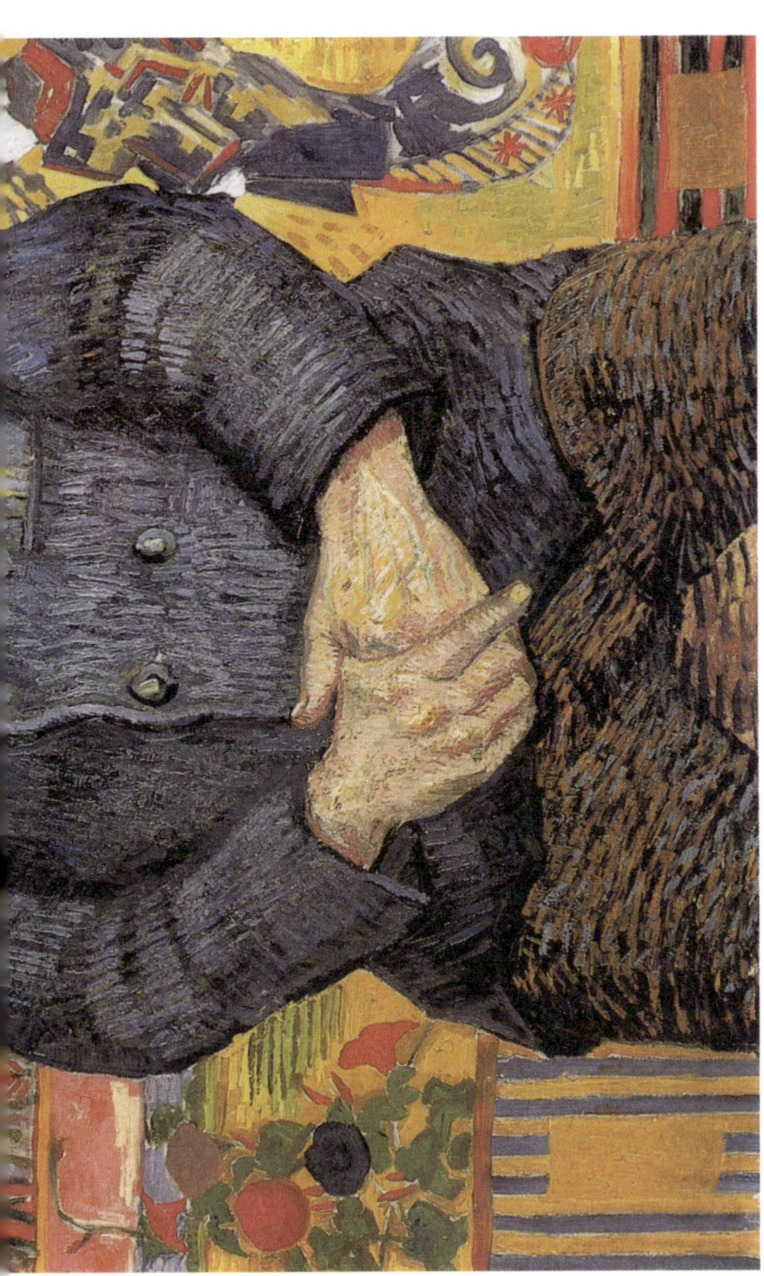

Self-Portrait with Grey Felt Hat

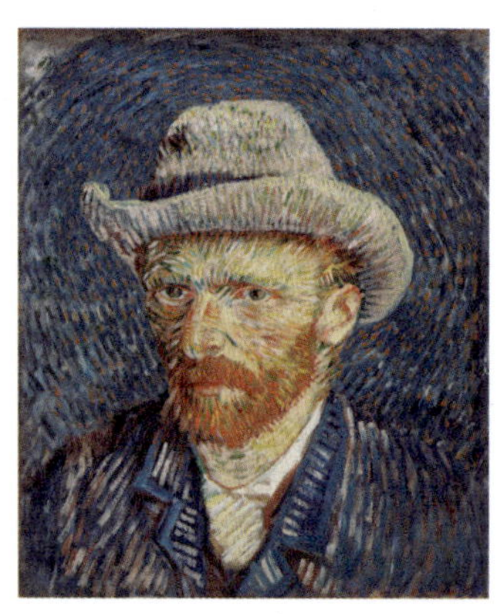

Oil on canvas
44.5 cm × 37.5 cm
(17½ in × 14¾ in)

Winter 1887
Paris

Viewing this self-portrait, from the latter part of 1887, alongside *Self-Portrait with Dark Felt Hat at the Easel* (page 44) from the previous winter, shows just how much Van Gogh's style changed during this period.

Three years earlier in Nuenen, Van Gogh had already expressed interest in contemporary colour theory, which he was able to read about in books. His stay in Antwerp introduced him to Rubens' rich colourism. Now in Paris, Van Gogh could see, in person, the expressive potentials of colour theory manifested in the paintings of Eugène Delacroix and of the Impressionists and Post-Impressionists.

Self-Portrait with Grey Felt Hat fuses these influences into a style that is all Van Gogh's own. The application of Pointillist russet dots upon the blue ground, which creates an unsettling vortex effect, gives way to longer dashes of complementary colours in the construction of Van Gogh's head and clothing. While his serious expression furthers a sense of disquiet, we cannot help but be struck by the portrait's new boldness and its confident proficiency of execution.

Self-Portrait with Grey Felt Hat

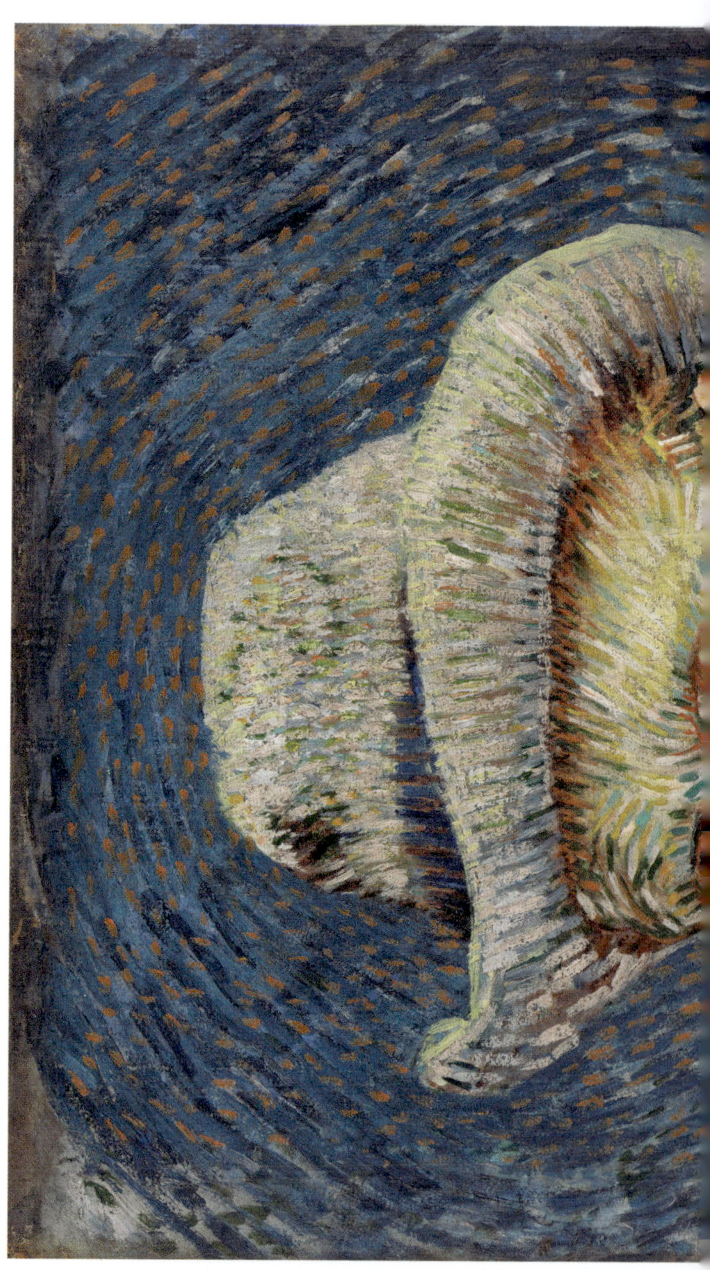

Winter 1887
Paris

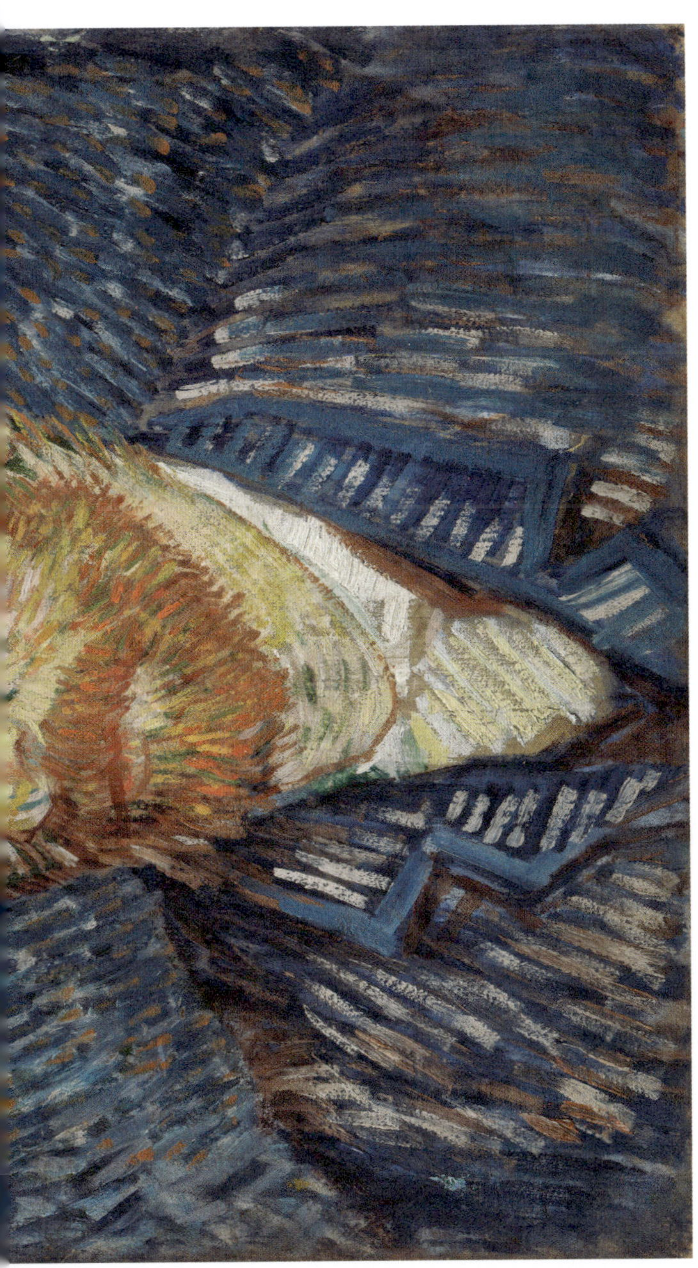

The Langlois Bridge at Arles with Women Washing

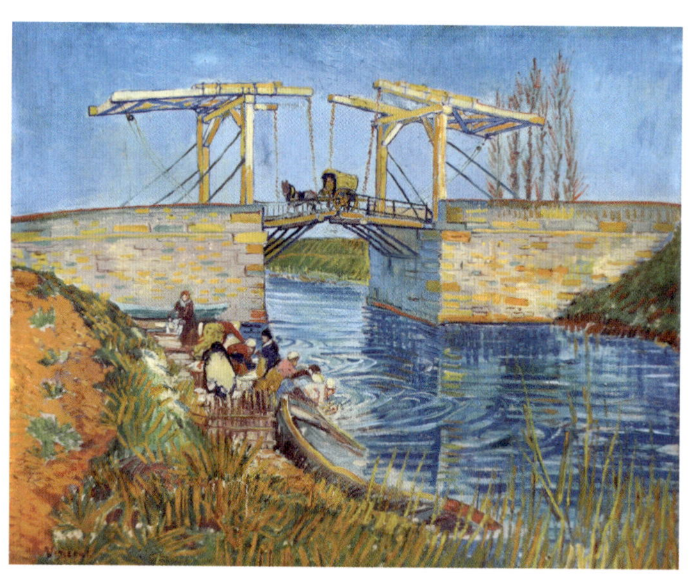

Oil on canvas
54 cm × 65 cm
(21¼ in × 25⅝ in)

March 1888
Arles

As early as autumn 1886 Van Gogh considered moving to the south of France. He wrote to his painter friend Horace Mann Livens: 'In spring – say February or even sooner – I may be going to the south of France, the land of the *blue* tones and gay colours.' (569) By the time Van Gogh left Paris for Arles in February 1888, he was physically and mentally exhausted. Relocation to Provence gave him the chance to recuperate from the pressures of Paris. As this painting shows, it also gave him 'the *blue* tones and gay colours' he was searching for.

In the first few months in Arles, Van Gogh painted a series of landscape paintings, including several studies of the Langlois drawbridge. This version – an early Arles masterpiece – shows a horse and carriage crossing the bridge and washerwomen on the canal bank. Both the sky and water are painted in vivid shades of blue. The former is calmly uniform; the latter's depth and movement are conveyed through a series of varying hues and brushstrokes. Particularly captivating are the deep blue and yellow-green dashes representing the stone bridge's reflection in the water and the energetic swirls of paint that convey the water's disturbance.

The Langlois Bridge at Arles with Women Washing

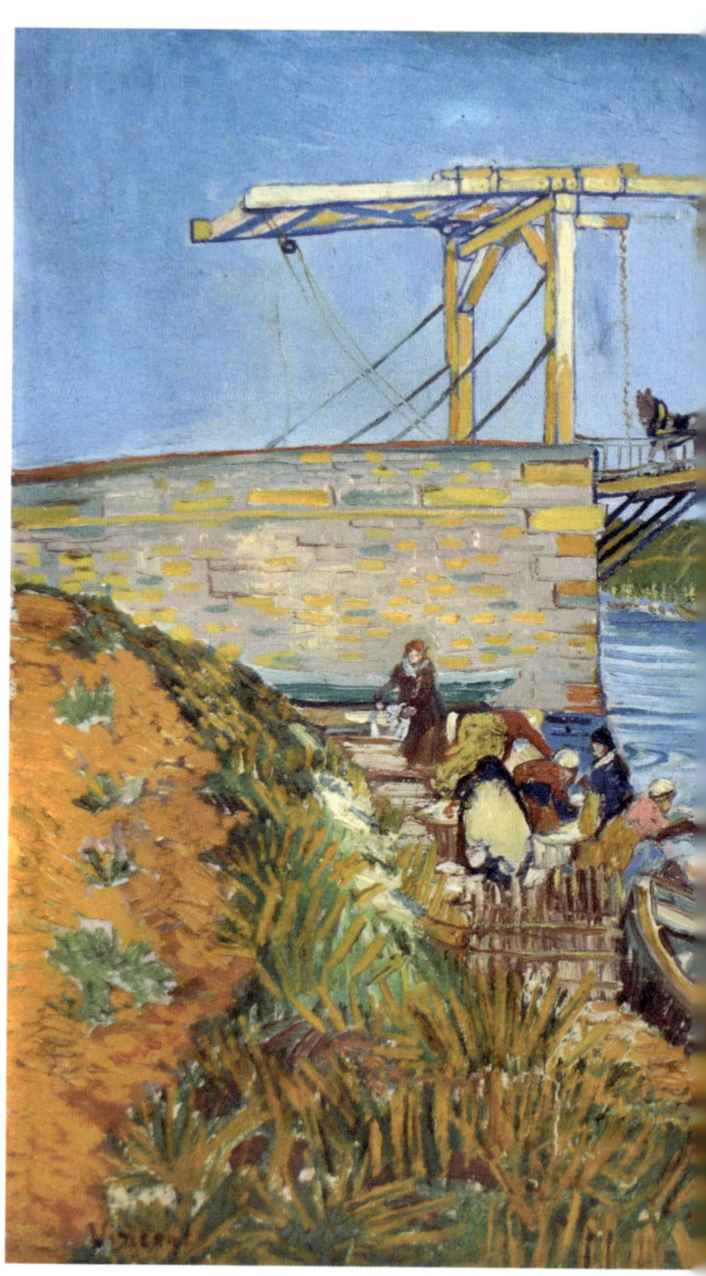

March 1888
Arles

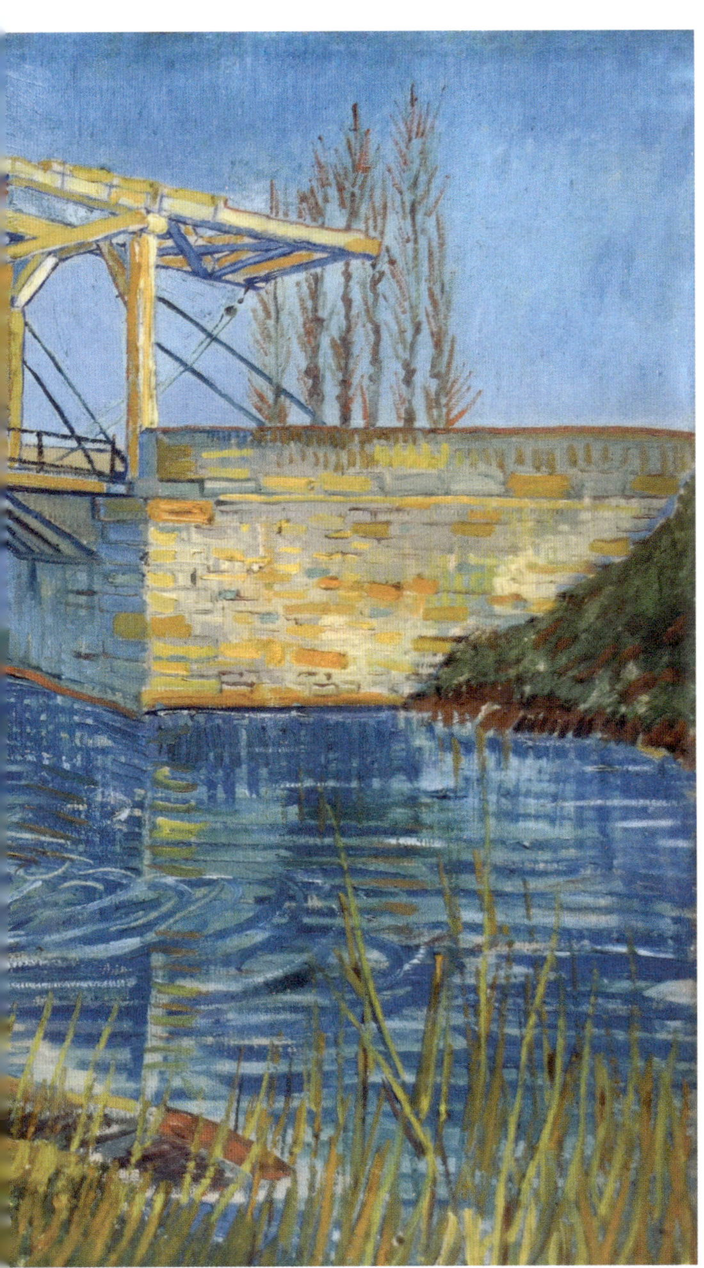

The Flowering Orchard

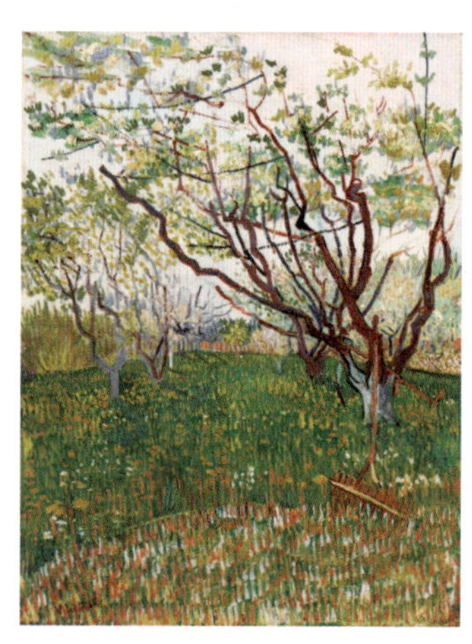

Oil on canvas
72.4 cm × 53.3 cm
(28½ in × 21 in)

March-April 1888
Arles

Spring in Arles presented Van Gogh, who so greatly loved nature, with a subject he embraced with unbridled enthusiasm. At the beginning of April 1888, he wrote to Theo: 'I'm in a fury of work as the trees are in blossom and I wanted to do a Provence orchard of tremendous gaiety' (592).

Fifteen paintings of orchards have come down to us, all created in the brief period when the trees – including plum, peach, apricot, cherry, pear, apple and almond – were in bloom. In Van Gogh's 'fury of work', several of these studies were worked on simultaneously. Some are Impressionist in their quality of light, but others, like the present canvas, are more vibrantly coloured: the meadow is a mass of vertical strokes and the blossoms are painted daubs.

Van Gogh regarded Japan as a 'painters' paradise' (691) and thought that Provence was the closest he could get to reach that ideal. It is, then, revealing to compare the angularity of the trees in *The Flowering Orchard* with *Japonaiserie: Flowering Plum Tree (after Hiroshige)* (page 64), which Van Gogh painted in Paris. It would seem that in the springtime profusion of the south, Van Gogh found his Japan.

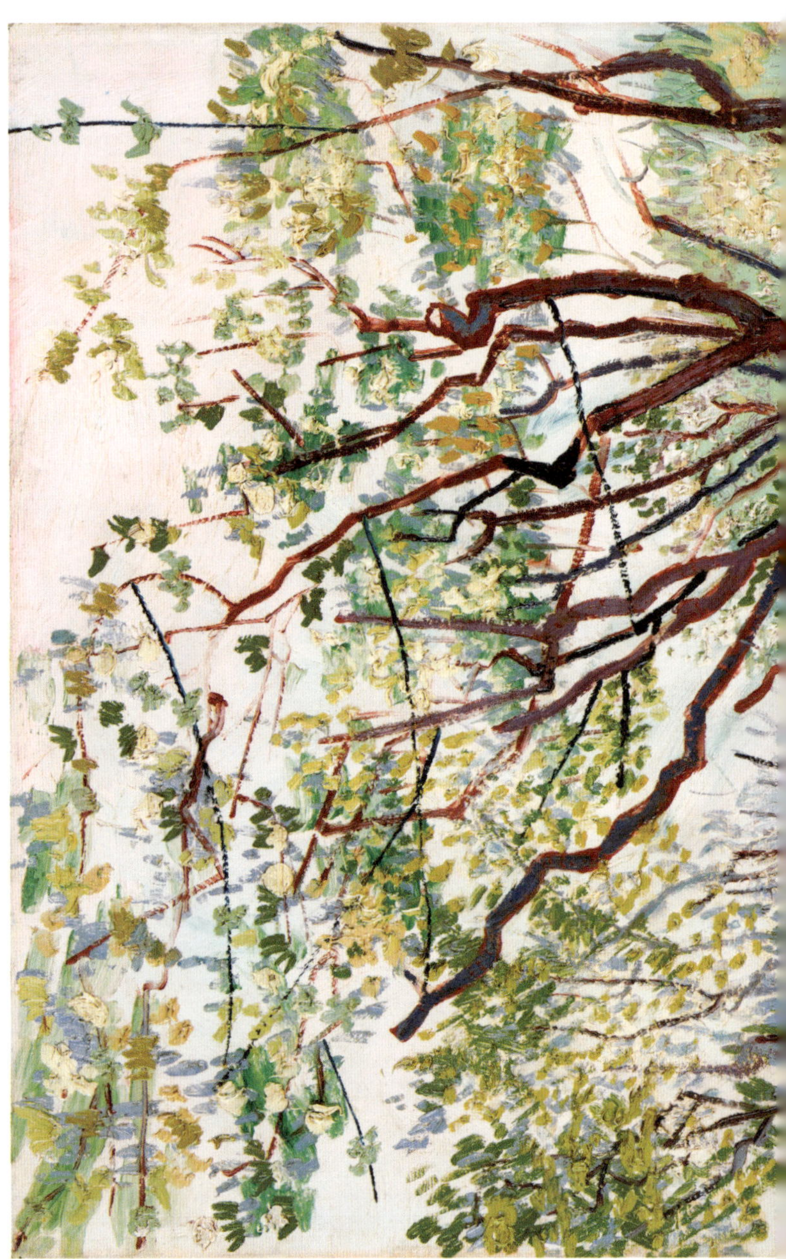

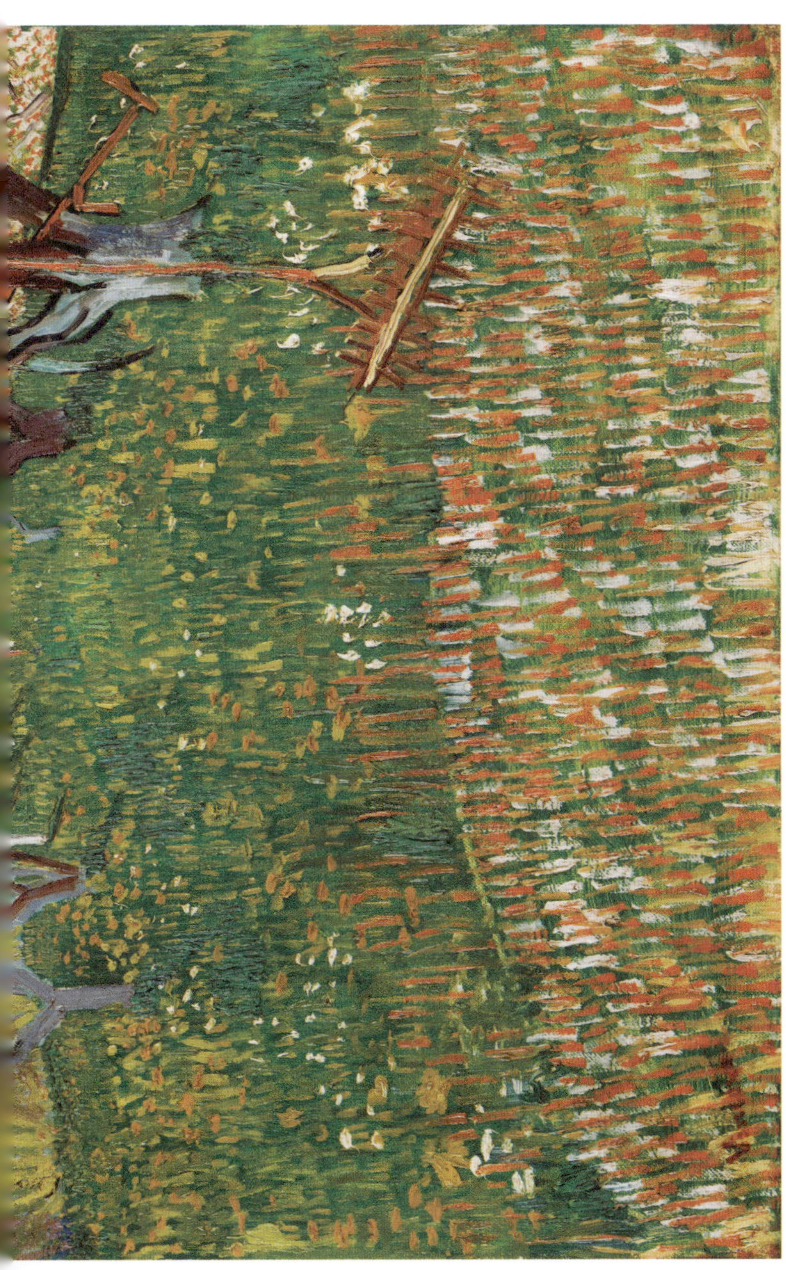

Sower with Setting Sun

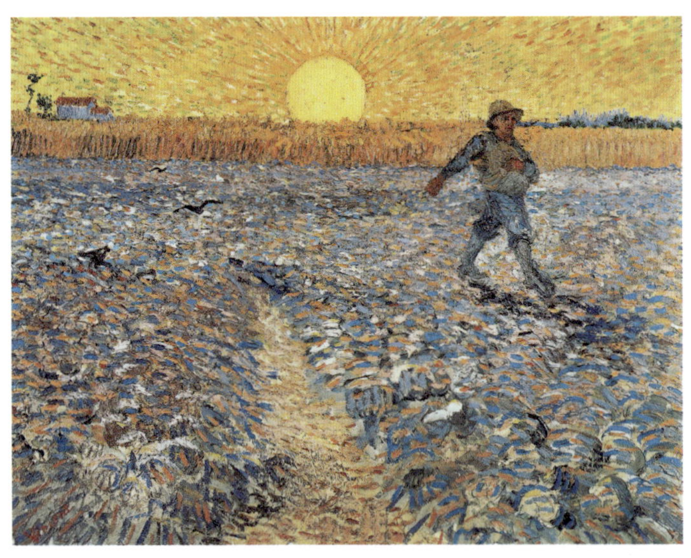

Oil on canvas
64.2 cm × 80.3 cm
(25¼ in × 31⅝ in)

June 1888
Arles

On 21 June 1888, Van Gogh wrote to Theo that he'd 'had a week of concentrated hard work in the wheatfields right out in the sun, the result was some studies of wheatfields, landscapes and – a sketch of a sower.' (629) This was not a new subject for Van Gogh. He'd copied Millet's *The Sower* (1850) during his early artistic training and painted his own depictions while in the Netherlands. But now, in the south of France, the figure was to be transformed by colour.

While the sketch would become this commanding painting, the magnitude of the task was clear. Van Gogh initially put the sketch aside, 'hardly daring to think about it.' (629) A week later, though, he reported that he had begun the painting. The clear intention was to make a work of the same consequence as Millet's:

'Millet's sower is colourless *grey*. ... Can we now paint the sower with colour, with simultaneous contrast between yellow and purple for example ... yes or no? *Yes* – definitely. So do it then! – yes – that's what [the art dealer] *père* Martin says too, "you must make the masterpiece".' (634) And so Van Gogh did.

Sower with Setting Sun

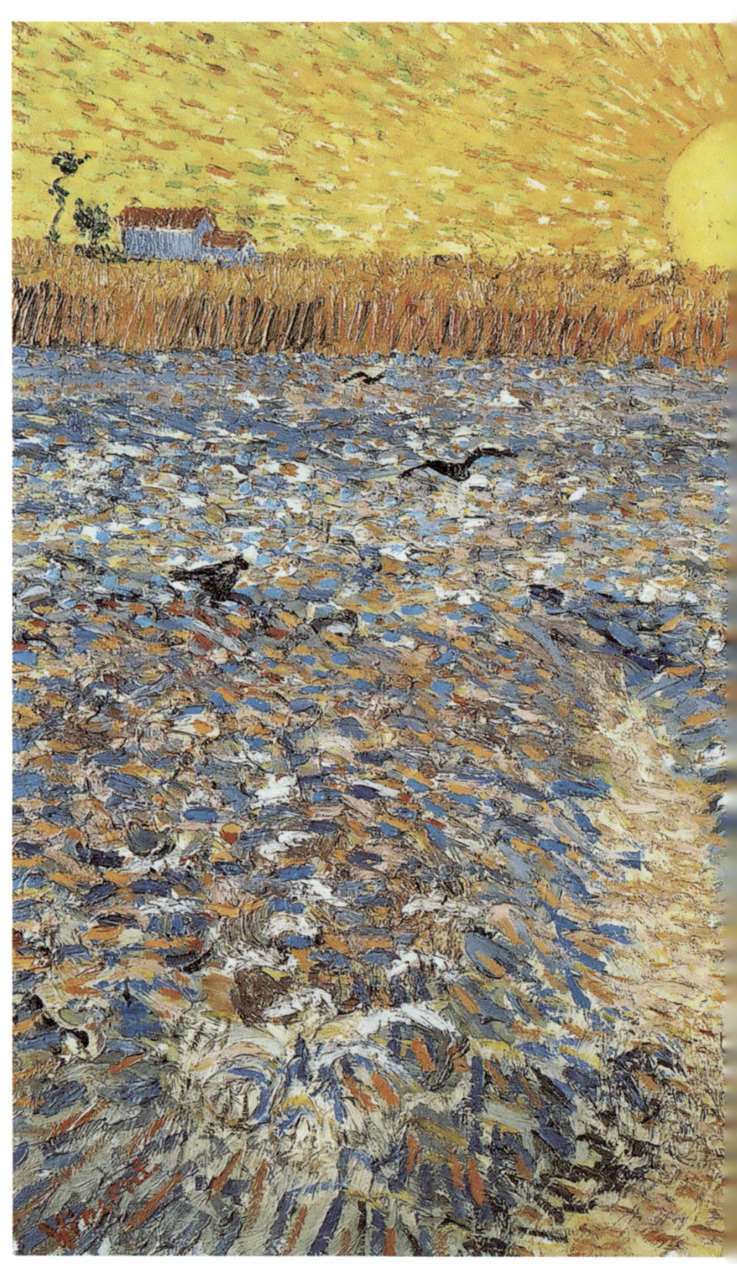

June 1888
Arles

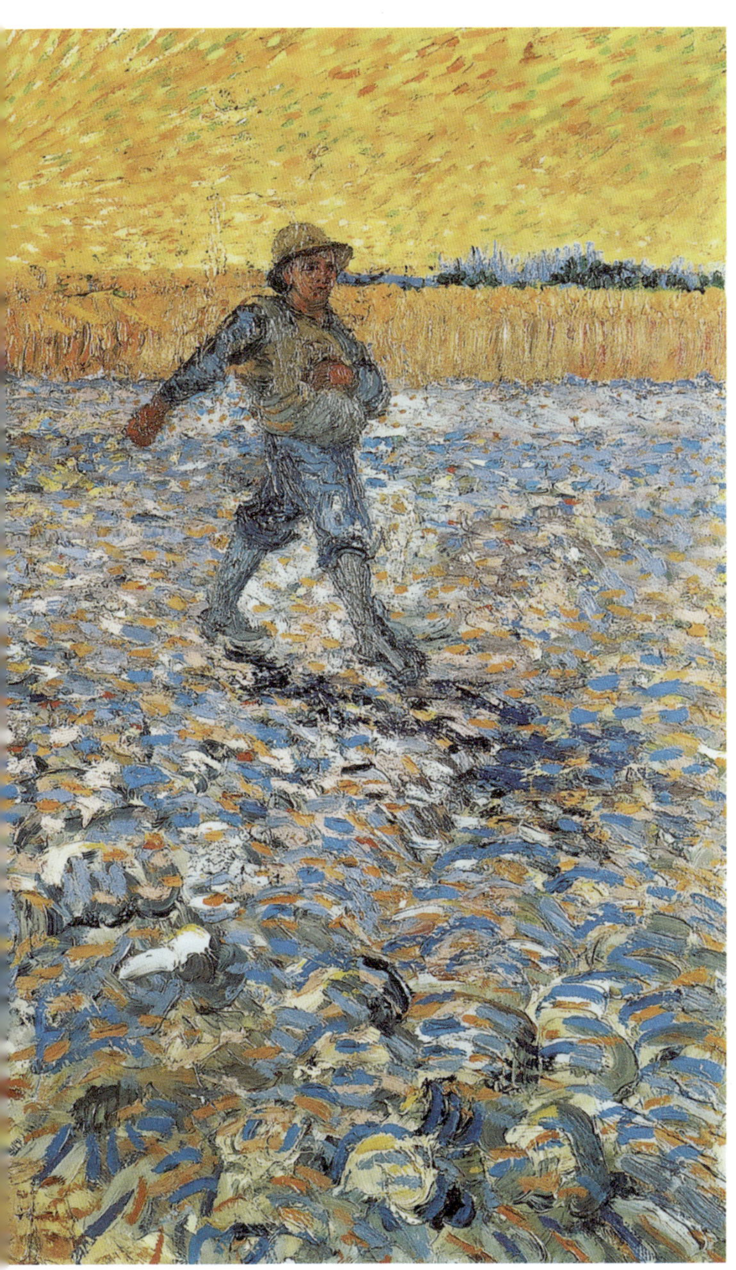

Portrait of the Postman Joseph Roulin

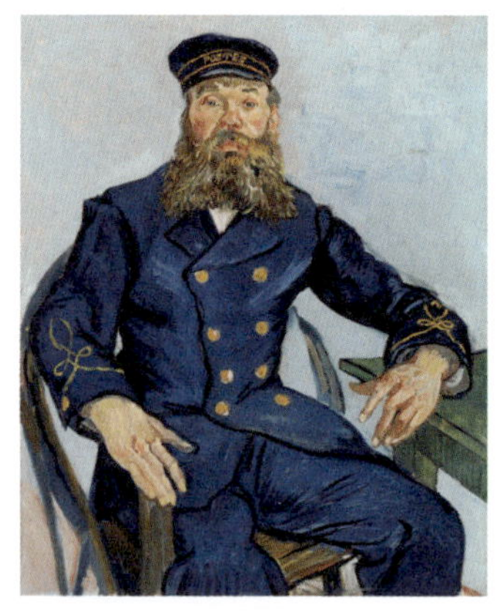

Oil on canvas
64.4 cm × 55.2 cm
(25⅜ in × 21¾ in)

July 1888
Arles

The deep blue and vivid yellow Van Gogh used in his early Provence painting *The Langlois Bridge at Arles with Women Washing* (page 76) are here picked up in the uniform of the postman Joseph Roulin. Represented against a pale blue background that reveals the white canvas, it is a wonderful portrait, full of character and warmth.

Van Gogh and Roulin met in Arles, and they became good friends. This is perhaps not surprising as Van Gogh described him to the artist Émile Bernard as 'a fierce republican, *like père Tanguy*' (655; see *Portrait of Père Tanguy* on page 68). Van Gogh painted Roulin several times and also made portraits of his wife and children.

In the same letter to Bernard, Van Gogh wrote that Roulin was a 'Socratic type, no less Socratic for being something of an alcoholic, and with a high colour as a result.' (655) Van Gogh captures the postman's ruddy complexion in the russet hues modelling his cheeks and nose. His full Socratic beard is created through a panoply of lively, earth-toned strokes. These features, alongside the depiction of his thoughtful eyes and large hands (his right rather roughly sketched), and that striking uniform, radiate both a powerful human and pictorial presence.

Portrait of the Postman Joseph Roulin

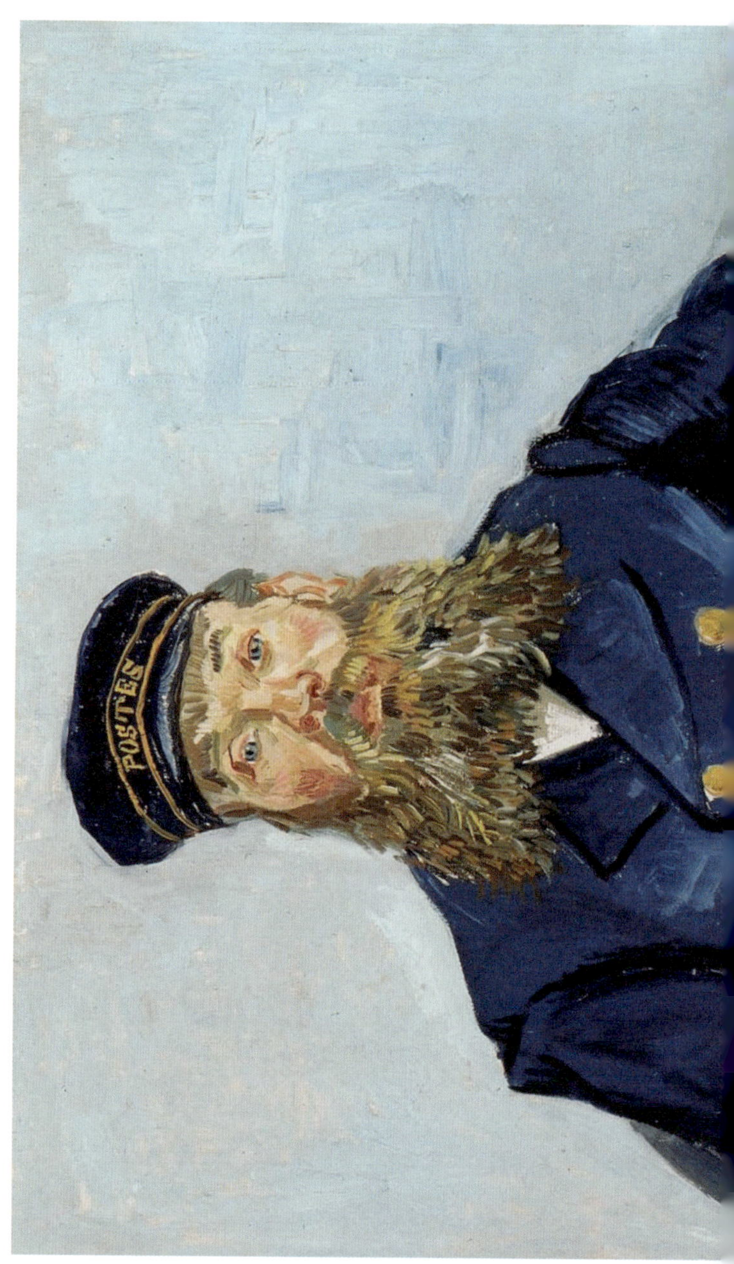

July 1888
Arles

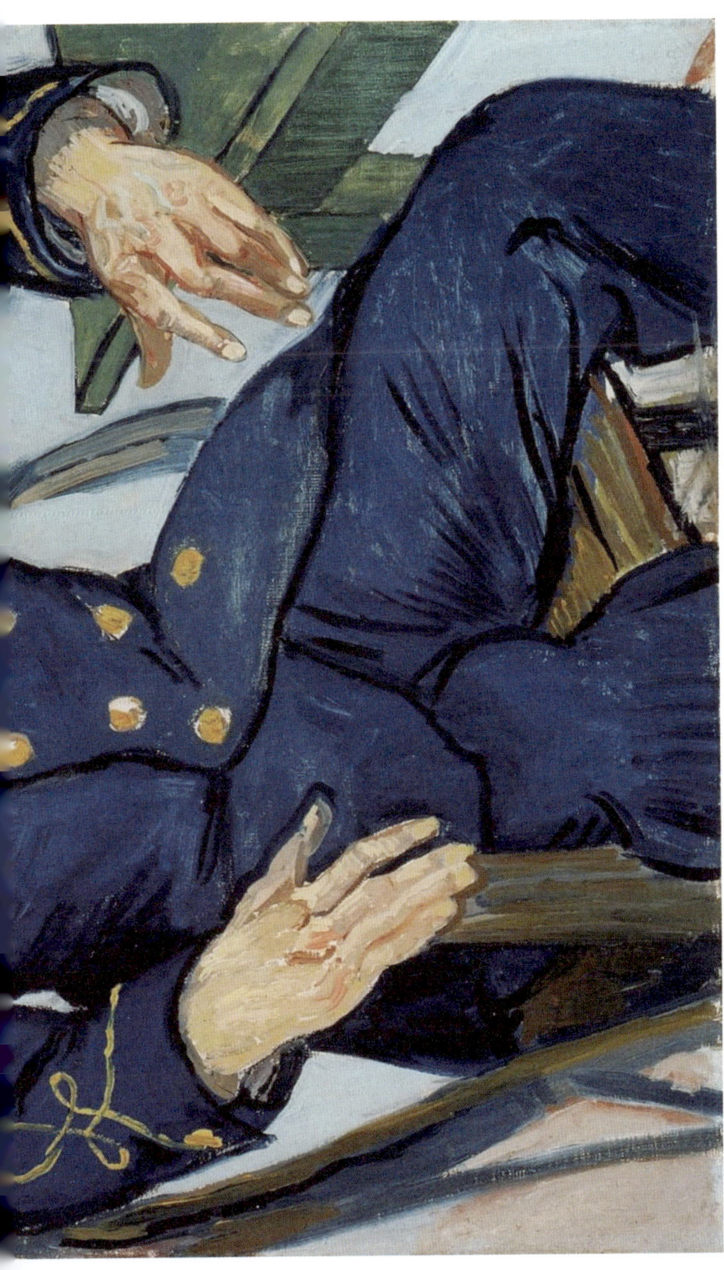

Sunflowers

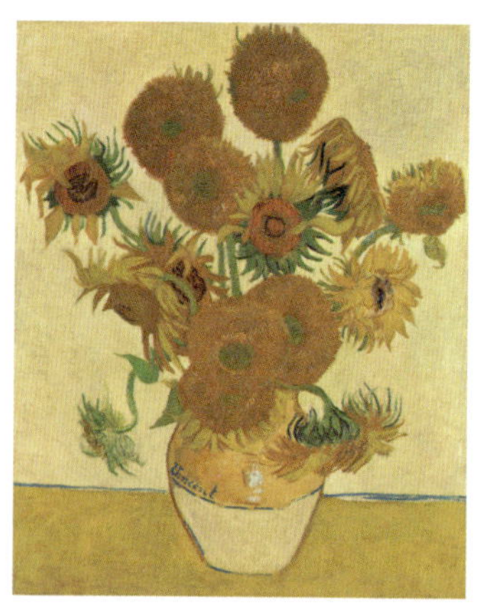

Oil on canvas
95 cm × 73 cm
(37⅜ in × 28¾ in)

August 1888
Arles

'I'm painting with the gusto of a Marseillais eating bouillabaisse, which won't surprise you when it's a question of painting *large SUNFLOWERS*.' (666) So wrote Van Gogh to his brother Theo in August 1888. Van Gogh had painted sunflowers in Paris, but it was in Provence that he created the versions that would become icons of his unique expressive style.

He made four different sunflower still lifes in August 1888, and three replicas in January 1889. They were intended for the Yellow House, which Van Gogh had rented in early May as a home and artist's studio. It was to be decorated in '*Nothing but large Sunflowers*' hung on blue backgrounds, creating 'a symphony in blue and yellow.' (666)

This painting of a vase of fifteen sunflowers at different stages of life is its own yellow symphony of varied tones and textures. The impasto of the seed heads is especially tactile. A lively rhythm is created by the vibrant green of the stalks and leaves, and by the blue used as a thin contour line and for the artist's prominent signature. In the south of France, where Van Gogh went to seek 'gay colours' (569), his sunflowers were odes to painterly possibilities.

August 1888
Arles

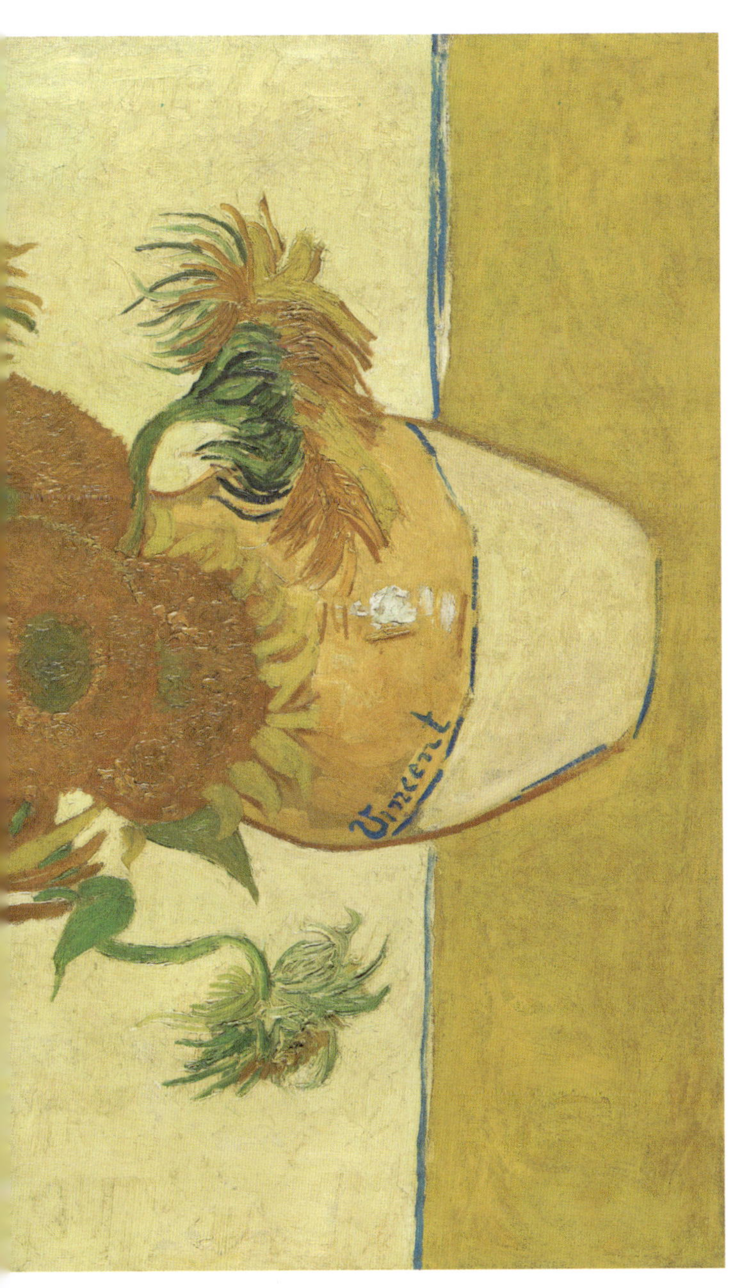

Shoes

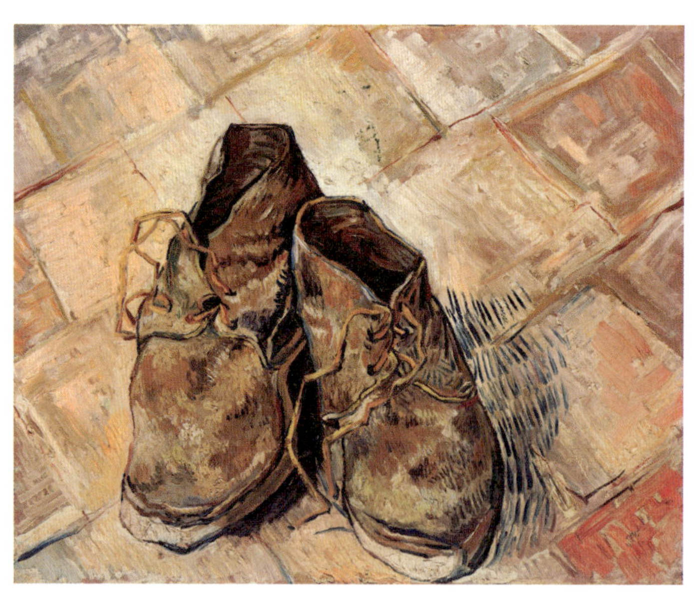

Oil on canvas
45.7 cm × 55.2 cm
(18 in × 21¾ in)

August 1888
Arles

For this 'still life of a pair of old shoes' (671), Van Gogh returned to a subject he had painted several times in Paris. The subject's meaning in Van Gogh's work is one of considerable debate among art historians. Old boots and shoes could represent the manual worker Van Gogh identified with, or it could be a reference to his wanderings and search for a place to settle. Or, more existentially, these old shoes might symbolise humankind's struggle and inevitable end.

In this painting the setting, at least, is clear. It is the russet tiled floor of *The Yellow House* (page 112), as can also be seen in *Van Gogh's Chair* (page 120). The tiles and shoes seem to be tipped towards us, the flooring in particular forming a decorative screen. Against this, the empty shoes appear highly animated. In part, this is achieved by their rumpled appearance, but this is accentuated by the shoelaces' rapidly worked strokes of yellow, orange, red and black. The deep blue parallel dashes to the right further this effect. Is this a shadow or a sign of vibrating movement? Certainly, in these shoes, there is still life!

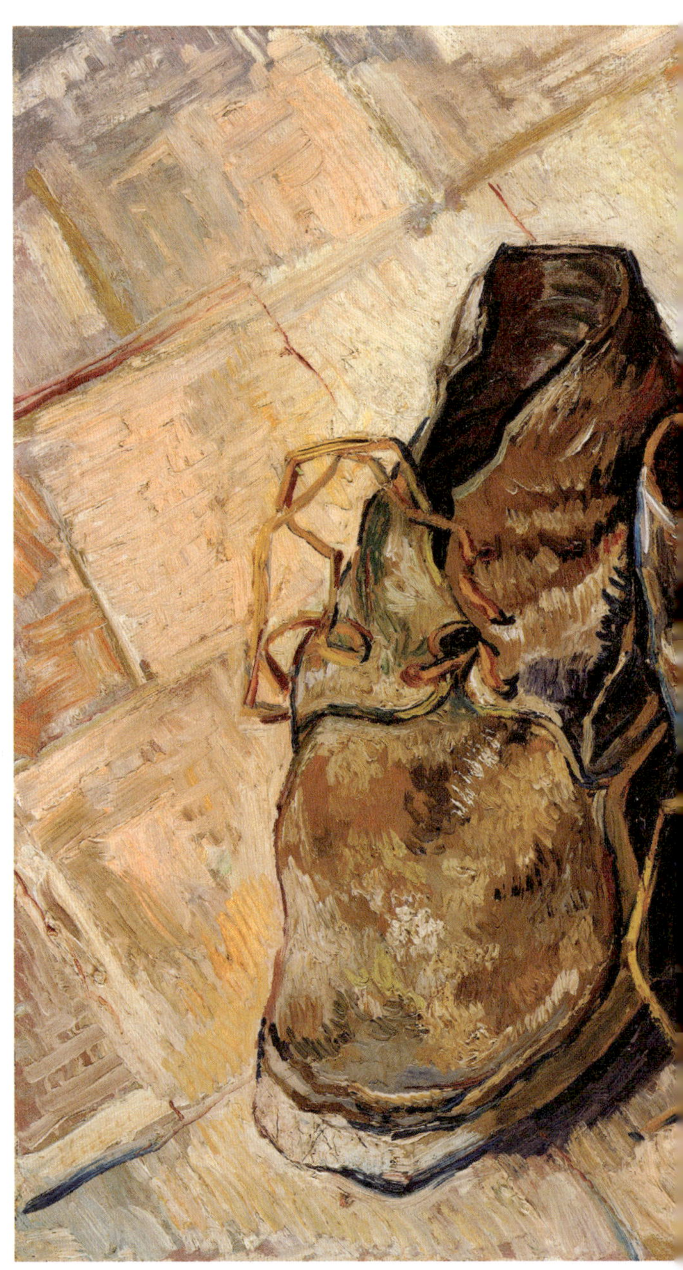

August 1888
Arles

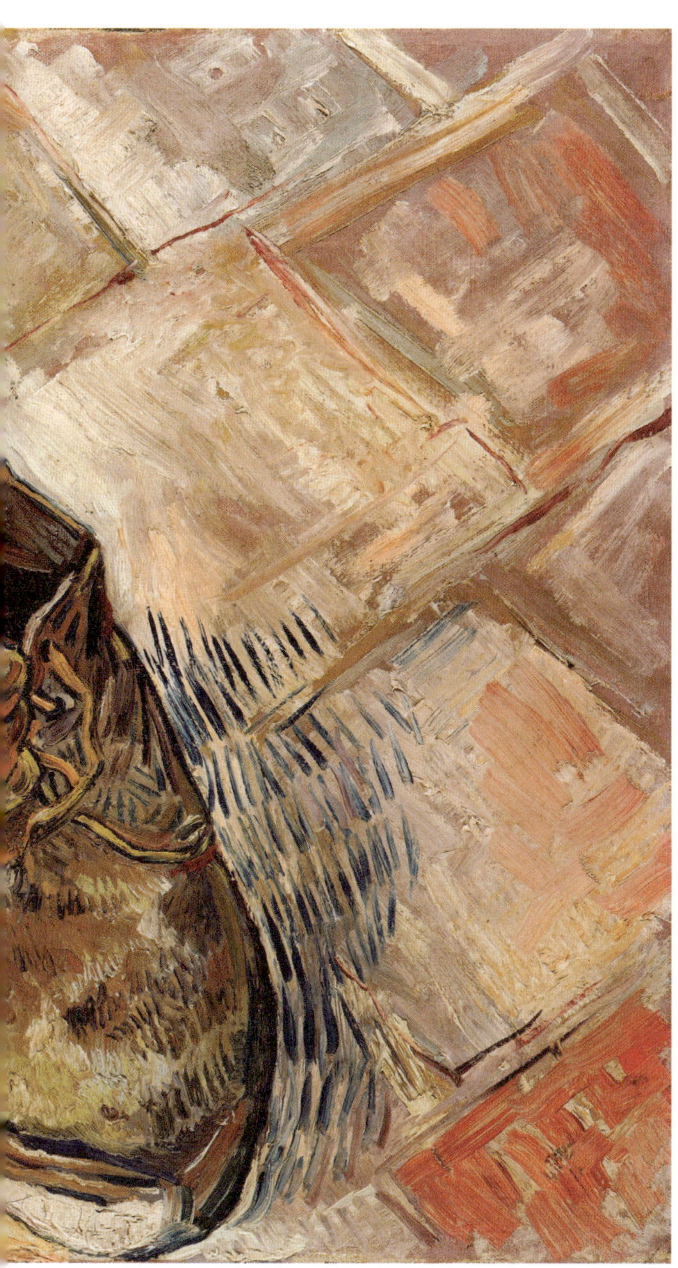

The Night Café

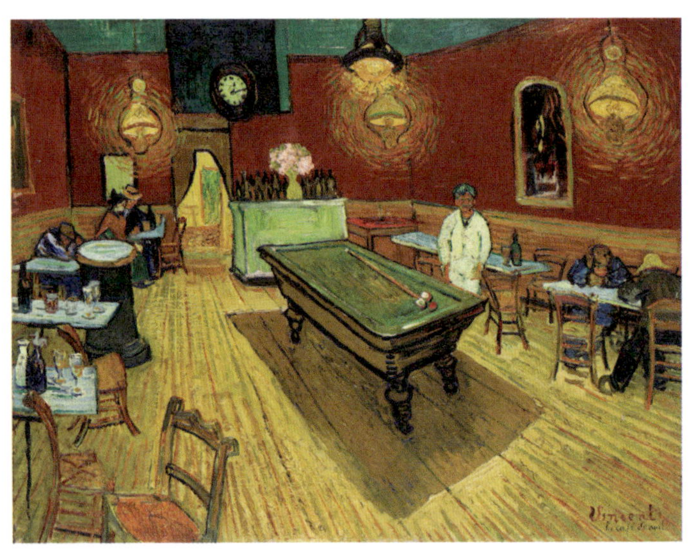

Oil on canvas
72.4 cm × 92.1 cm
(28½ in × 36¼ in)

September 1888
Arles

From early May until mid-September 1888, Van Gogh rented a room at the Café de la Gare. Before he left, he painted this Arles 'café de nuit' over the course of three nights. Van Gogh eloquently described the resulting picture, its paint loosely worked and thickly applied, in a letter to Theo: 'I've tried to express the terrible human passions with the red and the green. The room is blood-red and dull yellow, a green billiard table in the centre, 4 lemon yellow lamps with an orange and green glow.' (676)

The bold compositional layout, which seems to suck the viewer into the space, heightens this menacing quality, as does the figure of the landlord, whose 'white clothes ... become lemon yellow, pale luminous green'. In another letter, Van Gogh explains the painting's colour effects even more vividly:

'I've tried to express the idea that the café is a place where you can ruin yourself, go mad, commit crimes. Anyway, I tried with contrasts of delicate pink and blood-red and wine-red. Soft Louis XV and Veronese green contrasting with yellow greens and hard blue greens. All of that in an ambience of a hellish furnace, in pale sulphur.' (677)

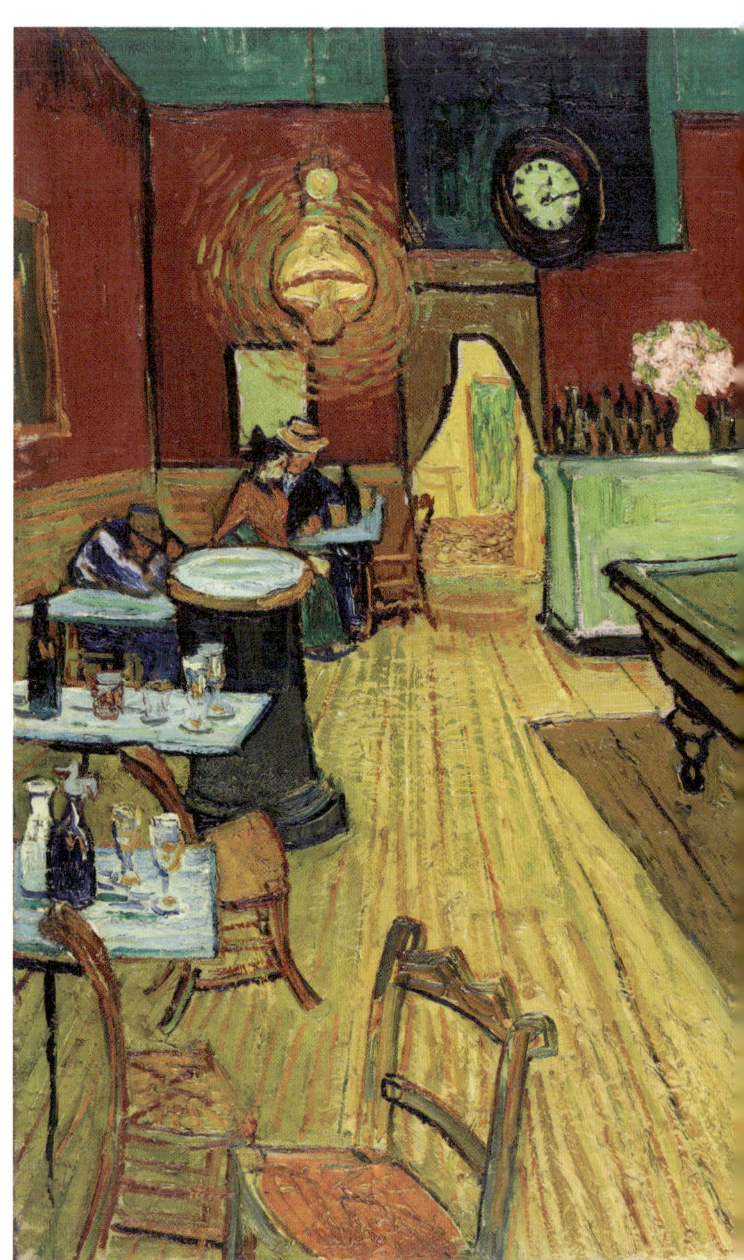

September 1888
Arles

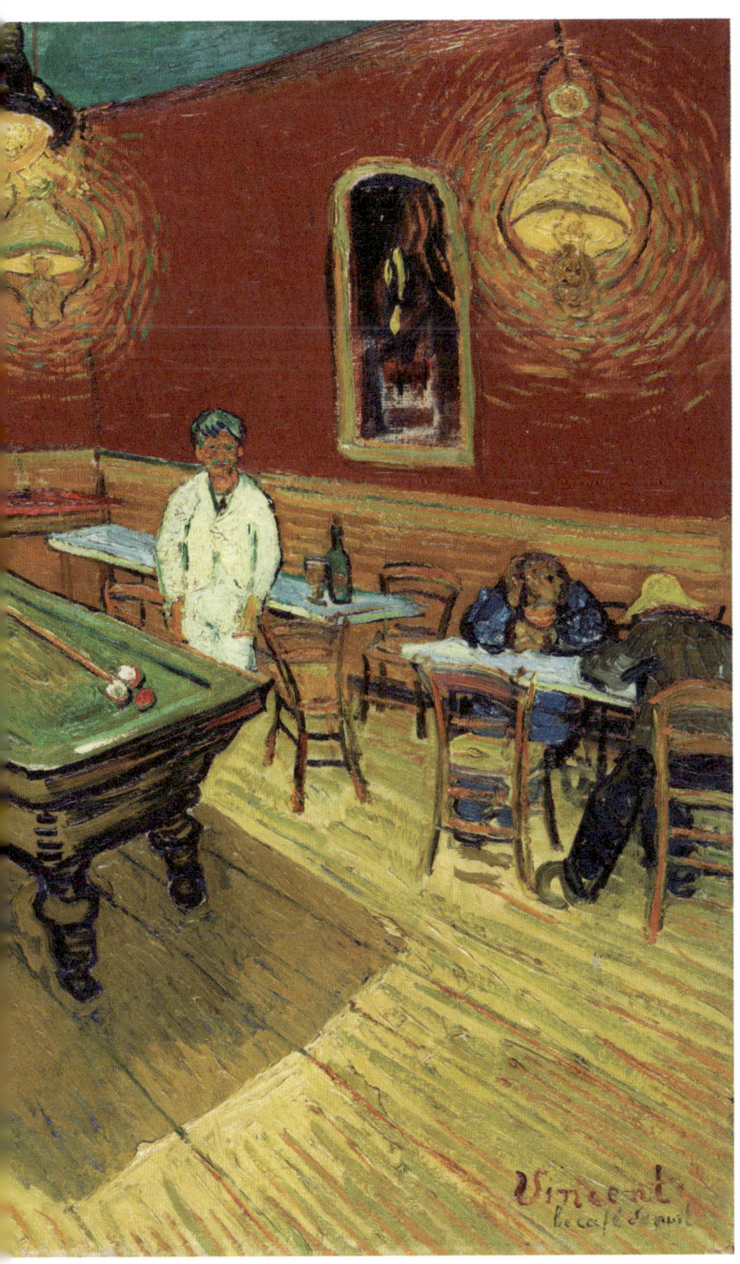

Café Terrace at Night

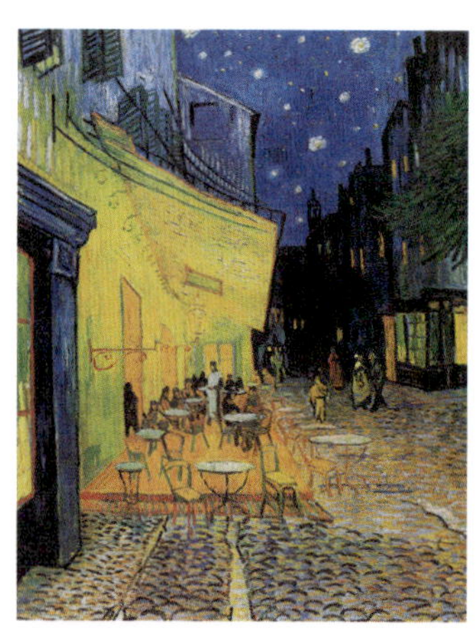

Oil on canvas
80.7 cm × 65.3 cm
(31¾ in × 25¾ in)

September 1888
Arles

Writing of *The Night Café* (page 100), Van Gogh observed 'It often seems to me that the night is much more alive and richly coloured than the day.' (676) Just after completing that canvas, he painted *Café Terrace at Night*. In contrast to the slightly earlier interior scene, this painting takes us into the evening streets of Arles.

Van Gogh would have seen representations of modern nightlife by artists like Manet, Degas and Toulouse-Lautrec. His vast reading – in Dutch, French, English and German – also informed his body of work. In the case of *Café Terrace*, there is a quite precise literary analogy. He told his sister Wil that a Parisian evening scene at the beginning of Guy de Maupassant's novel *Bel-Ami*, which describes 'the lighted cafés of the boulevard', is 'something like the same subject that I've painted just now.' (678)

Aside from depicting a quintessential subject of modern life, *Café Terrace* furthers Van Gogh's explorations of the expressive possibilities of colour. As he wrote in the letter to Wil: 'Now there's a painting of night without black. With nothing but beautiful blue, violet and green, and in these surroundings the lighted square is coloured pale sulphur, lemon green.' (678)

Café Terrace at Night

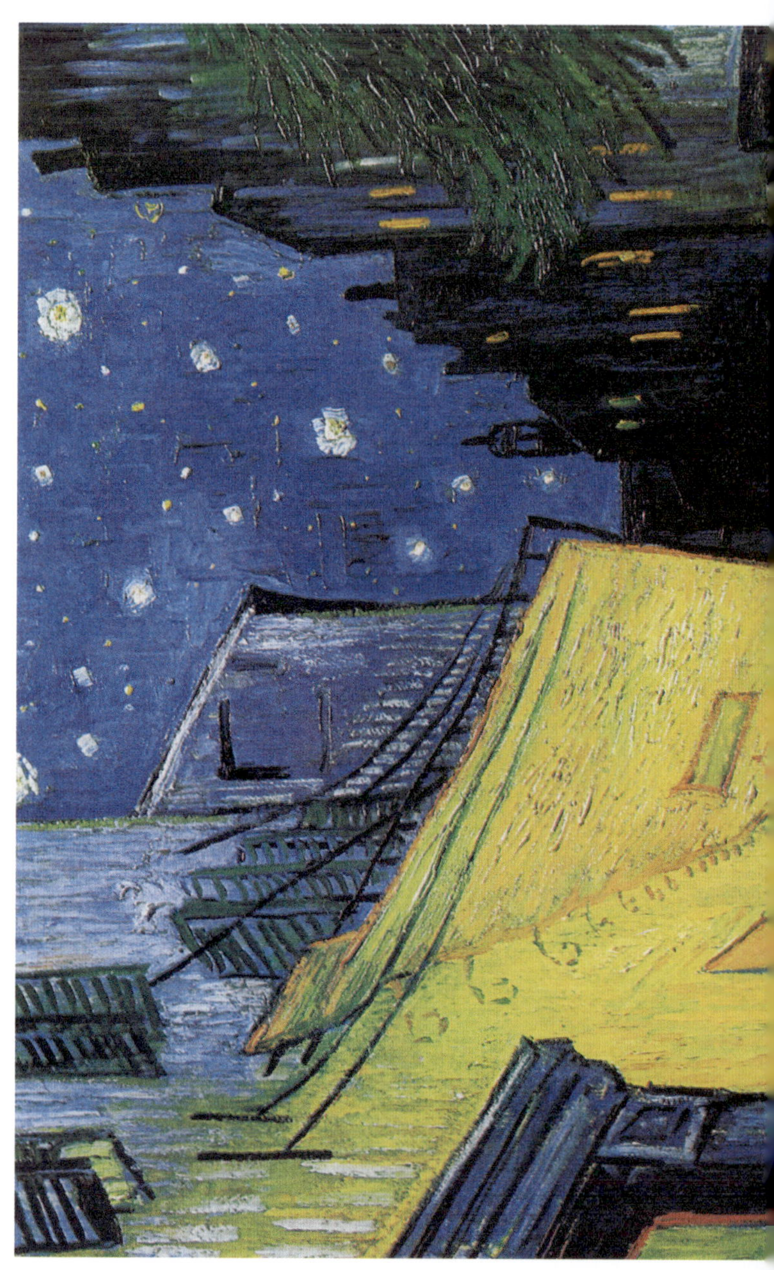

September 1888
Arles

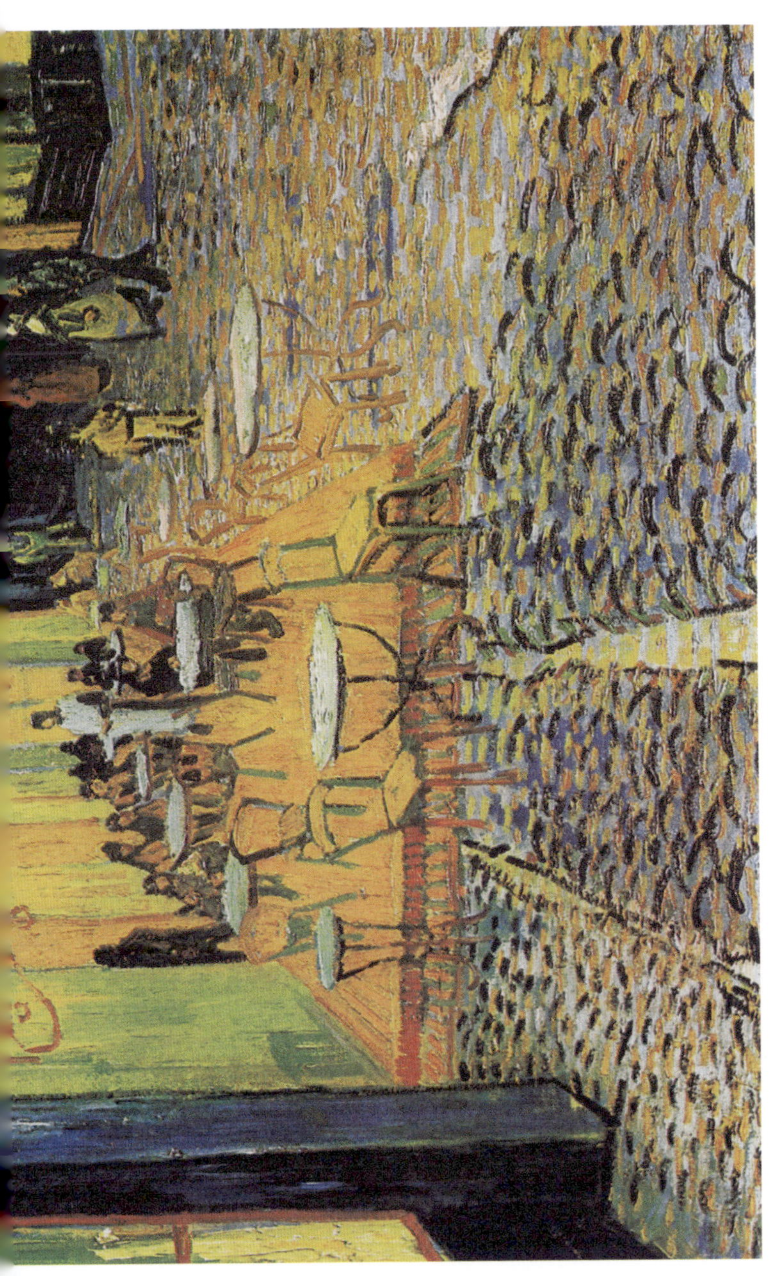

Starry Night Over the Rhône

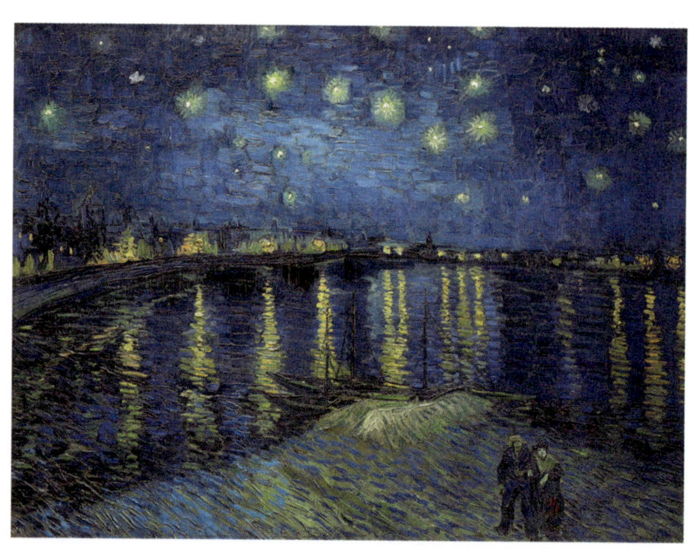

Oil on canvas
72 cm × 92 cm
(28¾ in × 36¼ in)

September 1888
Arles

While living in Provence, Van Gogh expressed interest in painting a starry sky several times, but it wasn't until September 1888 that this came about. Night scenes were of particular interest for the artist at that time, having first completed *The Night Café* (page 100). He then told his sister Wil, 'I definitely want to paint a starry sky now.' (678) He did this with haste, painting *Café Terrace at Night* (page 104) within the week and the current picture shortly thereafter. Each of these three works were painted 'on the spot and actually at night' (681), which Van Gogh said he enjoyed immensely.

Like the earlier cityscape, *Starry Night Over the Rhône* is an innovative 'painting of night without black.' (678) But the passage of deep blue sky and yellow and white stars of *Café Terrace* has here been expanded to fill the entire upper third of the canvas. The faintly glowing, slightly green stars contrast with the deep yellow of the city's gaslights. Their reflections reach across the water to the shore, where a couple look up towards the viewer. Painted with impasto and brushstrokes of different sizes and directions, the entire canvas pulsates.

Starry Night Over the Rhône

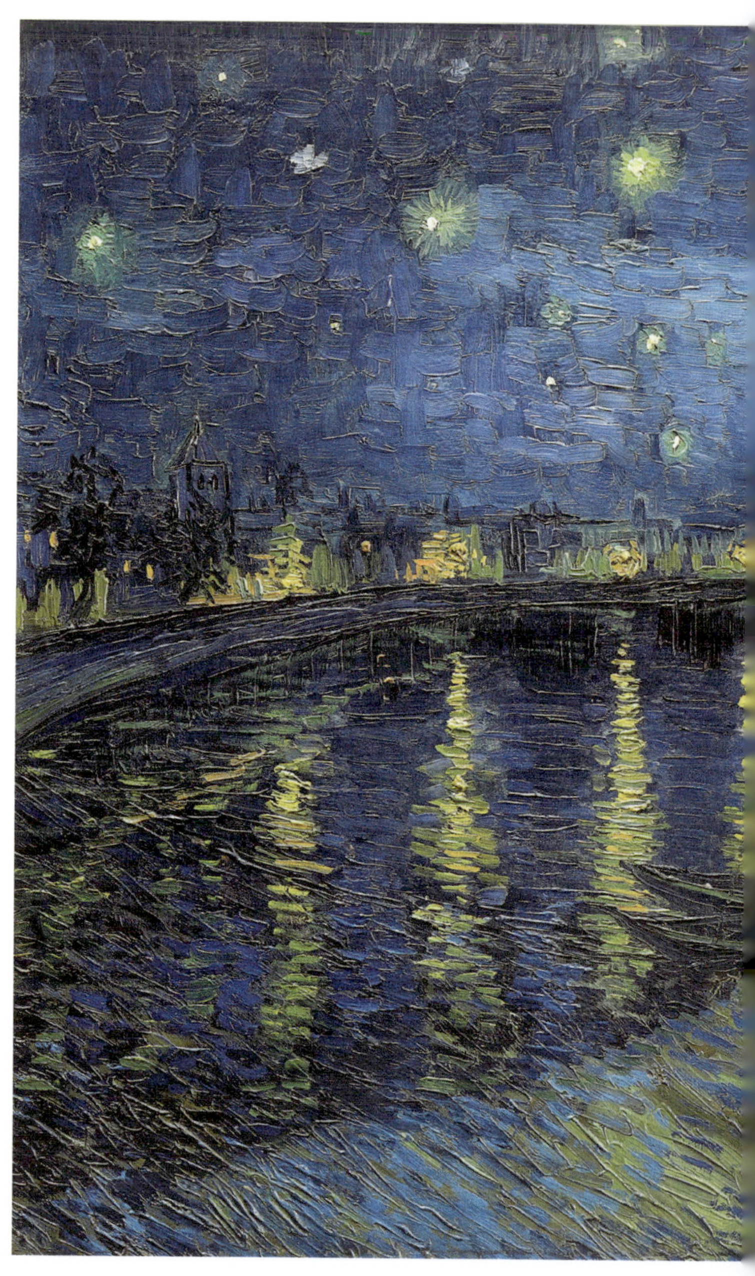

September 1888
Arles

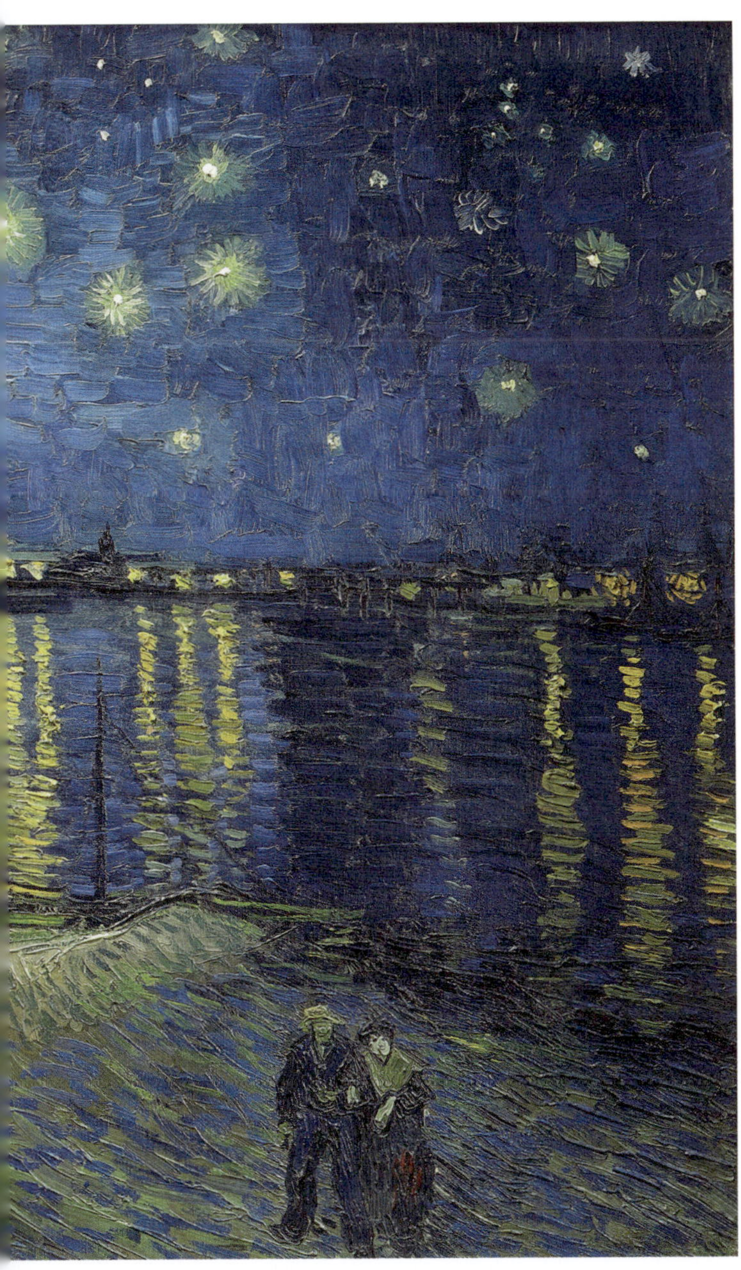

The Yellow House

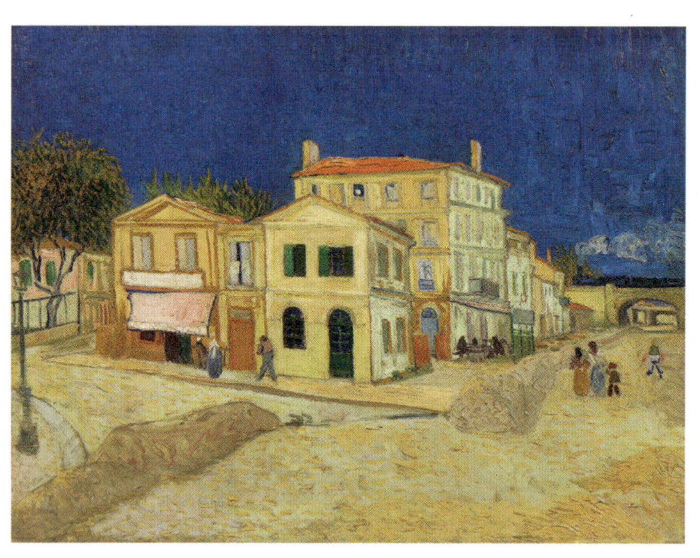

Oil on canvas
72 cm × 91.5 cm
(28⅝ in × 36 in)

September 1888
Arles

Van Gogh rented the Yellow House at 2 Place Lamartine on 1 May 1888. However, as he didn't then have the funds to furnish the property, he didn't move in until September. After lodging in cafés since arriving in Arles, the allure of his own place was understandably strong. It's clear from this painting, and from a letter he wrote to Wil:

'My house here is painted outside in the yellow of fresh butter, with garish green shutters, and it's in the full sun on the square, where there's a green garden of plane trees, oleanders, acacias. And inside, it's all whitewashed, and the floor's of red bricks. And the intense blue sky above. Inside, I can live and breathe, and think and paint.' (678)

But the Yellow House was to be more than a home for Van Gogh; it was to be a place where other artists could visit and work. With the picture's figures and details summarily sketched – the smoke of the passing train is particularly captivating – the blue sky and the green shutters stand out in this field of yellow. Indeed, it recalls Van Gogh's *Sunflowers* (page 92), which he painted especially for his artist's retreat.

The Yellow House

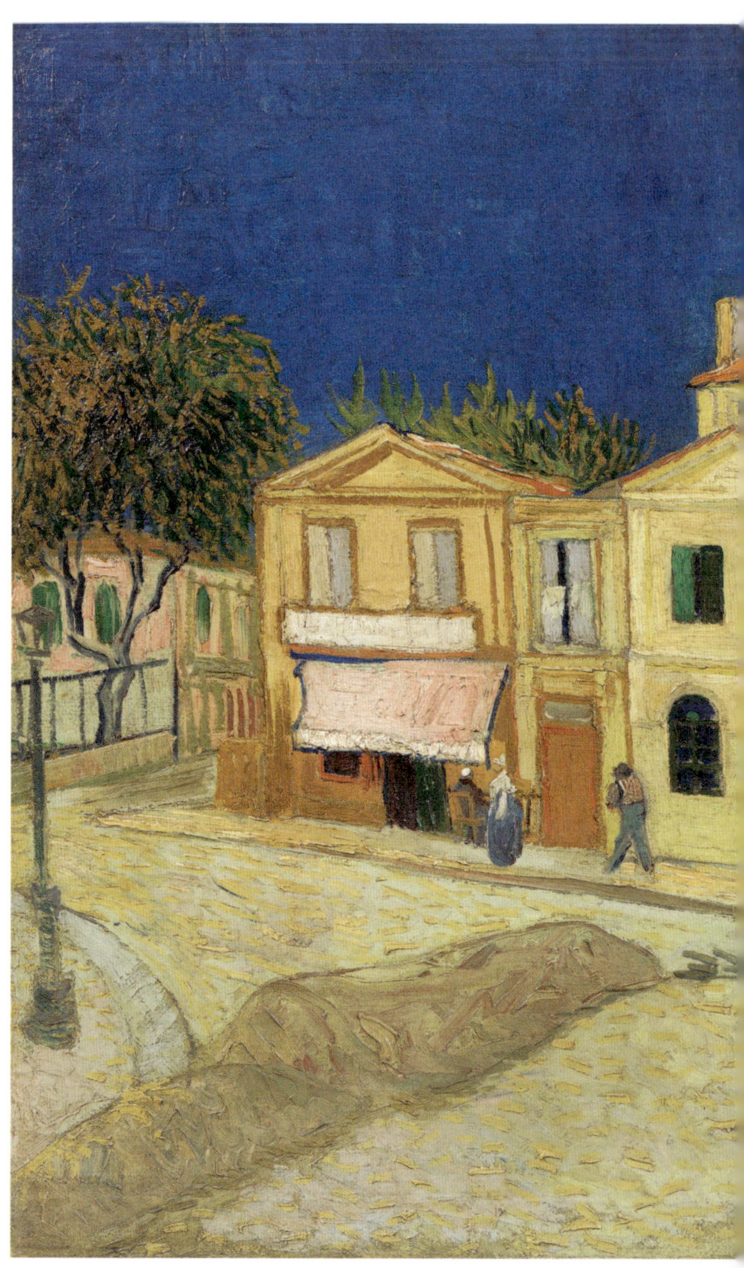

September 1888
Arles

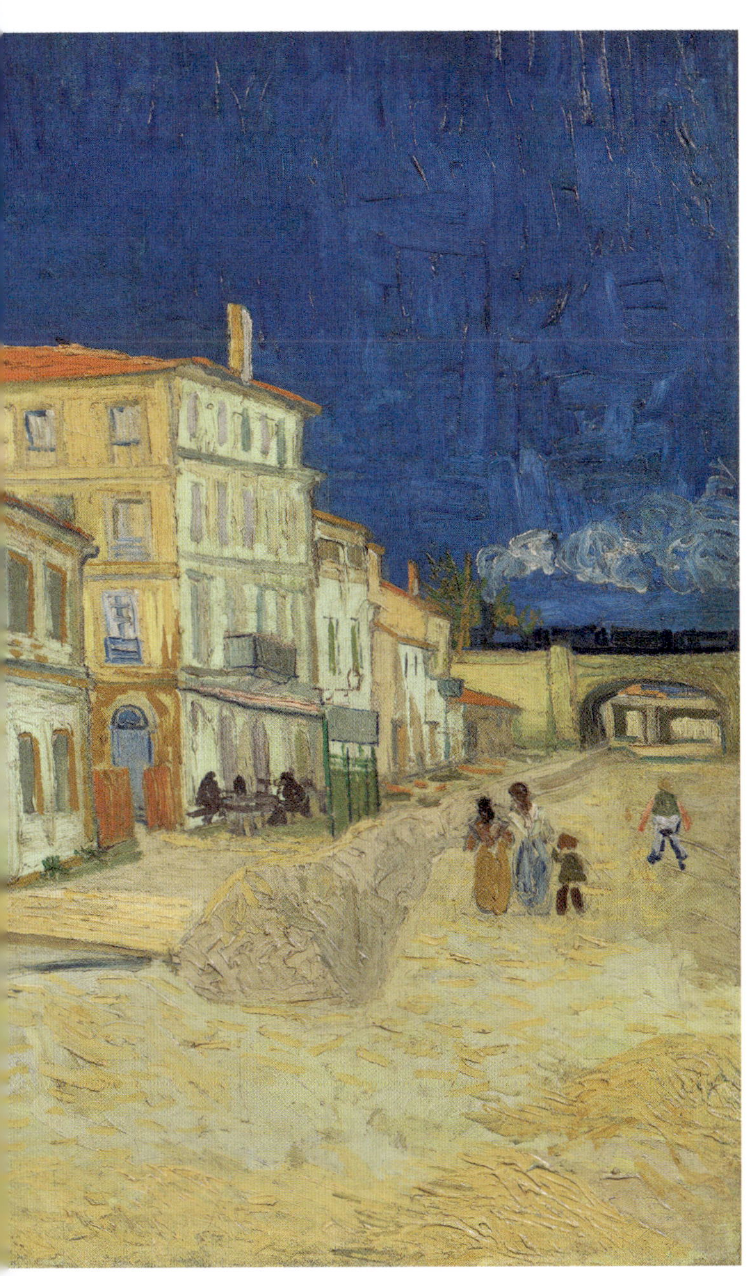

The Bedroom

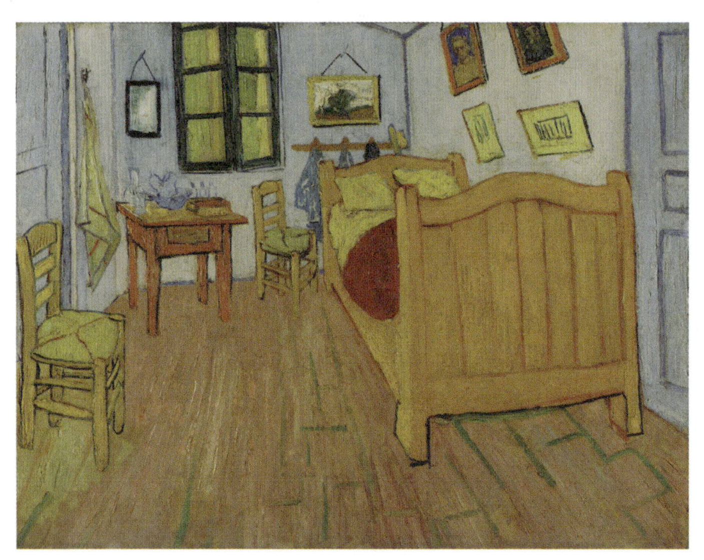

Oil on canvas
72.4 cm × 91.3 cm
(28½ in × 36 in)

October 1888
Arles

Van Gogh was an incredibly prolific artist who worked quickly. In October 1888, having moved into the Yellow House, he painted to exhaustion and had to rest for a few days. When recovered, he created the first version of his *Bedroom*. He would paint two slightly different versions the following year.

While we may view this as a rather lively picture, Van Gogh's letters make it clear that he felt the range of colour tones, 'coarsely brushed in full impasto', suggested '*utter repose*' (706). 'In short, looking at the painting should *rest* the mind, or rather, the imagination.' (705) He also noted that 'the shadows and cast shadows are removed; it's coloured in flat, plain tints like Japanese prints.' (705)

The influence of Japanese art was already evident in paintings Van Gogh made in Paris (see *Japonaiserie: Flowering Plum Tree (after Hiroshige)* on page 64) and his move south was partly prompted by his hope 'that looking at nature under a brighter sky can give us a more accurate idea of the Japanese way of feeling and drawing.' (801) With its bold, shadowless colour complements, *The Bedroom* symbolises the home he found, now seen 'with a more Japanese eye' (620).

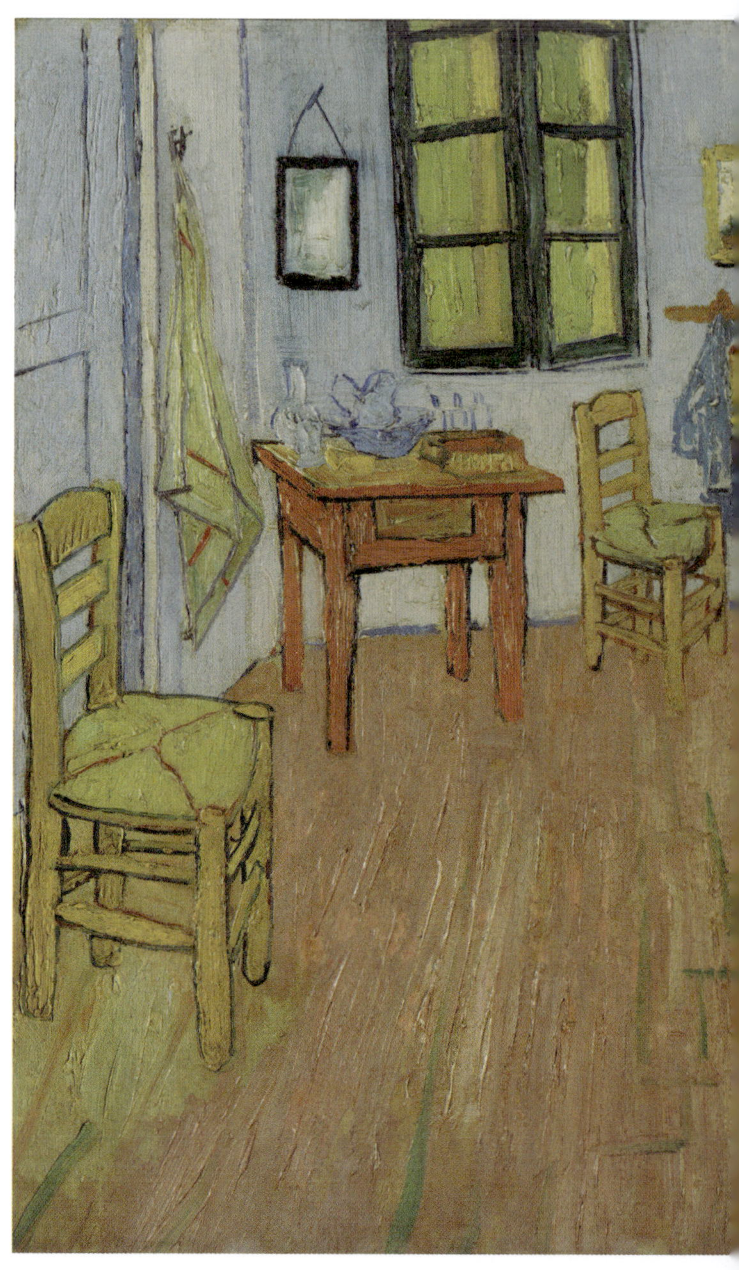

October 1888
Arles

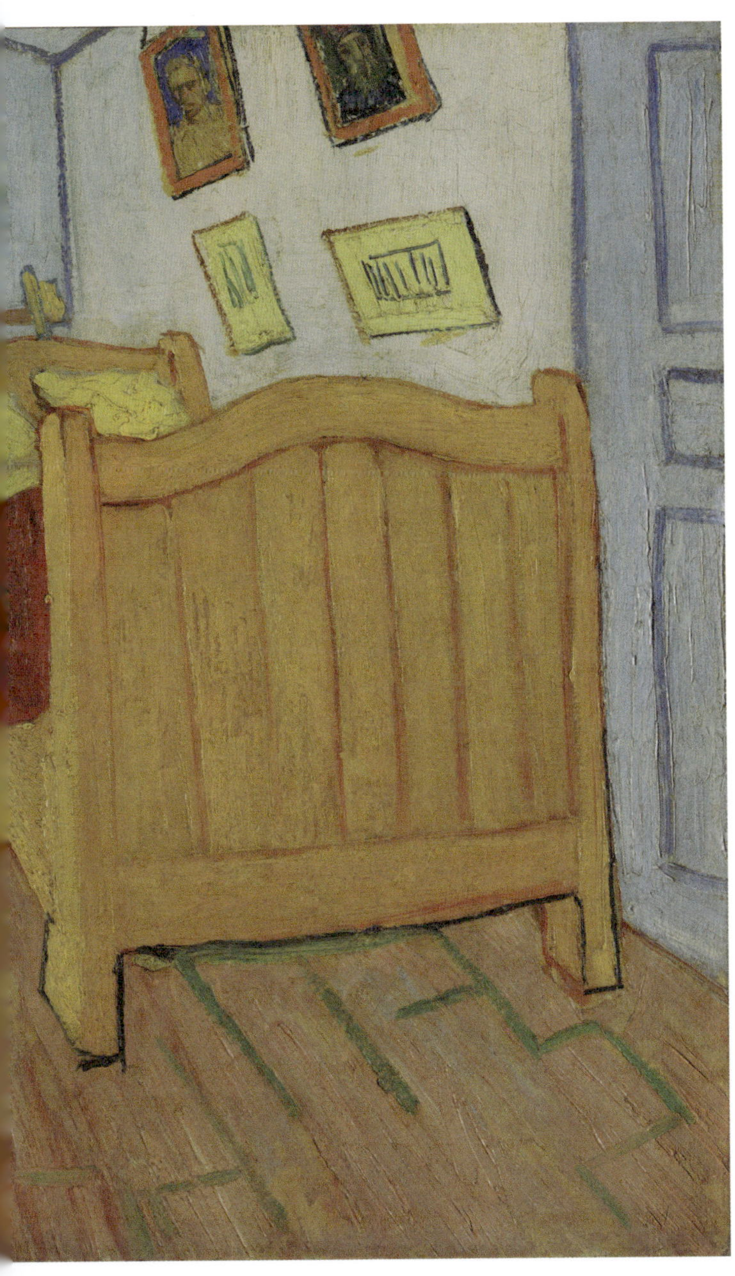

Van Gogh's Chair

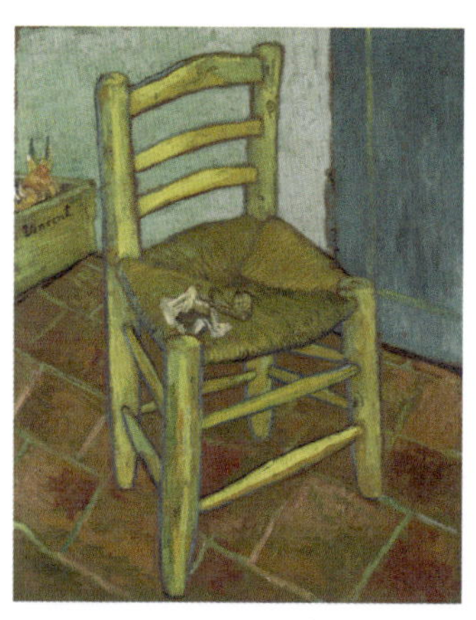

Oil on canvas
91.8 cm × 73 cm
(36⅛ in × 29¾ in)

November 1888
Arles

This iconic image is actually one of a pair. Around 19 November 1888, Van Gogh described his recently completed works to Theo: 'a wooden and straw *chair* all yellow on red tiles against a wall (*daytime*). Then Gauguin's armchair, red and green, night effect, on the seat two novels and a candle. On sailcloth in thick impasto.' (721)

Van Gogh had met Paul Gauguin (1848-1903) in Paris in November 1887 and they exchanged paintings. They remained in touch, as did Gauguin and Theo, who owned and dealt the French artist's works. When Van Gogh rented the Yellow House and conceived of it becoming a 'studio in the south' (674; 702), he invited Gauguin to join him. While Gauguin kept postponing, he eventually arrived in Arles on 23 October 1888.

The pendant portraits are powerful indicators of the two artists' different temperaments. In contrast to Gauguin's rather elegant chair, Van Gogh's is rustic, recalling those depicted in *The Bedroom* (page 116). His pipe and tobacco pouch are found on the chair's rush seat, and his tie to the rural land indicated by the box of shallots or onions, where Van Gogh has signed his name. The presence of this humble chair's one-time occupant is palpable.

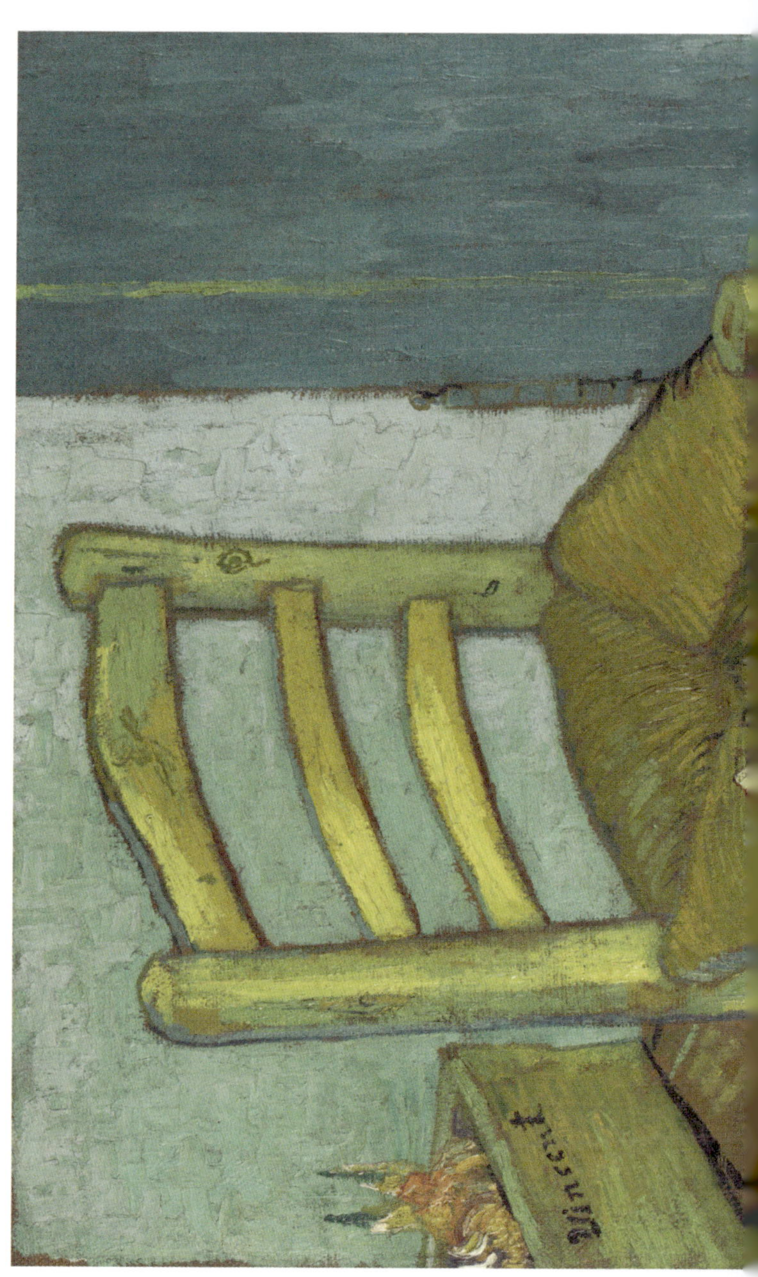

November 1888
Arles

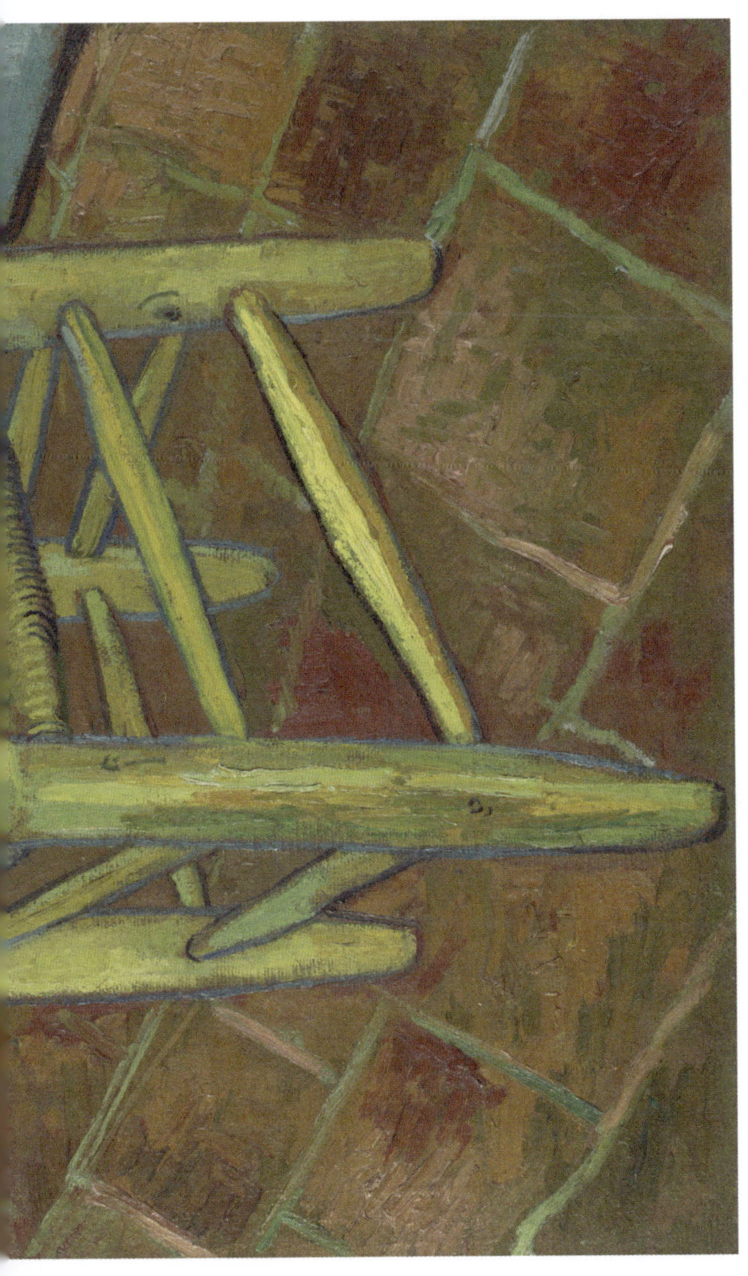

The Red Vineyard

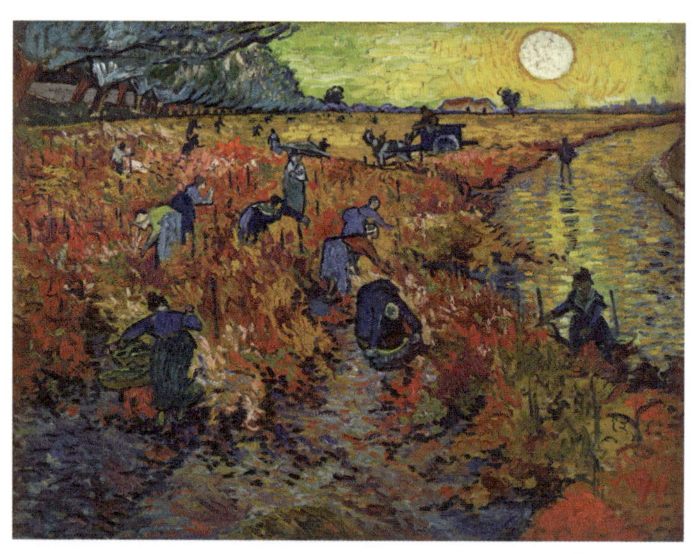

Oil on canvas
75 cm × 93 cm
(29½ in × 36⅝ in)

November 1888
Arles

In autumn 1888 Van Gogh described to Theo a walk he took with Gauguin in the Arles countryside: 'We saw a red vineyard, completely red like red wine. In the distance it became yellow, and then a green sky with a sun, fields violet and sparkling yellow here and there after the rain in which the setting sun was reflected.' (717) Through this canvas's bountiful brushstrokes, freely and thickly applied in warm, luxuriant tones, Van Gogh preserved a record of that vital, bustling scene.

The Red Vineyard was one of only a few paintings that Van Gogh sold during his lifetime, but the frequent claim that he was an unrecognised artist when he died is not quite true. His works were included in several group exhibitions, and *The Red Vineyard* was one of six of his canvases shown at the annual Les XX (Les Vingt) exhibition in Brussels in 1890. In January that same year an article about Van Gogh by the art critic G-Albert Aurier was published in the respected literary magazine the *Mercure de France*. Van Gogh's genius had begun to be recognised.

The Red Vineyard

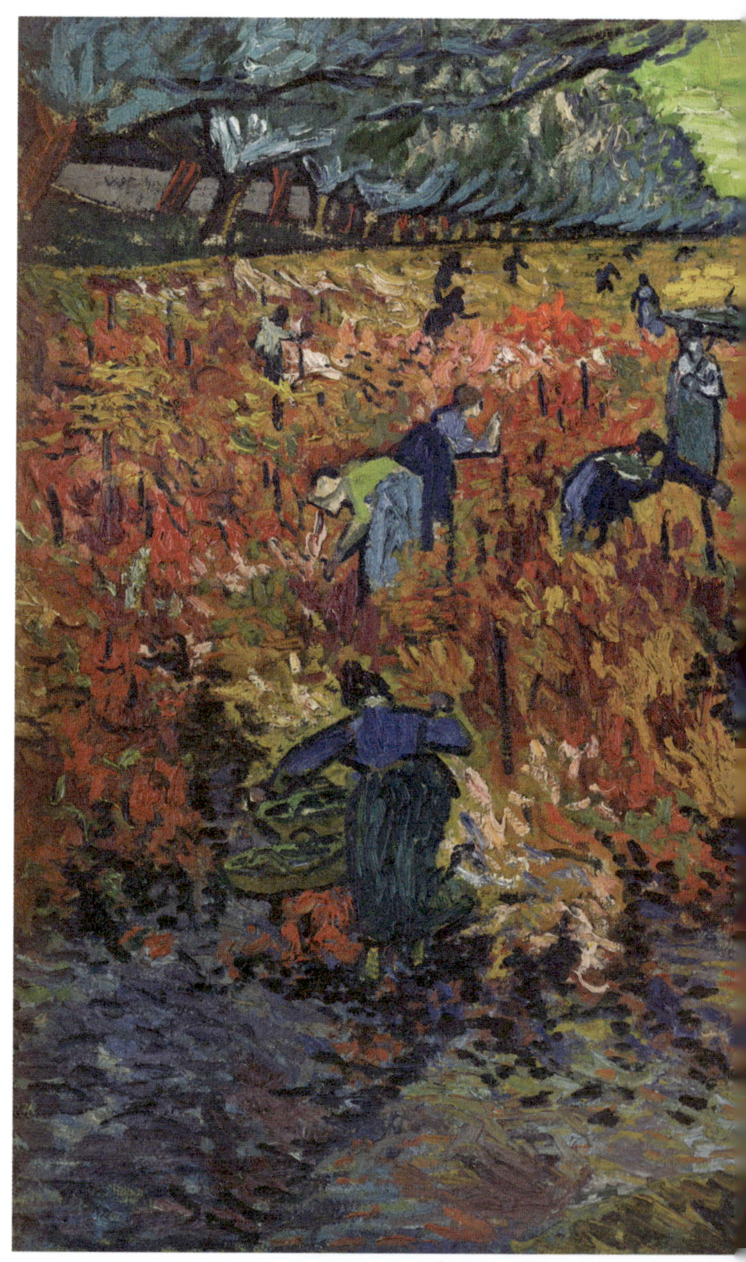

November 1888
Arles

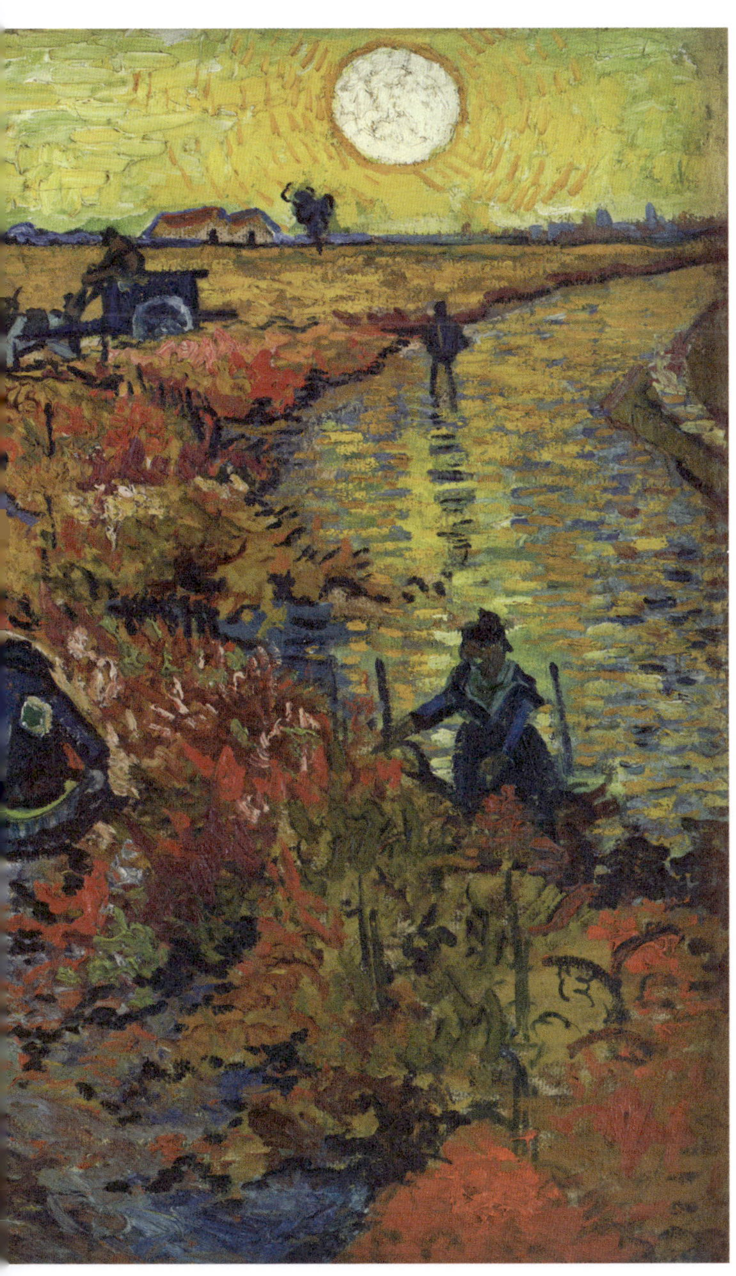

L'Arlésienne: Madame Ginoux

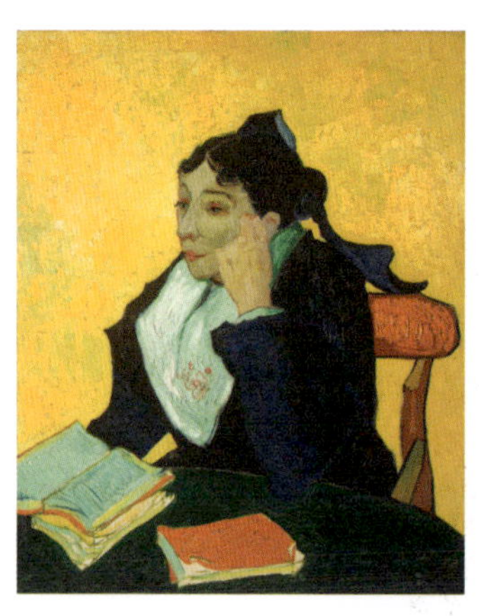

Oil on canvas
91.4 cm × 73.7 cm
(36 in × 29 in)

November 1888
Arles

The model for this astounding painting was Marie Ginoux. She and her husband were the proprietors of the Café de la Gare, which Van Gogh depicted in *The Night Café* (page 100). As *L'Arlésienne* (the woman from Arles), she is represented wearing the regional costume, its deep blue-black an invigorating foil to the background's flat field of startling yellow.

Integrating the aesthetic of Japanese woodblock prints and the 'gay colours' (569) Van Gogh found in the south, the canvas is a scintillating pattern of bold colour contrasts. The table's dark green reappears as a lighter tone in the white of the woman's clothing and in the pages of the books on the table. These objects also repeat the yellow of the background and the orange of the chair, the colour of which is then used to highlight the sitter's facial features.

Amidst this rhythm of hues, Madame Ginoux is a figure of calm as she sits thoughtfully, having just looked up from reading. The work is an example of the 'modern portrait' that Van Gogh sought to create, not by way of realistic representation, but 'by way of colour' (879).

L'Arlésienne: Madame Ginoux

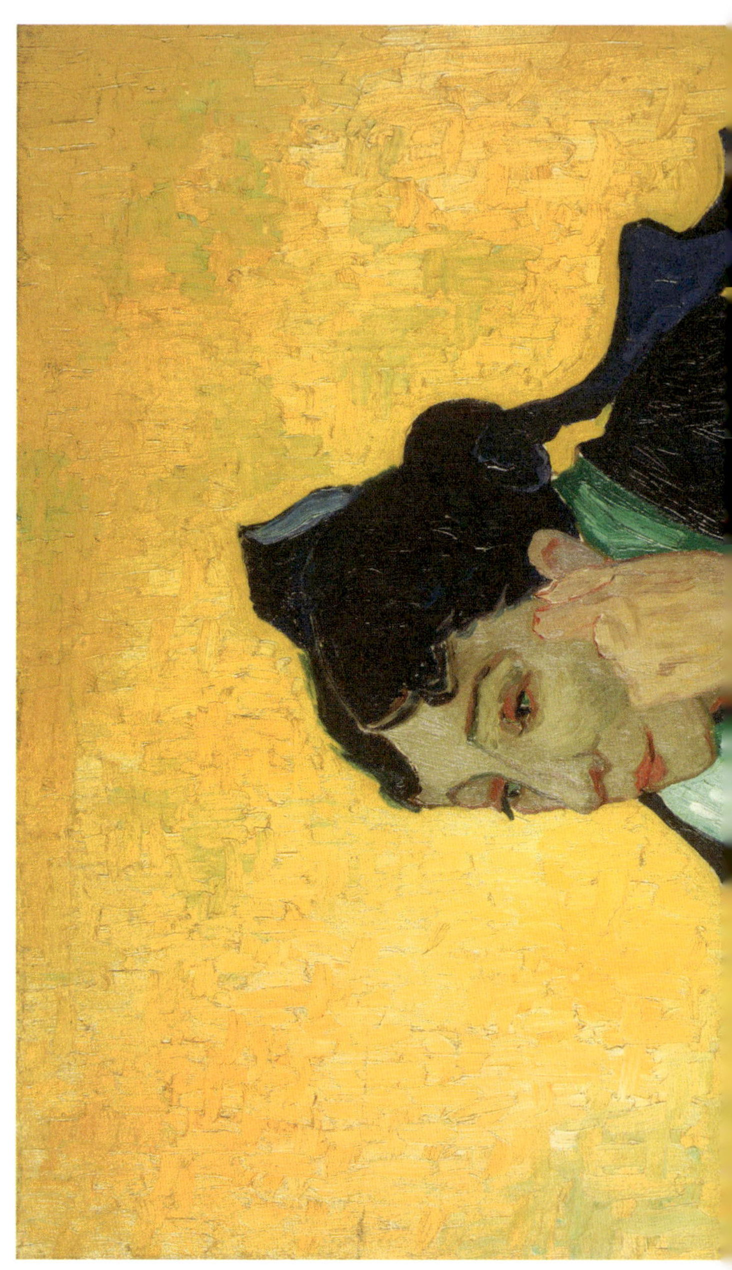

November 1888
Arles

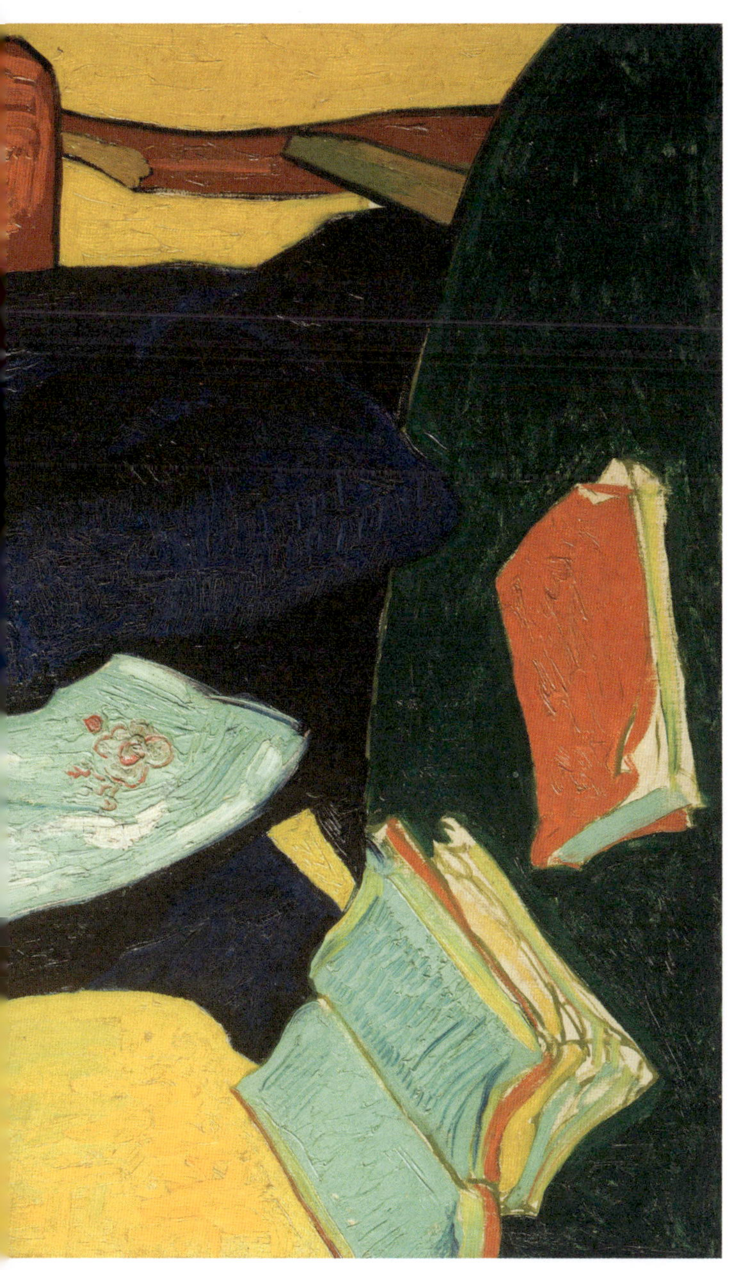

Self-Portrait with Bandaged Ear and Pipe

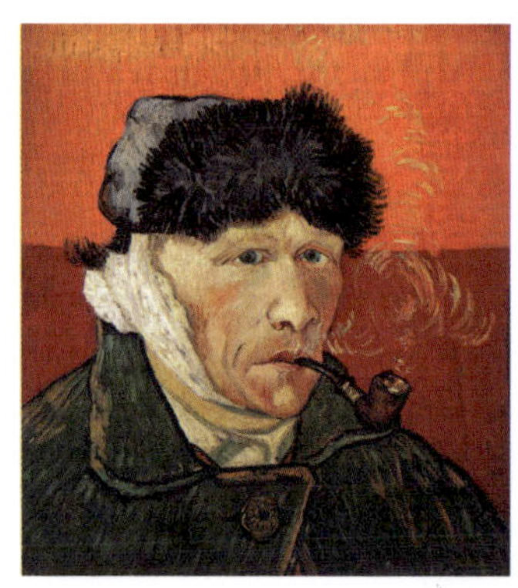

Oil on canvas
51 cm × 45 cm
(20⅛ in × 17¾ in)

January 1889
Arles

The nine weeks Van Gogh and Gauguin spent together at the Yellow House is one of the most storied periods in art history. It seems that after a short period of conviviality, the two artists began to disagree, particularly about approaches to art. On 23 December 1888, Van Gogh had a severe mental breakdown and cut off his left ear, which he took to a prostitute in a local brothel. He was hospitalised the next day, Theo came to join him in Arles and Gauguin left for Paris.

After Van Gogh returned home from the hospital in January 1889, he painted two mirror-image self-portraits with his bandaged ear. What makes this work astonishing is how Van Gogh has portrayed himself with such candour while still strongly advancing his singular pictorial program.

The background consists of two fiery blocks of colour, suggesting the anguish of Van Gogh's breakdown. These contrast vividly with their complements in the foreground – the orange with the artist's blue hat and the red with his green coat. Among these cool, calm colours, Van Gogh's eyes look out tiredly, but he takes resigned comfort in his cherished pipe (see *Van Gogh's Chair* on page 120).

Self-Portrait with Bandaged Ear and Pipe

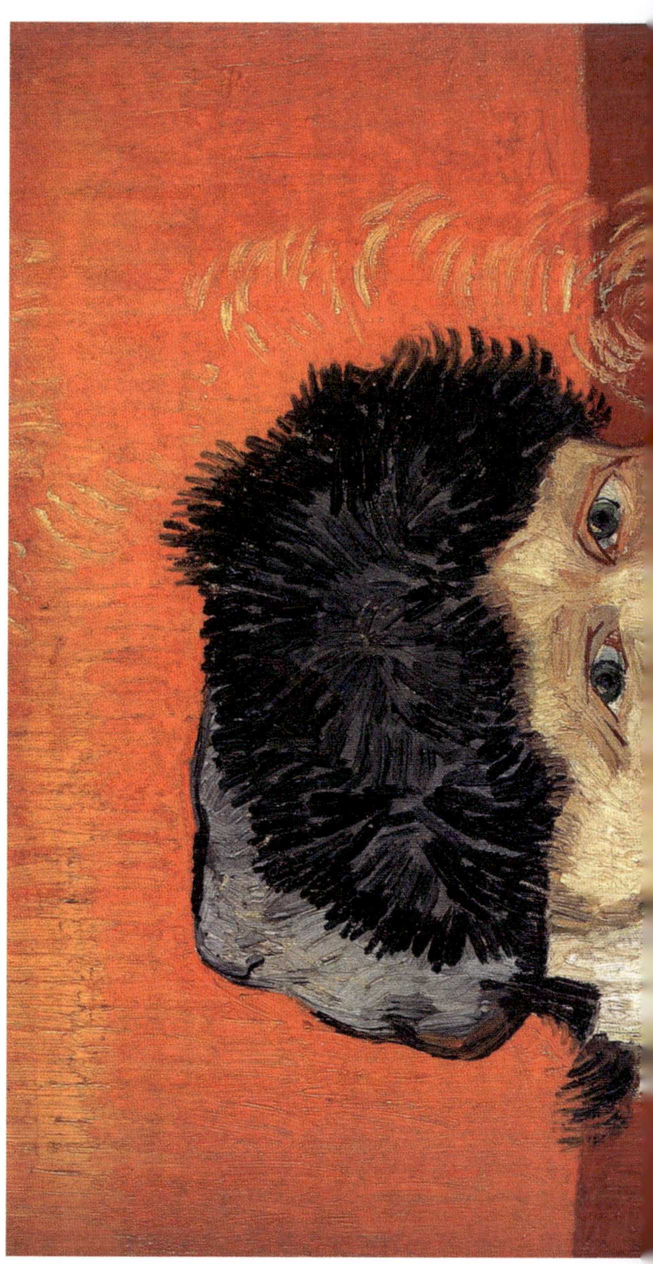

January 1889
Arles

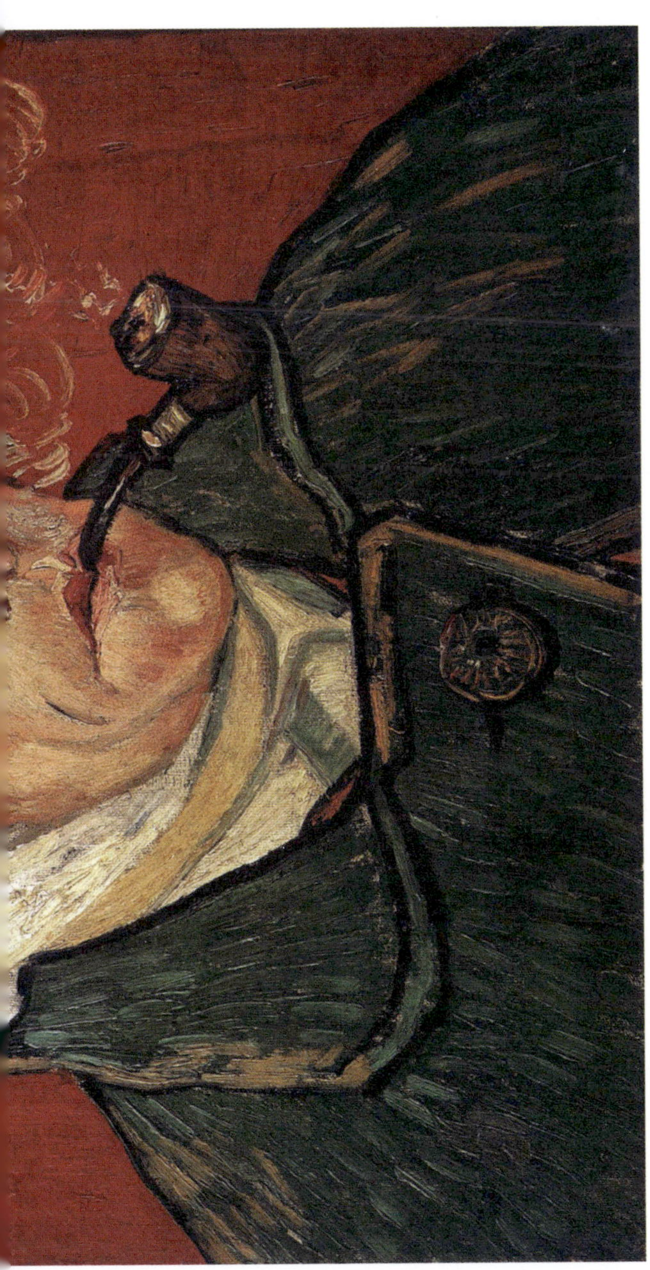

La Berceuse (Woman Rocking a Cradle)

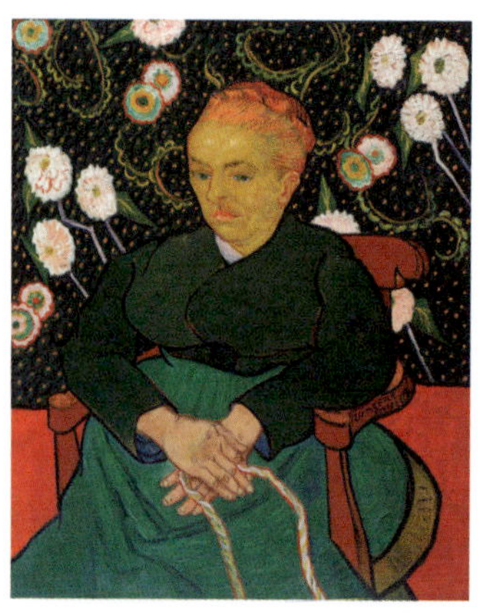

Oil on canvas
92.7 cm × 73.8 cm
(36½ in × 29 in)

January 1889
Arles

After recovering from his breakdown (see *Self-Portrait with Bandaged Ear and Pipe* on page 132), Van Gogh completed several versions of this striking painting. The sitter is Augustine Roulin, whose husband Van Gogh had previously painted (see *Portrait of the Postman Joseph Roulin* on page 88).

Augustine Roulin is here transformed from an individual woman into an icon. She has become 'La Berceuse', meaning '"our lullaby", or the woman by the cradle' (740), and is pictured holding the rope of this unseen object. Van Gogh envisages her as a patron saint of fishermen and the painting as a 'lullaby with colour'.

Recalling the Cloisonnism technique developed by Émile Bernard and Louis Anquetin, Van Gogh employs flat planes of red and green outlined in black. Against these forms the wallpaper strikes a lively, decorative note, though the pink dahlias' impasto – a texture mirrored in Roulin's orange hair – playfully subverts its quality as flat decoration.

While Gauguin left Arles after Van Gogh's breakdown, the two artists remained in touch. Van Gogh wrote to him of *La Berceuse*: 'As an Impressionist arrangement of colours, I've never devised anything better.' (739)

La Berceuse (Woman Rocking a Cradle)

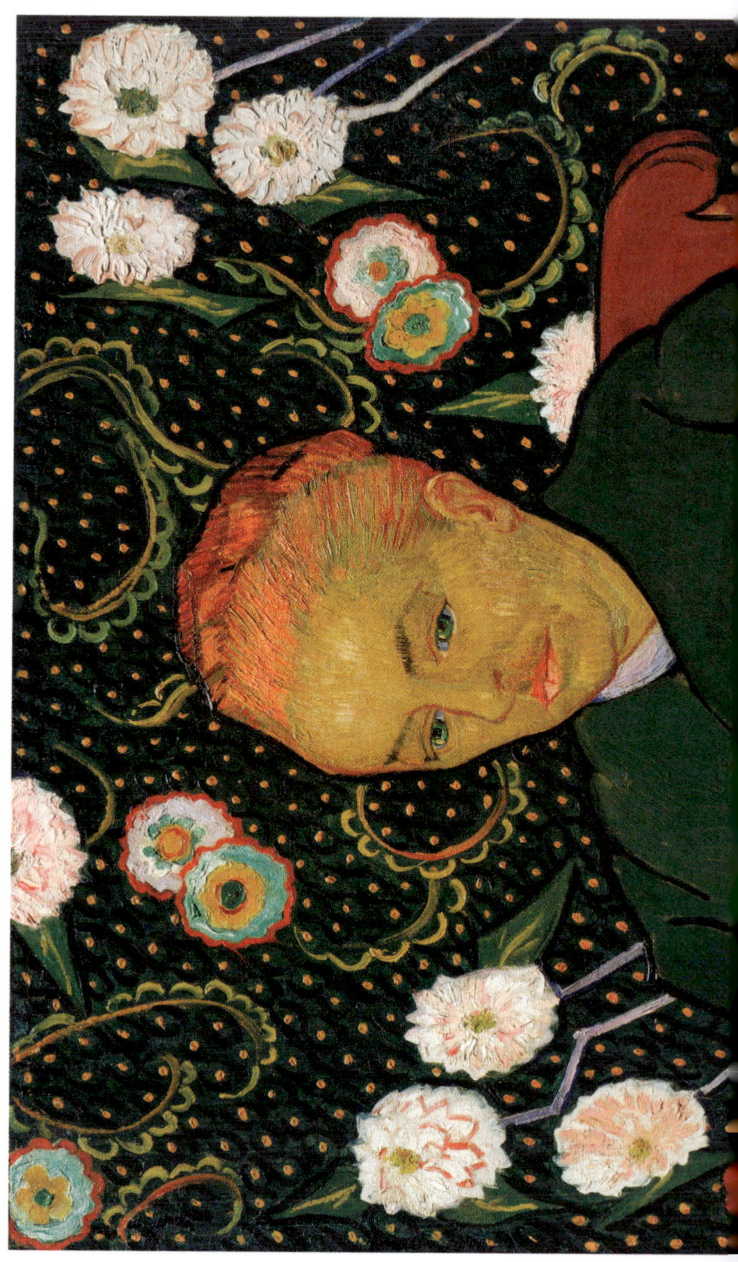

January 1889
Arles

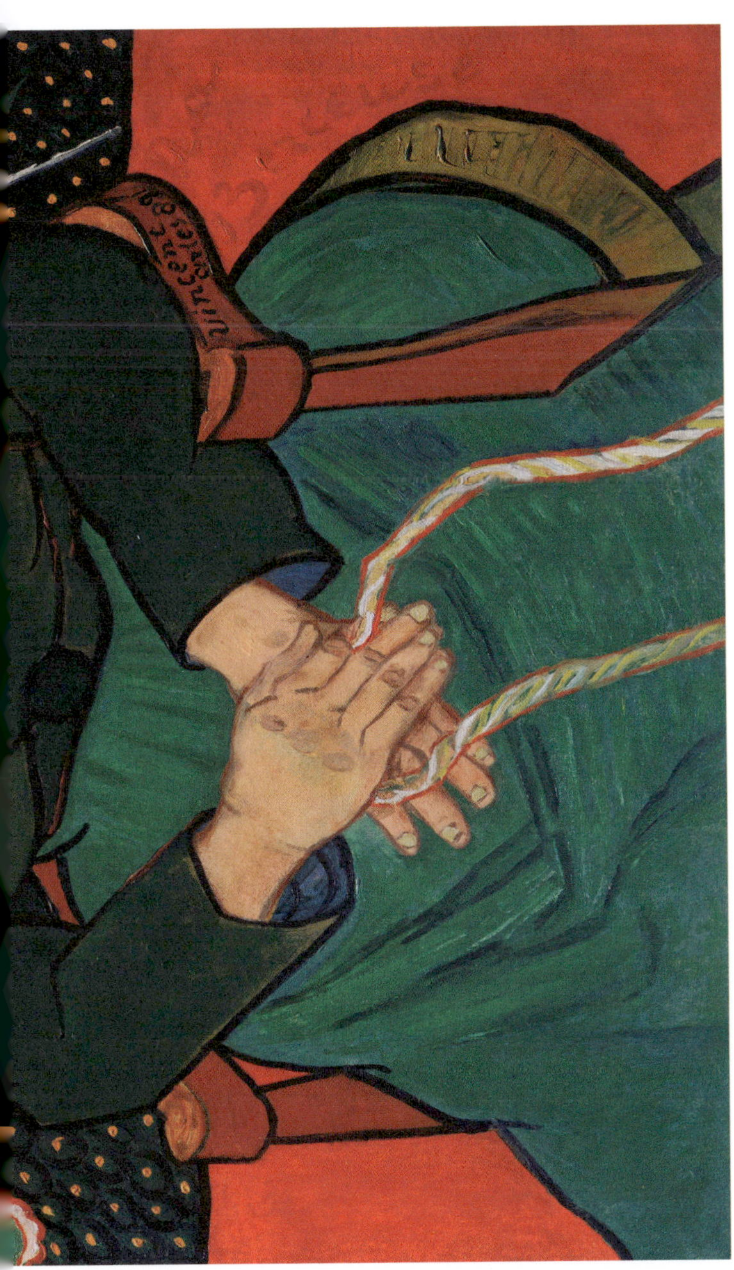

View of Arles, Flowering Orchards

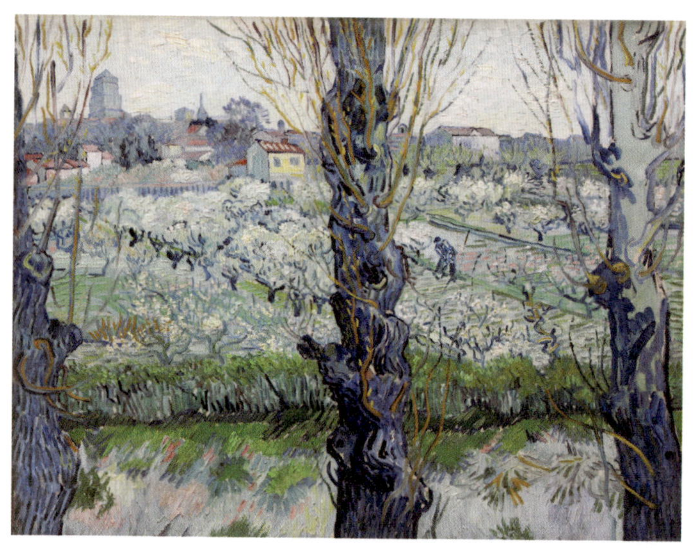

Oil on canvas
72 cm × 92 cm
(28⅜ in × 36¼ in)

April 1889
Arles

Van Gogh seemed to recover remarkably quickly from his mental collapse in late 1888. On 28 January 1889, he wrote to Theo that he knew people could recover from broken arms and legs, 'but I didn't know that one could break one's brain and that afterwards that got better too.' (743) Unfortunately, he was to have other attacks over the next few months, requiring further spells in hospital.

While Van Gogh was understandably worried and drained by his illness, he continued to paint between episodes. As early as his next hospitalisation in January 1889, he expressed his eagerness to resume painting orchards in bloom, a subject that had preoccupied him the previous spring (see *The Flowering Orchard* on page 80). He was able to paint at least three orchards in 1889, including the present work, where grey poplars cross the canvas foreground, a froth of pale blossoms visible between their trunks.

In one of the few extant letters from Theo, dated 16 November 1889, he told Vincent that *View of Arles* was in Père Tanguy's shop window, adding, 'I like it enormously. That truly is nature.' (819)

View of Arles, Flowering Orchards

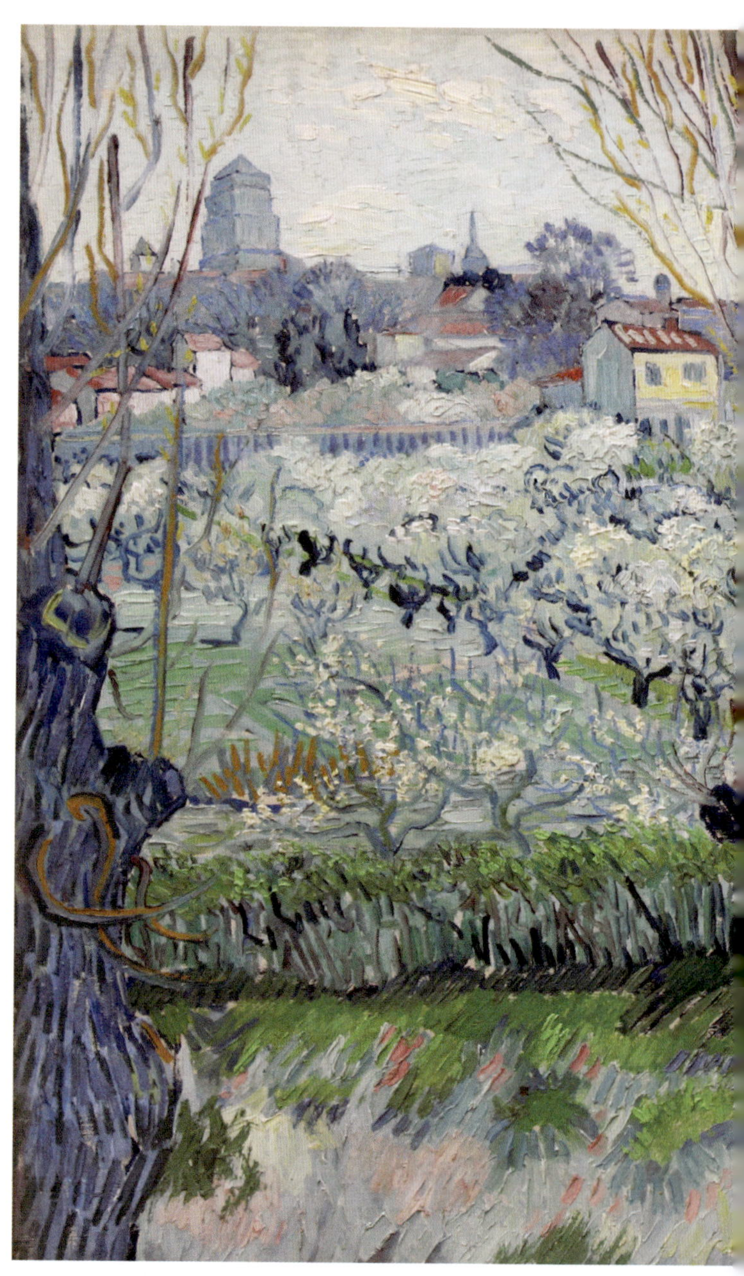

April 1889
Arles

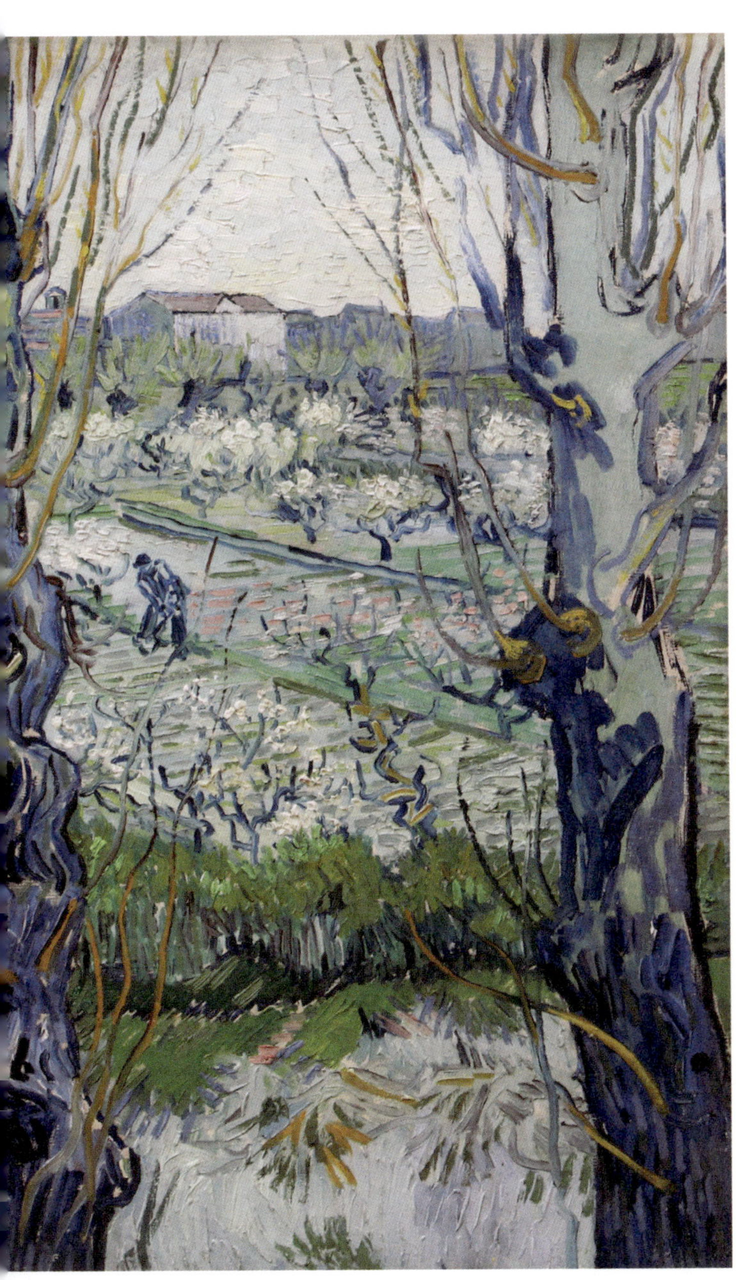

Lilac Bush

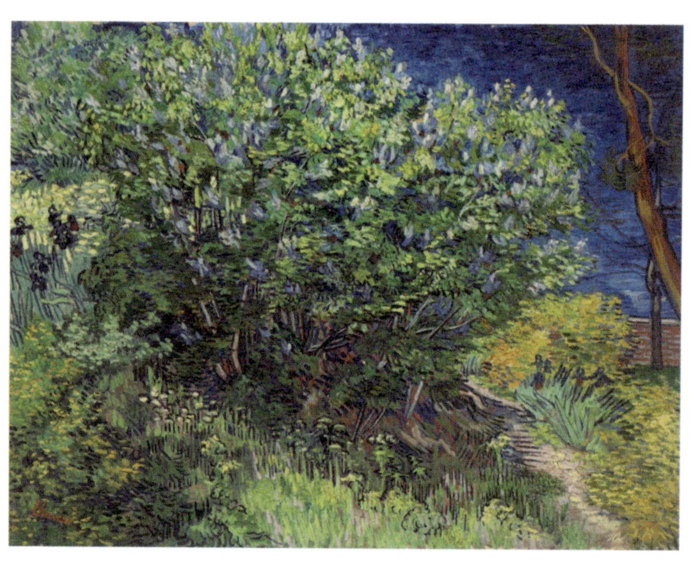

Oil on canvas
72 cm × 92 cm
(28⅜ in × 36¼ in)

May 1889
Saint-Rémy-de-Provence

Van Gogh was able to return to the Yellow House after his first episode of mental illness, but other attacks followed. In spring 1889, he wrote to Wil that 'in all I've had 4 big crises in which I hadn't the slightest idea of what I said, wanted, did.' (764) On 8 May, unable to manage on his own, Van Gogh admitted himself into Saint-Paul-de-Mausole, a psychiatric asylum northeast of Arles in Saint-Rémy-de-Provence.

The following day, Van Gogh wrote letters to Theo and to Theo's new wife, Jo van Gogh-Bonger (the wedding had taken place in April). He expressed his contentment on entering the asylum, remarking that 'little by little I can come to consider madness as being an illness like any other.' (772) He also mentioned that he had already begun working on two new paintings – 'violet irises and a lilac bush. Two subjects taken from the garden.'

For the first month of what would be a year-long stay, Van Gogh could not leave the hospital grounds. But his paintings *Irises* (page 148) and *Lilac Bush* reveal, in all their fresh vitality, how its walled garden was both a source of comfort and of inspired artistic production.

Lilac Bush

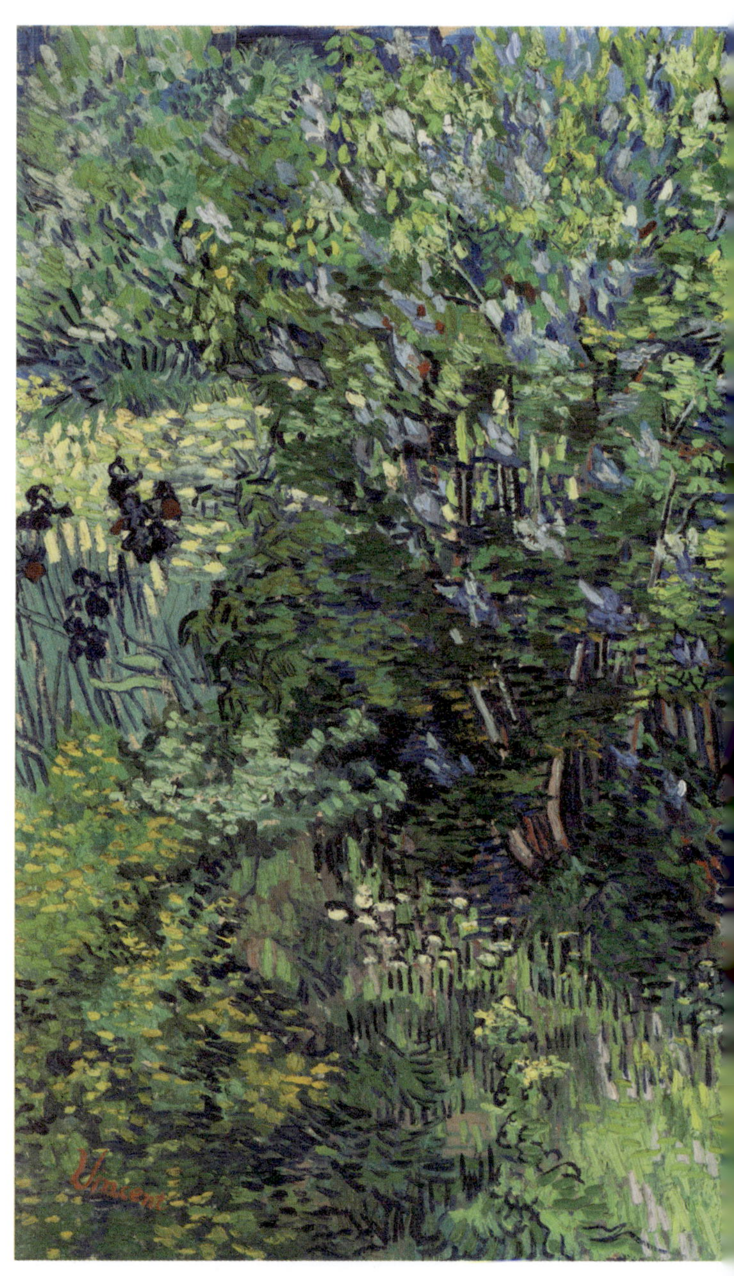

May 1889
Saint-Rémy-de-Provence

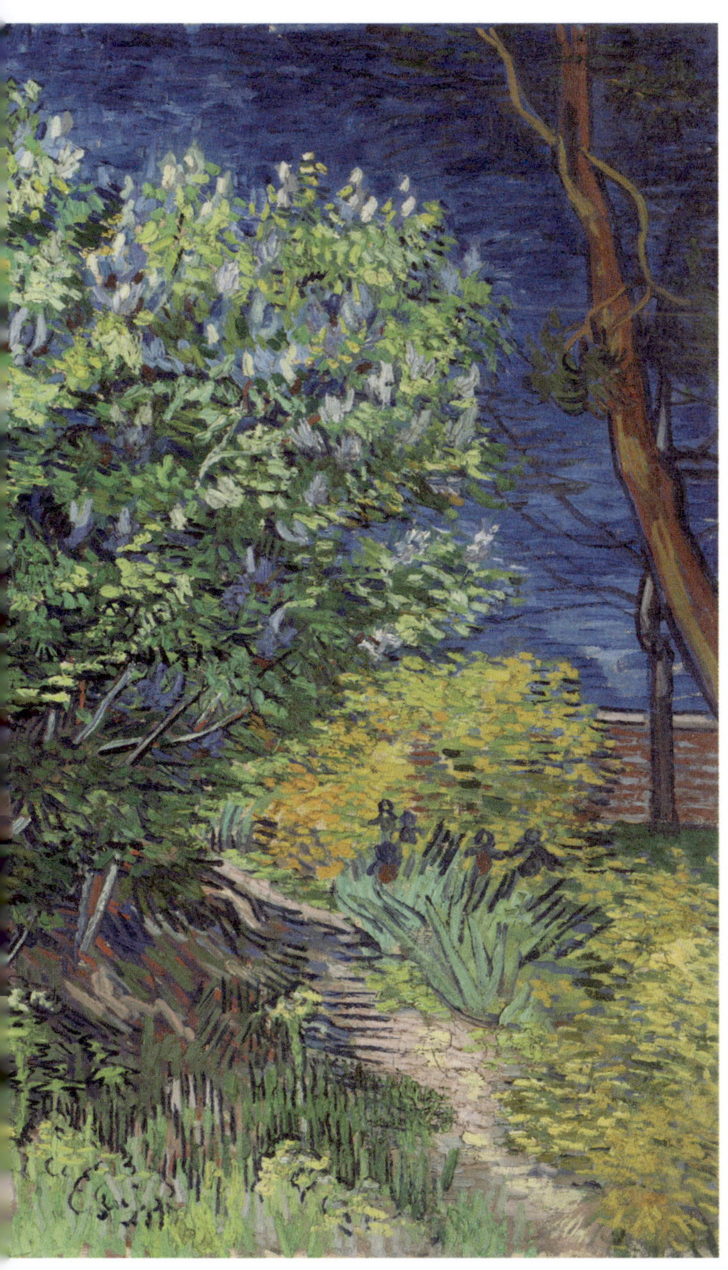

Irises

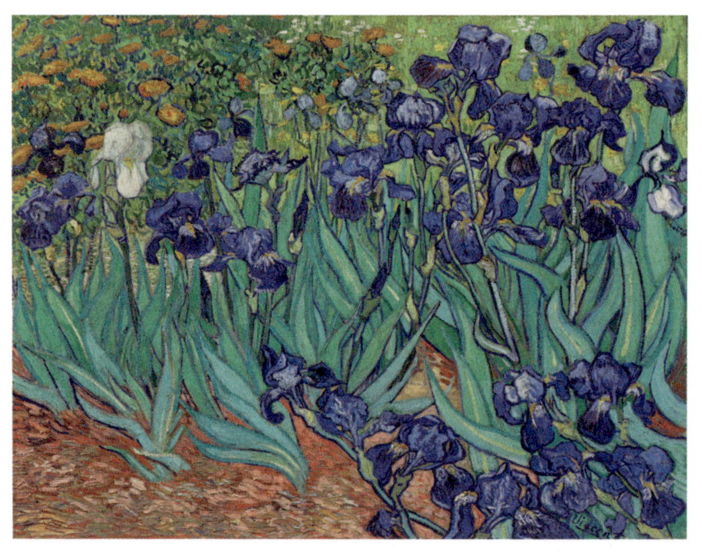

Oil on canvas
74.3 cm × 94.3 cm
(29¼ in × 37⅛ in)

May 1889
Saint-Rémy-de-Provence

The asylum in Saint-Rémy, where Van Gogh lived from May 1889 to May 1890, was housed in the ancient monastery of Saint-Paul-de-Mausole. Its overgrown walled garden was a tranquil haven for Van Gogh, and is the subject of many drawings, watercolours and oil paintings created during his stay. A couple of weeks after he arrived, Van Gogh wrote to Theo: 'When I send you the four canvases of the garden I have on the go you'll see that, considering that life happens above all in the garden, it isn't so sad.' (776)

Van Gogh had in fact begun two of these canvases – *Lilac Bush* (page 144) and the present *Irises* – as soon as he arrived at Saint-Paul. In this work, Van Gogh presents us with an extreme close-up of a section of life in the garden. Such is the crowding of the blue irises, particularly in the right foreground, we can sense Van Gogh stooping to study the flowers. He did this carefully, depicting the unique characteristics of each one. Encompassed by the warm russet of the soil and small orange flowers in the upper left, and by fresh tones of green, white and yellow, the irises seem to dance with life.

Irises

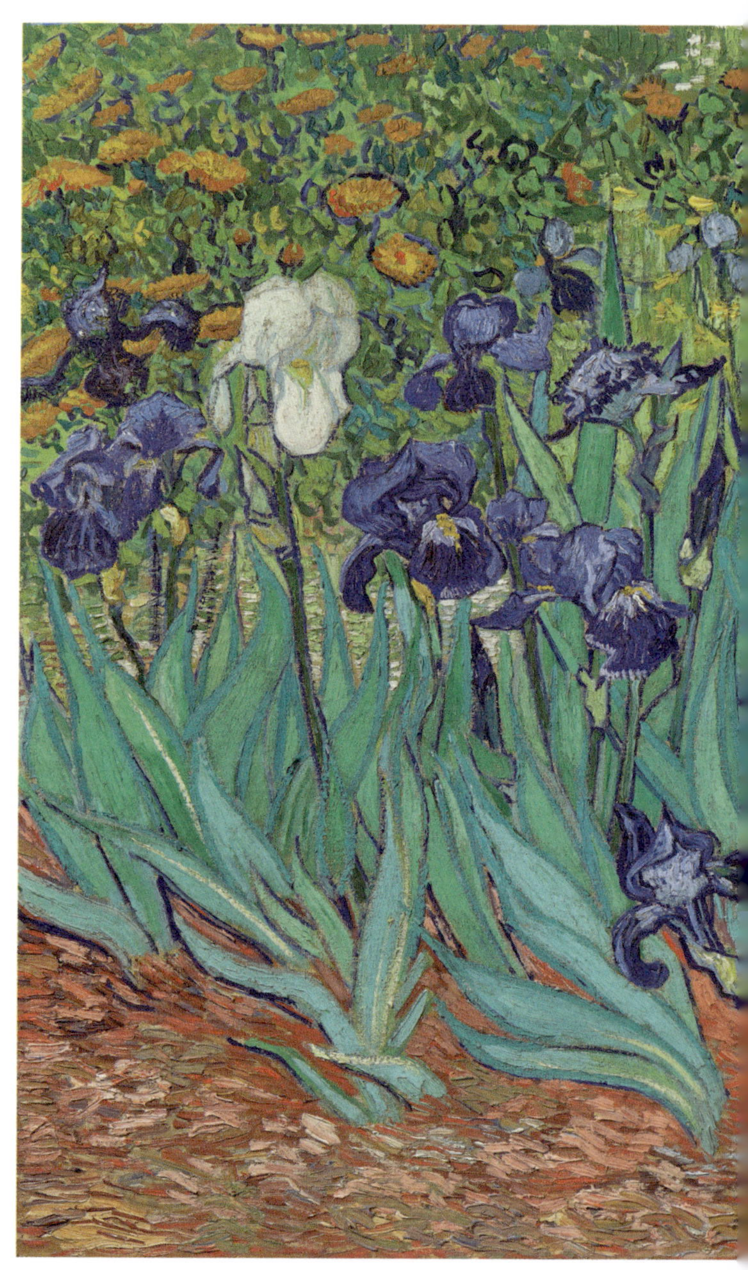

May 1889
Saint-Rémy-de-Provence

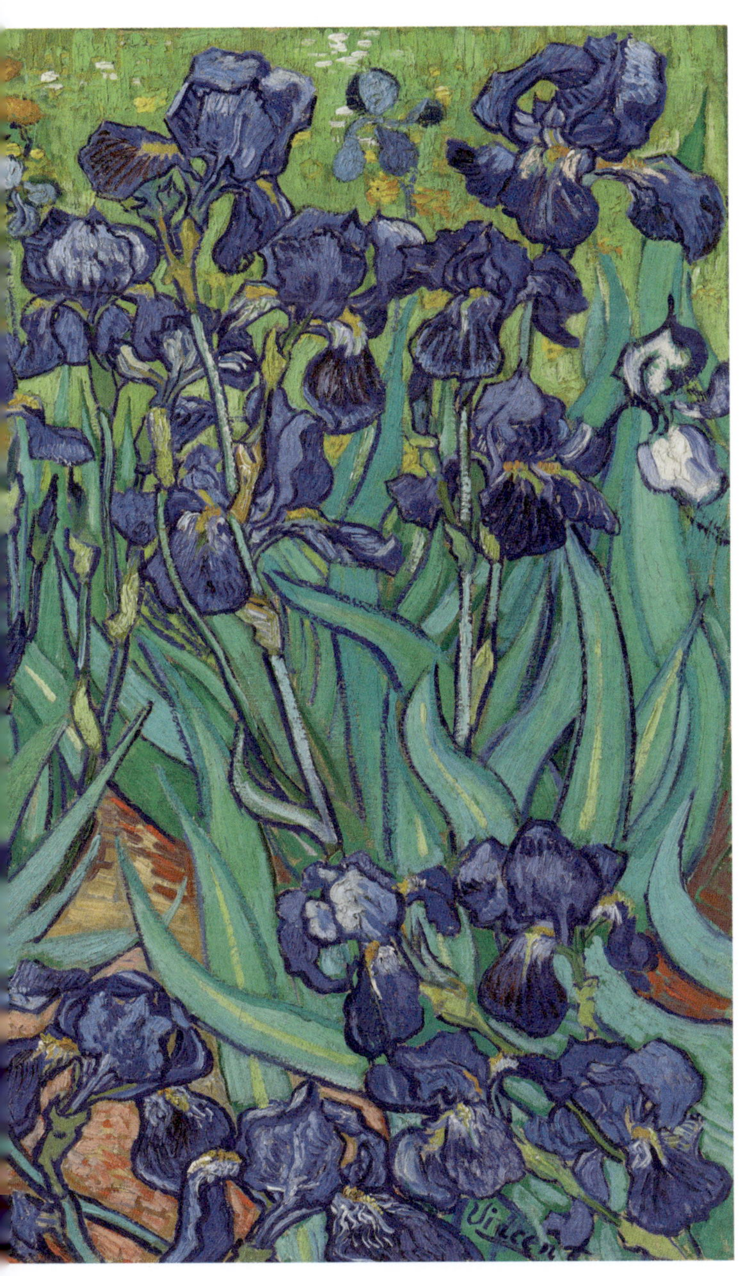

Green Wheat Field with Cypress

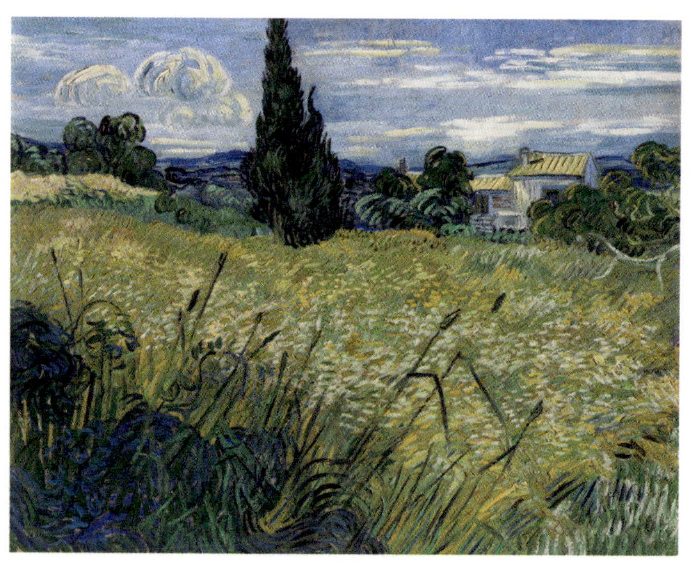

Oil on canvas
73 cm × 92.5 cm
(28¾ in × 36⅜ in)

June 1889
Saint-Rémy-de-Provence

At the Saint-Paul asylum, Van Gogh had a bedroom on the second floor and a room on the first where he could paint. Of the view from the former, he wrote: 'Through the iron-barred window I can make out a square of wheat in an enclosure ... above which in the morning I see the sun rise in its glory.' (776) Van Gogh made several drawings and paintings of this view, but by early June he was able to work outside the asylum accompanied by an escort. *Green Wheat Field with Cypress* was one of the first outcomes.

On 16 June 1889, he described the painting to Wil as 'a field of yellowing wheat surrounded by brambles and green bushes. At the end of the field a little pink house with a tall and dark cypress tree that stands out against the distant purplish and bluish hills and against a forget-me-not blue sky streaked with pink whose pure tones contrast with the already heavy, scorched ears, whose tones are as warm as the crust of a loaf of bread.' (780)

The cypress tree motif appears in several works from this time, including *The Starry Night* (page 156).

Green Wheat Field with Cypress

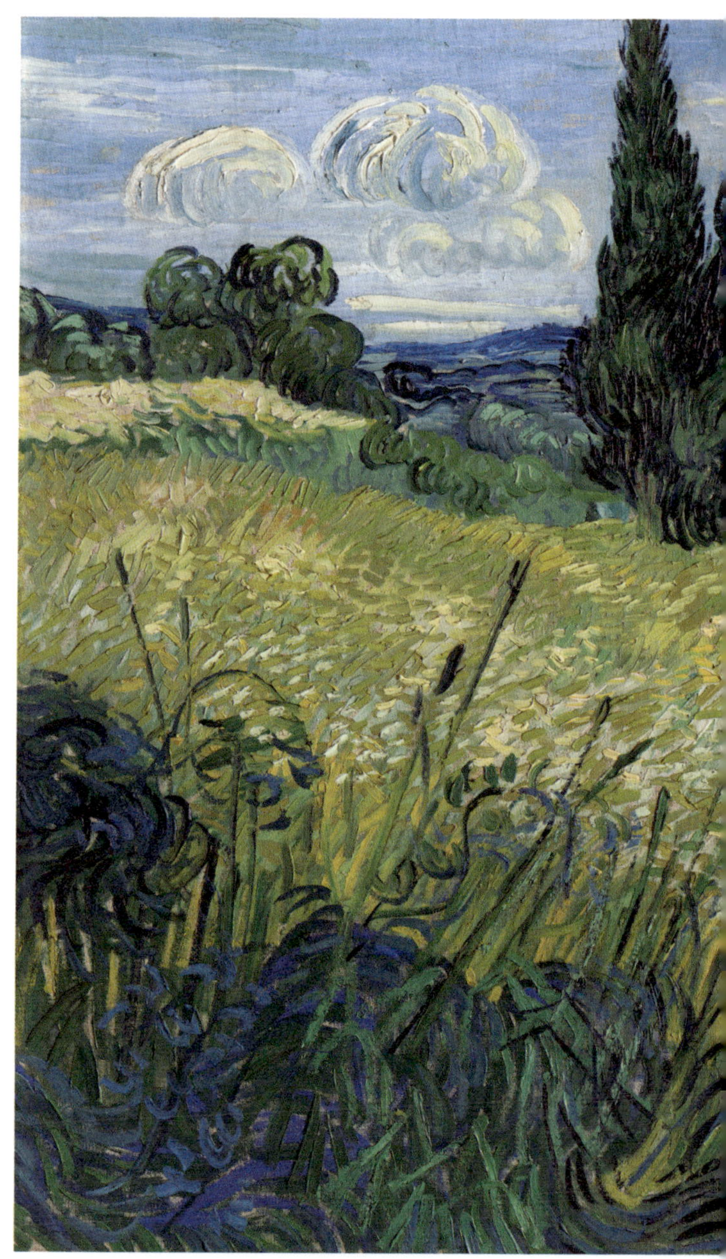

June 1889
Saint-Rémy-de-Provence

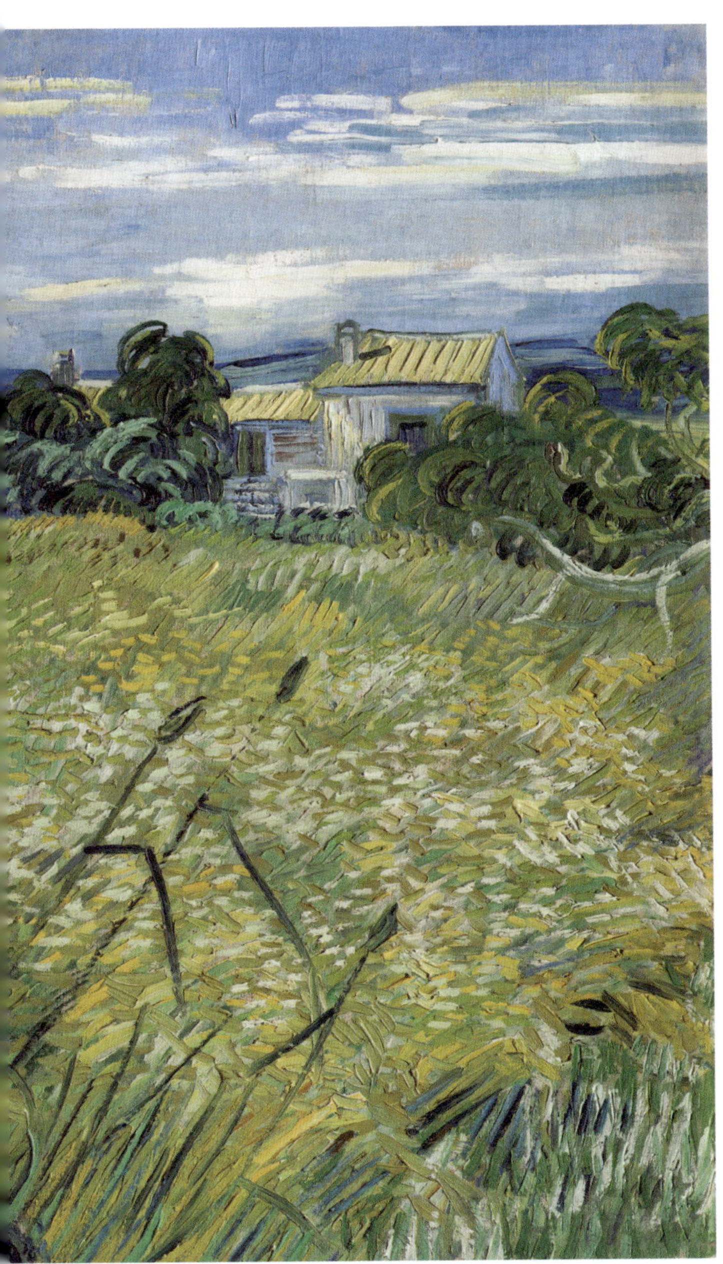

The Starry Night

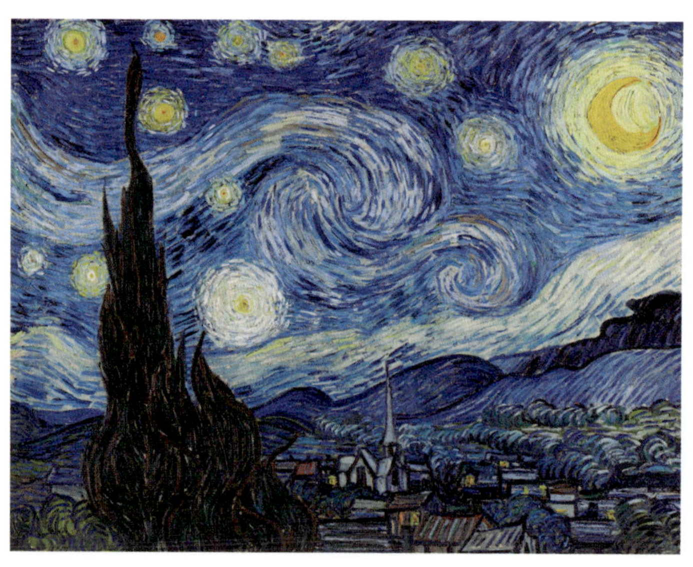

Oil on canvas
73.7 cm × 92.1 cm
(29 in × 36¼ in)

June 1889
Saint-Rémy-
de-Provence

When Van Gogh wrote to Theo from Arles in September 1888, enclosing a sketch of his recently completed *Starry Night Over the Rhône* (page 108), he said he had 'a tremendous need for, shall I say the word – for religion – so I go outside at night to paint the stars' (691).

For the former evangelist and trainee minister, religion was now found in nature. But this world did not have to be depicted realistically. In accord with the artistic theories of his friends Gauguin and Bernard and inspired, as always, by Delacroix, Van Gogh believed colour and line could be as truthfully expressive as any naturalistic representation. In Saint-Rémy, he created another *Starry Night* that demonstrates just that. It is one of his most famous works.

Painted with thick dashes of deep blue, yellow and white, the large, swirling sky, with its glowing crescent moon, almost overwhelms the quiet village below. The church steeple's verticality is mirrored by the tall cypresses, a motif that held special resonance for Van Gogh at this time (see *Wheat Field with Cypresses* on page 160). In Van Gogh's imaginative rendering of the night-time sky and of humans dwelling in nature, *The Starry Night* suggests wonderment.

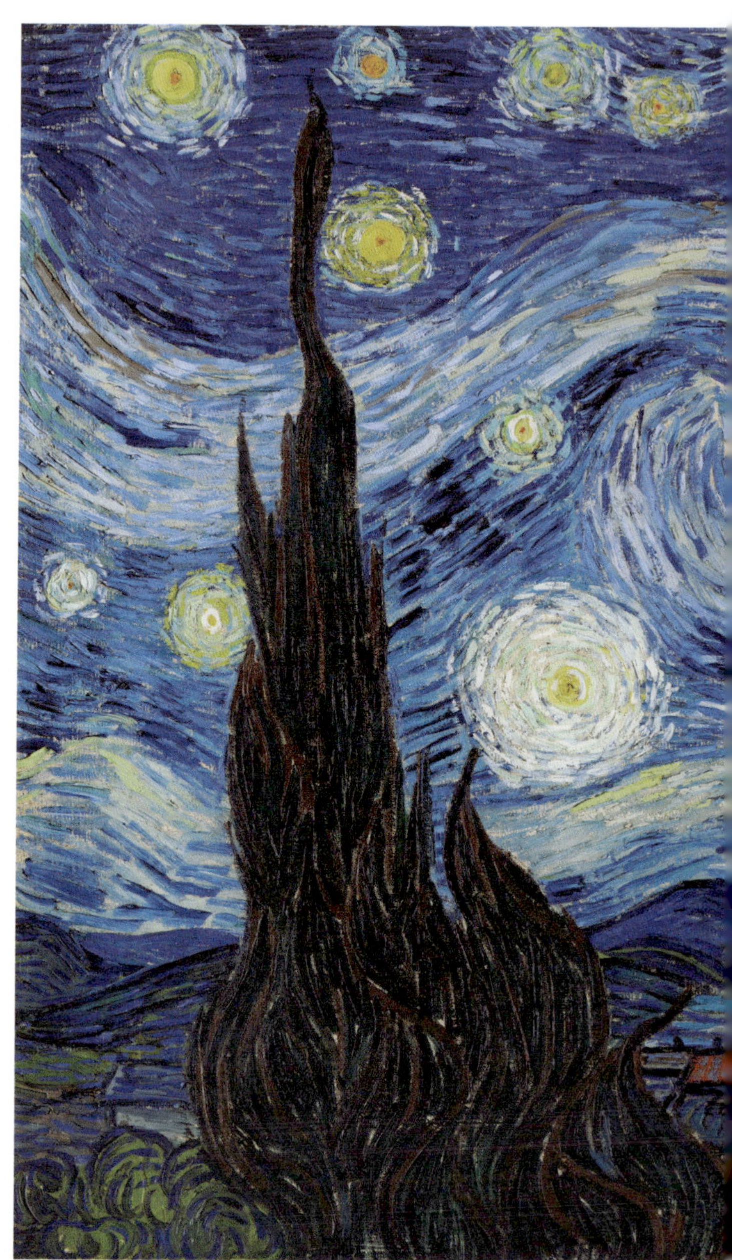

June 1889
Saint-Rémy-de-Provence

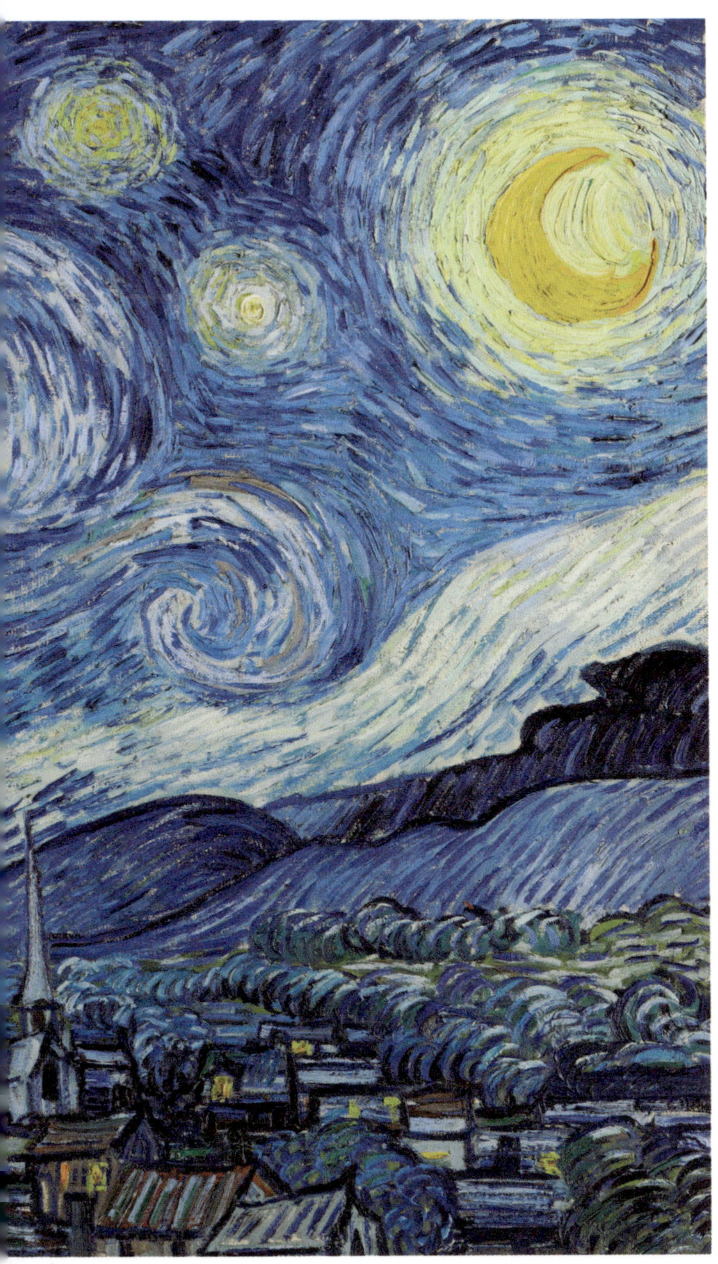

Wheat Field with Cypresses

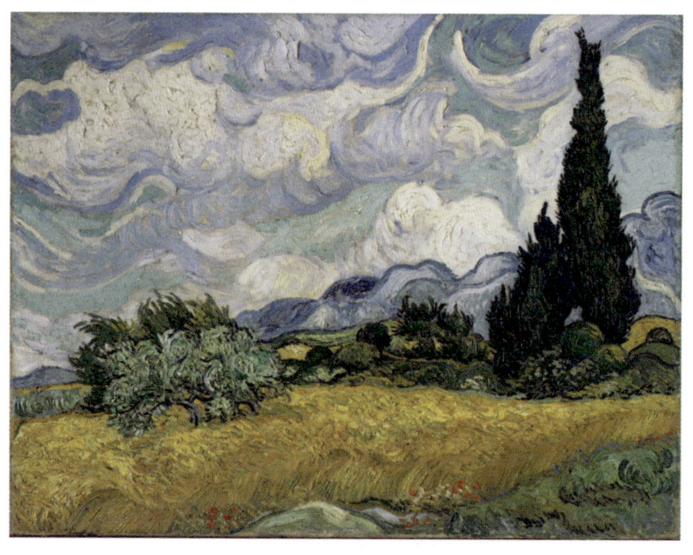

Oil on canvas
73.2 cm × 93.4 cm
(28⅞ × 36¾ in)

Late June-July 1889
Saint-Rémy-de-Provence

As demonstrated by the slightly earlier paintings *Green Wheat Field with Cypress* (page 152) and *The Starry Night* (page 156), cypress trees had a formal and symbolical importance for Van Gogh, and he painted several versions of the present work. He wrote to Theo on 25 June 1889:

'The cypresses still preoccupy me, I'd like to do something with them like the canvases of the sunflowers because it astonishes me that no one has yet done them as I see them. It's beautiful as regards lines and proportions, like an Egyptian obelisk. And the green has such a distinguished quality. It's the *dark* patch in a sun-drenched landscape, but it's one of the most interesting dark notes ... Now they must be seen here against the blue, *in* the blue, rather.' (783)

The blue sky of *Wheat Field with Cypresses* is a billowing mass of wind-blown clouds. Indeed, the whole landscape – the wheat field, the olive trees, even the blue Alpilles mountains – appears blown by southern France's mistral wind, which Van Gogh frequently mentions in his letters. Amongst all this movement, the cypresses, while still full of vital life, stand out as Van Gogh observed – as monumental obelisks.

Wheat Field with Cypresses

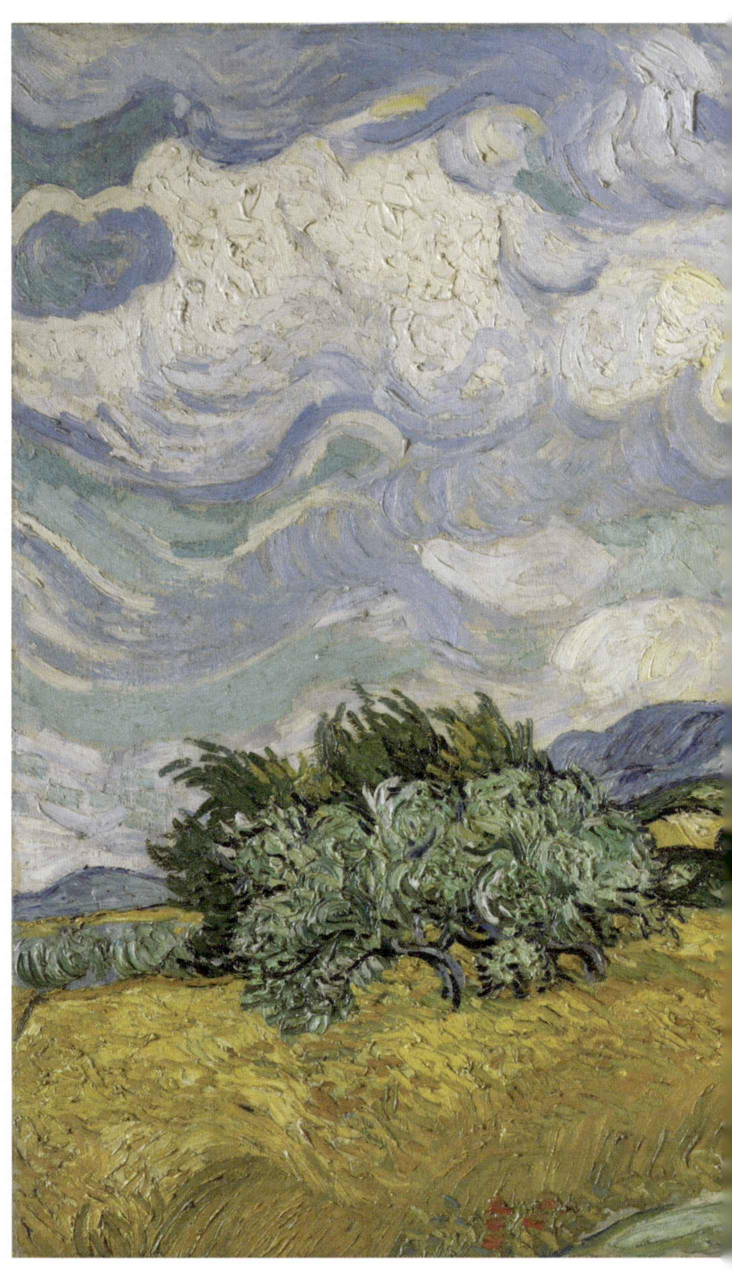

Late June-July 1889
Saint-Rémy-de-Provence

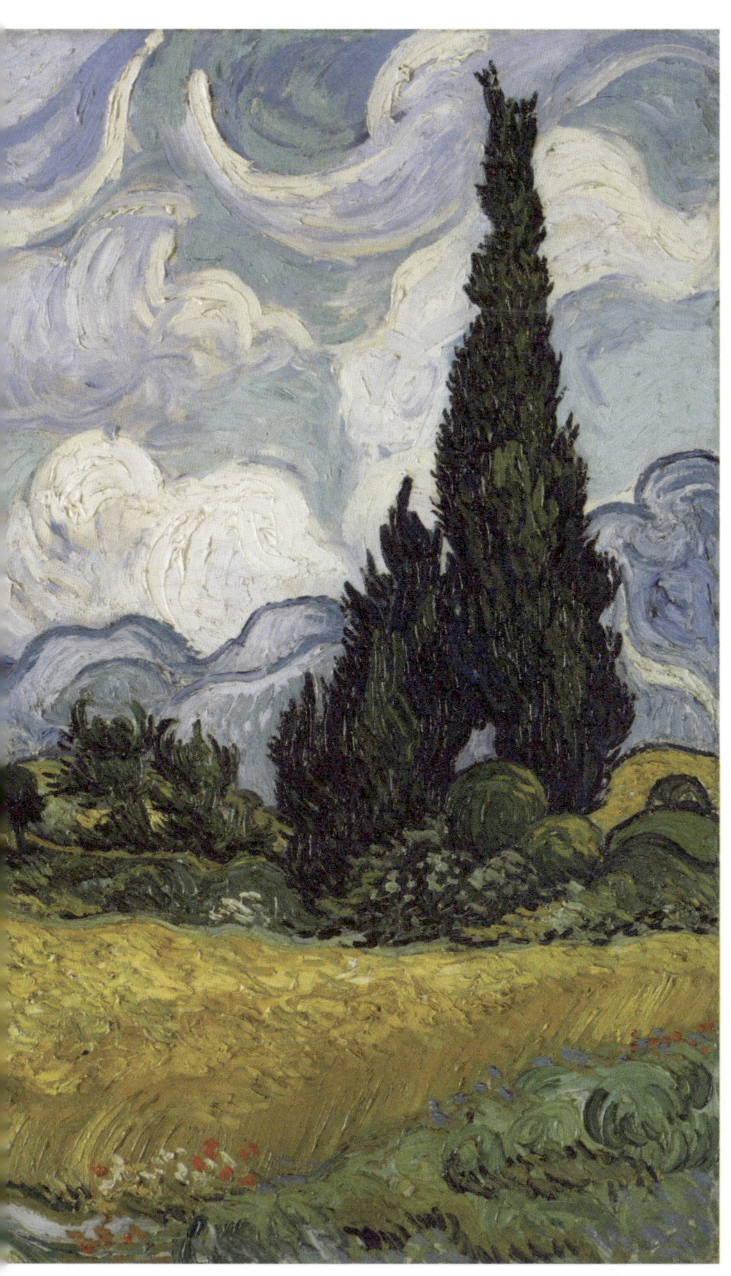

Self-Portrait

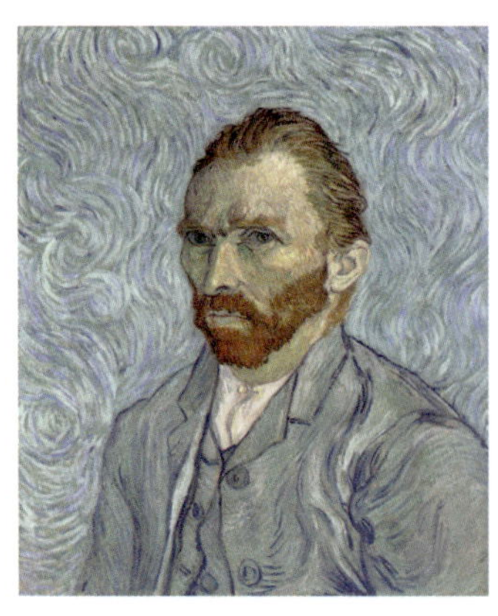

Oil on canvas
65 cm × 54.2 cm
(25⅝ in × 21⅜ in)

September 1889
Saint-Rémy-de-Provence

Comparing this painting with *Self-Portrait with Bandaged Ear and Pipe* (page 132), we can see how Van Gogh's artistic concerns changed when he moved to Saint-Rémy. There is less focus on bold colour contrasts and more emphasis on the expressive possibilities of brushwork. Not unlike *Wheat Field with Cypresses* (page 160), the entire canvas is suffused with movement. But the landscape of the former could be understood to be blown by the mistral wind. What causes the background eddies in this *Self-Portrait*? Or the animation of Van Gogh's clothes?

In the middle of July 1889 Van Gogh had another devastating attack and couldn't paint for six weeks. When he recovered, he threw himself back into his work – the thing he saw as 'quite necessary to me for my recovery' (797) – and created an astonishing number of artworks in a short period of time. One of the greatest was this penetrating *Self-Portrait*. Executed with masterful control, Van Gogh pictures himself gazing stilly and intently as these whirling forces assail him. Just as he discusses his illness so frankly in his letters, in this portrait his brushwork expresses the turmoil that can come from the mind.

Self-Portrait

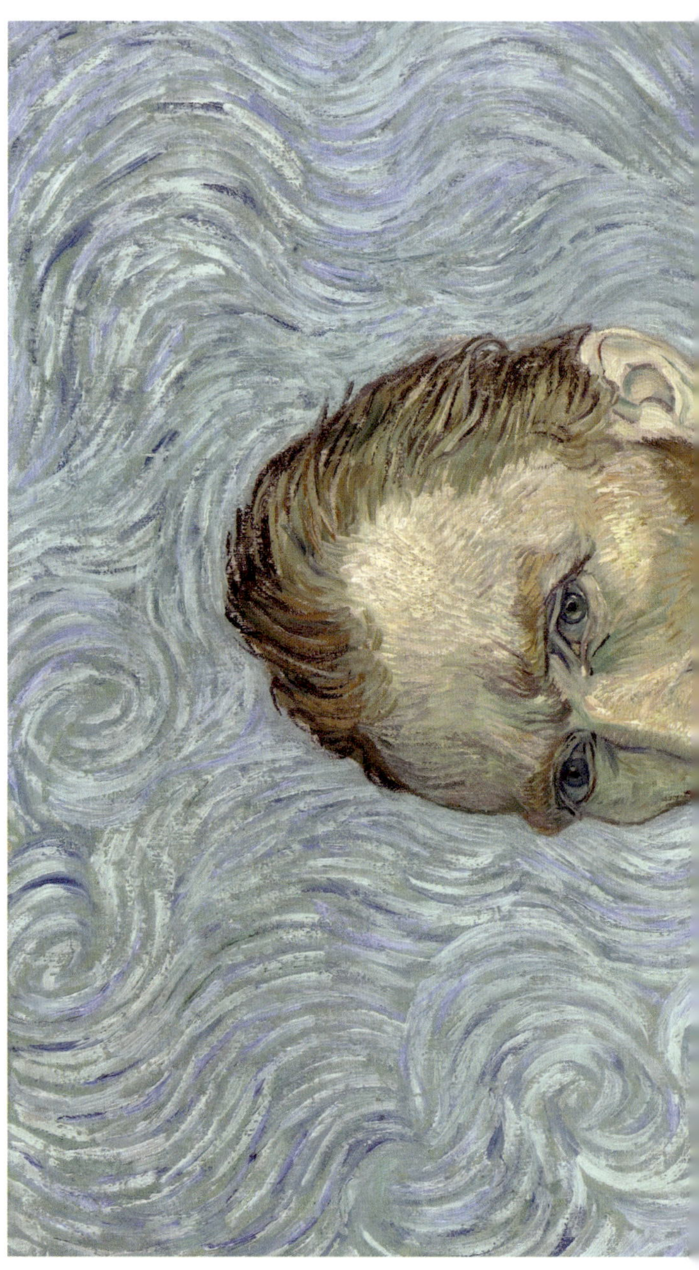

September 1889
Saint-Rémy-de-Provence

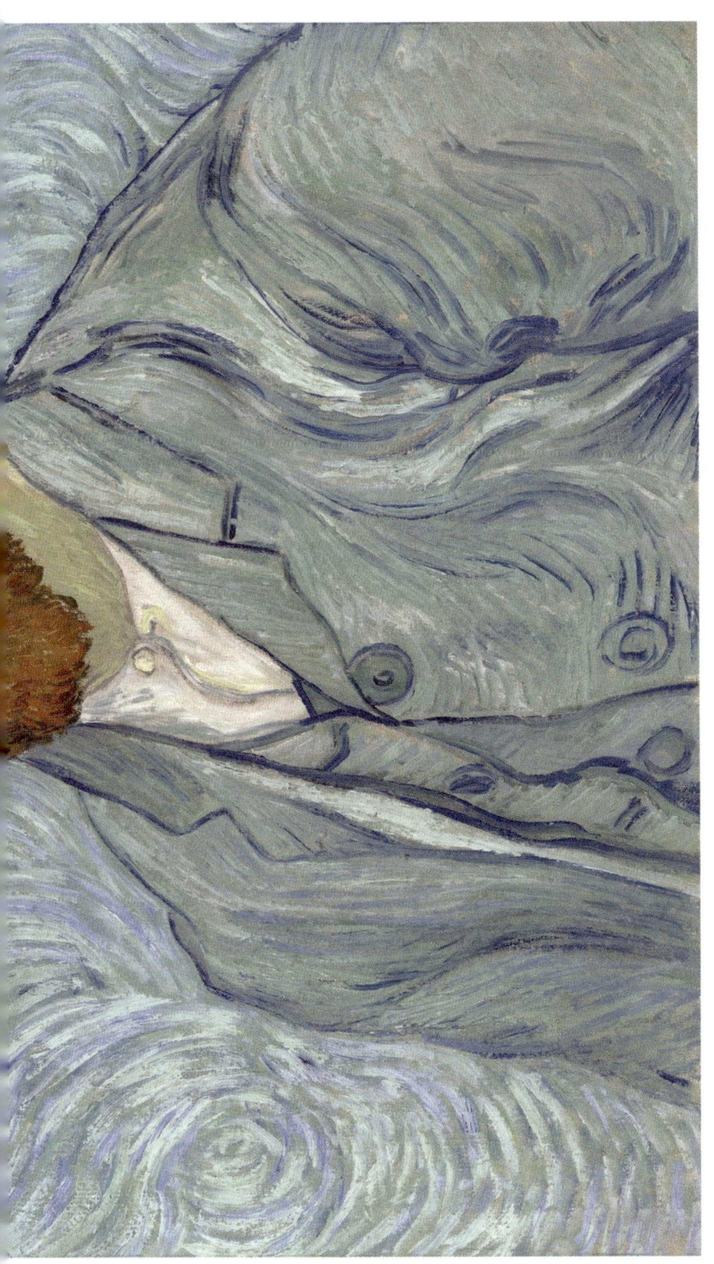

The Siesta

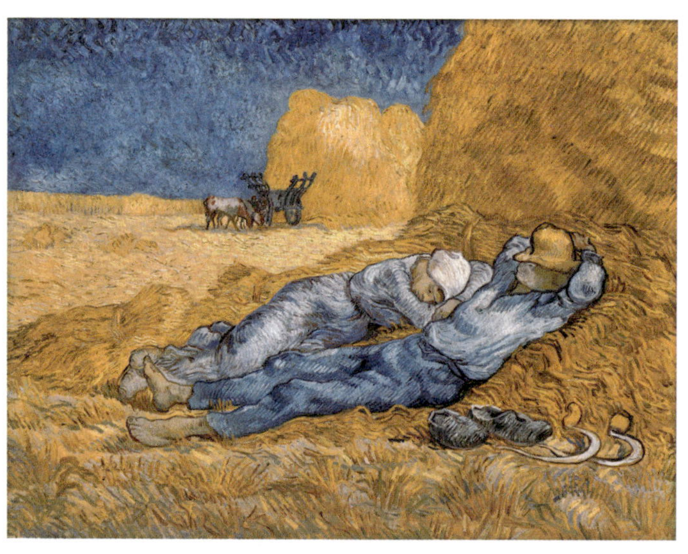

Oil on canvas
73 cm × 91 cm
(28¾ in × 35⅞ in)

January 1890
Saint-Rémy-
de-Provence

Van Gogh would have several attacks while a patient at the Saint-Paul asylum. In between were periods of recovery when he would pick up his work with resolve. When confined to the asylum due to health concerns or inclement weather, he would often make copies of his own paintings or those of others, particularly by the artists he most admired, including Rembrandt, Delacroix and Millet.

The Siesta was copied from an engraving by Adrien Lavieille after Millet's *Noonday Rest* (1866). Lavieille's engraving was part of the series *Four Times of the Day* and Van Gogh also made paintings after the other three prints. As he told Theo, his own works were not direct transcriptions of these: 'It is rather translating into another language, the one of colours, the impressions of chiaroscuro and white and black.' (839)

For *The Siesta*, Van Gogh carefully followed Millet's composition, including the details of the oxen and cart and the shoes and sickles, but the colouring and brushwork are distinctively his. The complementary colours of yellow and blue, which model forms through a multiplicity of short brushstrokes, create an image as warm and as restful as the subject matter it depicts.

The Siesta

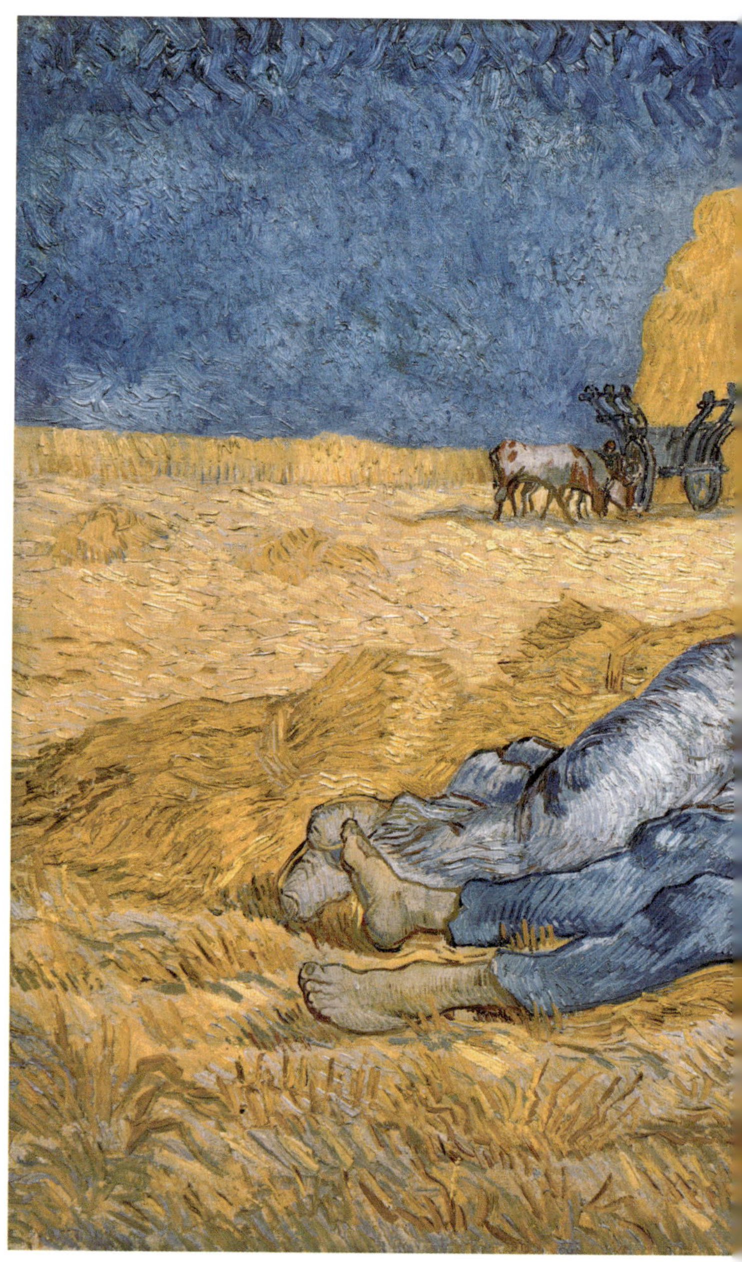

January 1890
Saint-Rémy-de-Provence

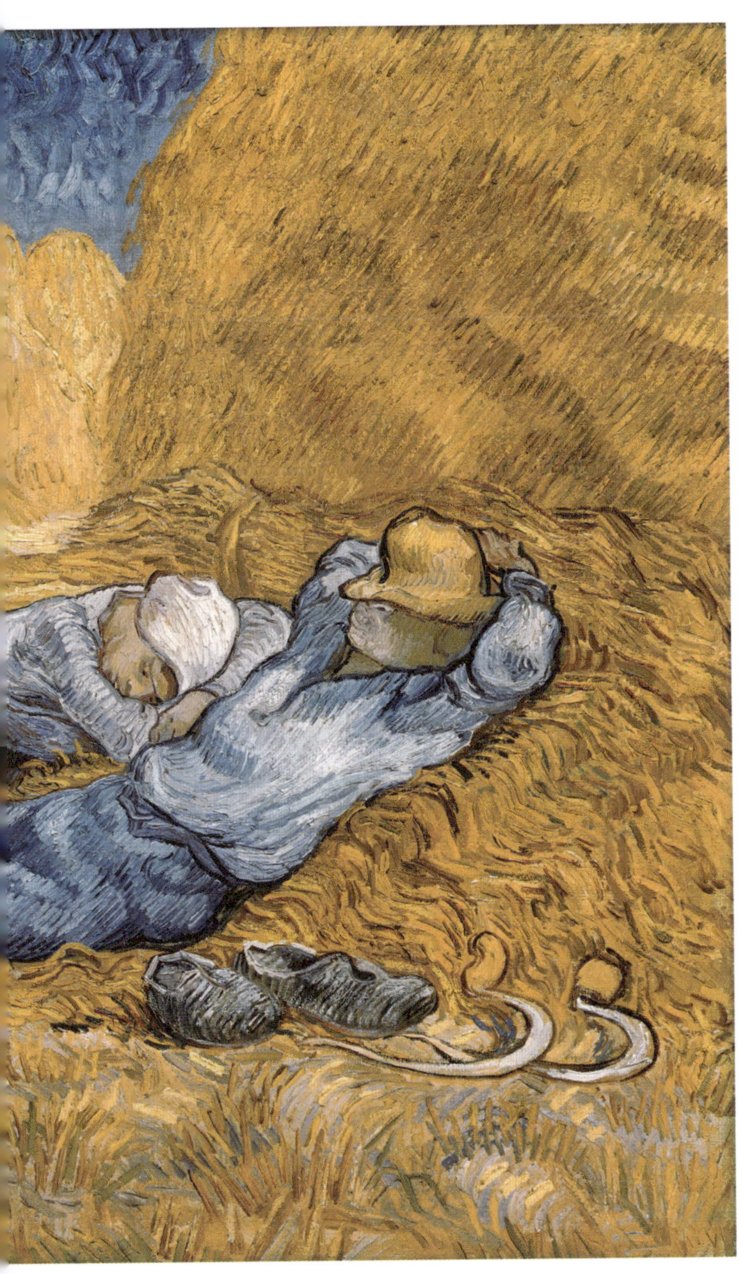

Prisoners Exercising

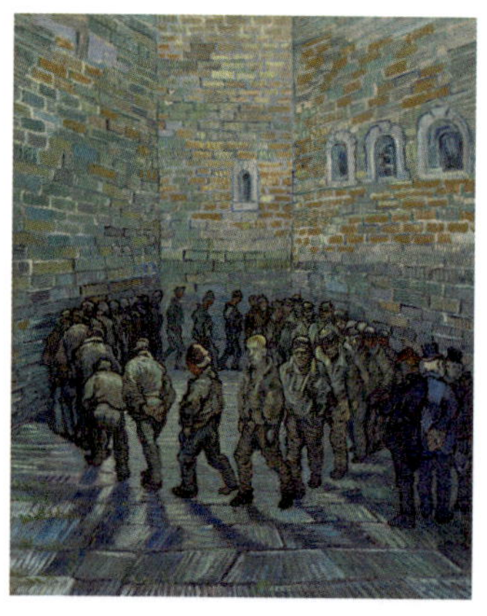

Oil on canvas
80 cm × 64 cm
(31½ in × 25¼ in)

February 1890
Saint-Rémy-
de-Provence

On 12 February 1890, Van Gogh wrote to Theo: 'I've tried to copy Daumier's Drinkers and Doré's Penitentiary, it's very difficult.' (854) Like *The Siesta* (page 168), these were 'translations' into his own colours and brushwork, though the two prints' subject matter is unusual for Van Gogh. Gustave Doré had made illustrations for the 1872 book *London: A Pilgrimage*, and the current work is after his *Penitentiary*, also known as *Newgate Prison Exercise Yard*.

The repetition of dark strokes of colour in the lower half of the canvas serves to intensify the scene's feeling of confinement and the terrible monotony of the men's lives. Their cast shadows indicate the sun above the walls. It has been suggested that the central prisoner with red hair is a self-portrait of Van Gogh. But even if that's not the case, it's not unreasonable to view *Prisoners Exercising* reflecting the tedium he felt living at the Saint-Paul asylum.

A little over two months later, Van Gogh wrote to Theo: 'The surroundings here are starting to weigh on me more than I could express – my word, I've waited patiently for over a year – I need air, I feel damaged by boredom and grief.' (868)

Prisoners Exercising

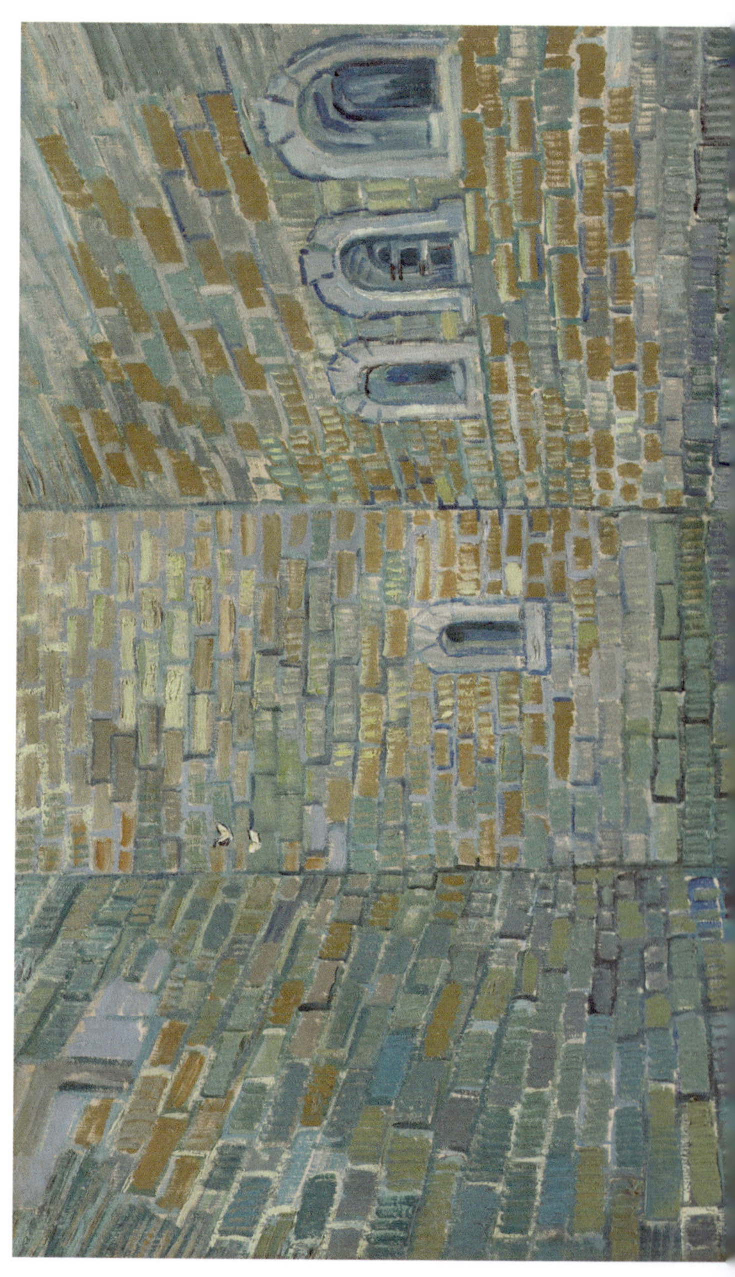

February 1890
Saint-Rémy-de-Provence

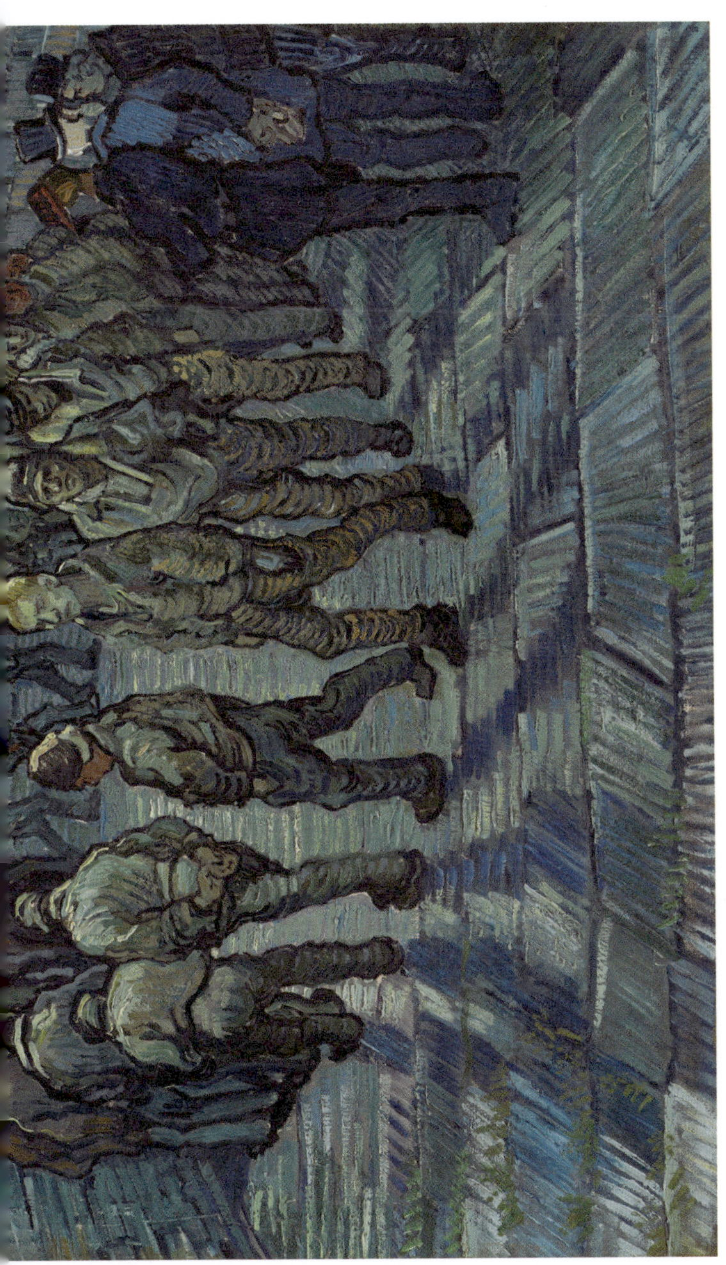

Almond Blossom

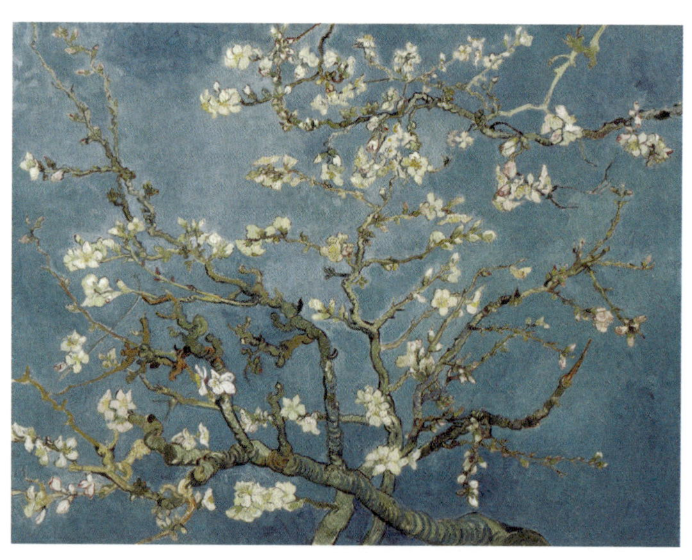

Oil on canvas
73.3 cm × 92.4 cm
(28⅞ in × 36⅜ in)

February 1890
Saint-Rémy-de-Provence

On 31 January 1890, Jo van Gogh-Bonger gave birth to a son. She and Theo named him Vincent after his uncle. Shortly thereafter, Van Gogh started work on this large canvas, which was to be a present for his nephew. An emblem of rebirth, the early flowering almond tree made the ideal subject for an artist who exulted in the new growth of spring (see *View of Arles, Flowering Orchards* on page 140).

This image transports the viewer to the foot of an almond tree. There we look up into the branches filled with white and pink blossoms and beyond to the blue sky. It is an exquisitely painted work, which in its decorative patterning is reminiscent of the Japanese prints that had so long inspired Van Gogh.

Sadly, for an image that symbolises so much hope, its completion marked the beginning of a two-month period of terrible illness for Van Gogh (see *Sorrowing Old Man (At Eternity's Gate)* on page 180).

Almond Blossom

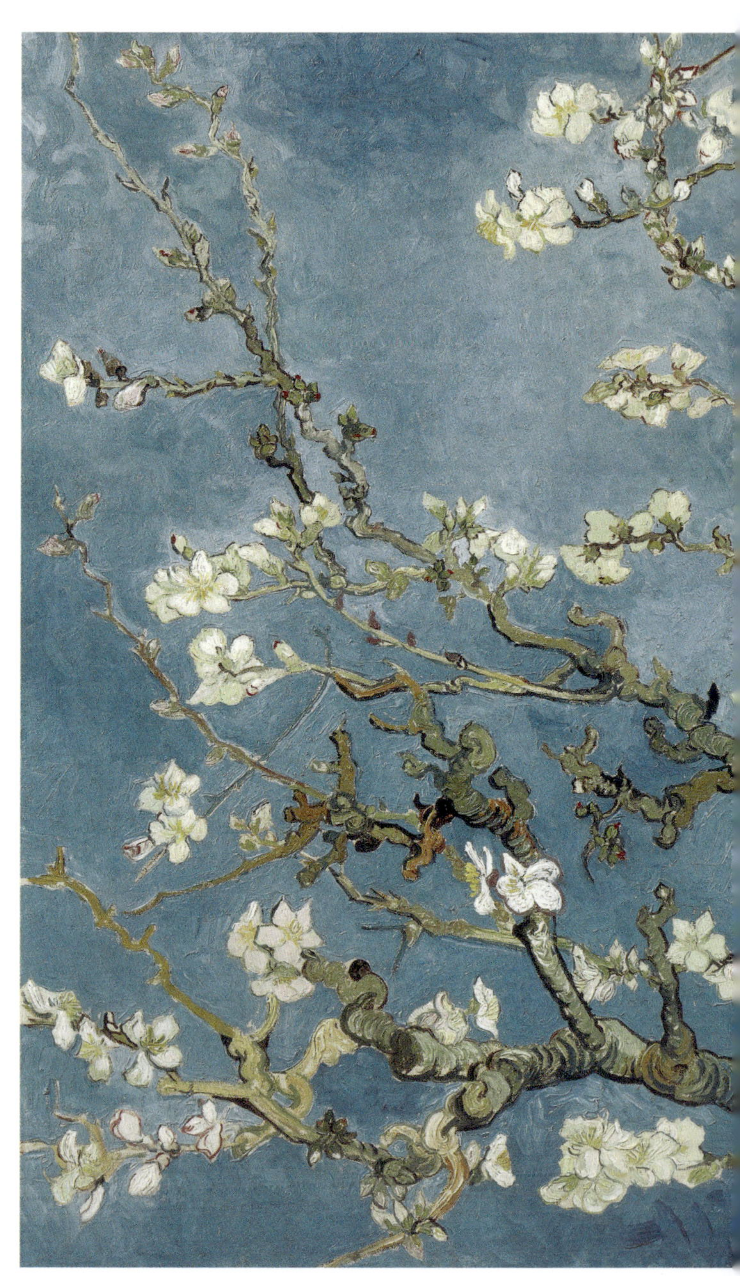

February 1890
Saint-Rémy-de-Provence

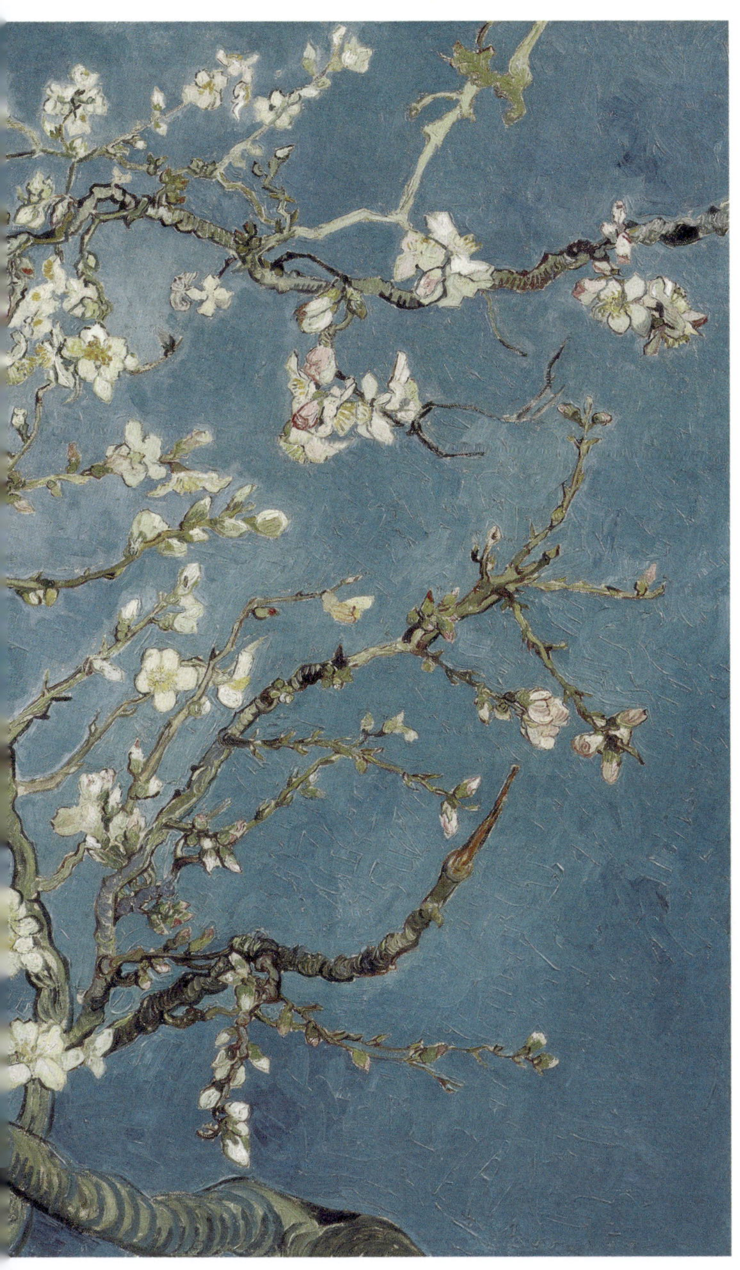

Sorrowing Old Man (At Eternity's Gate)

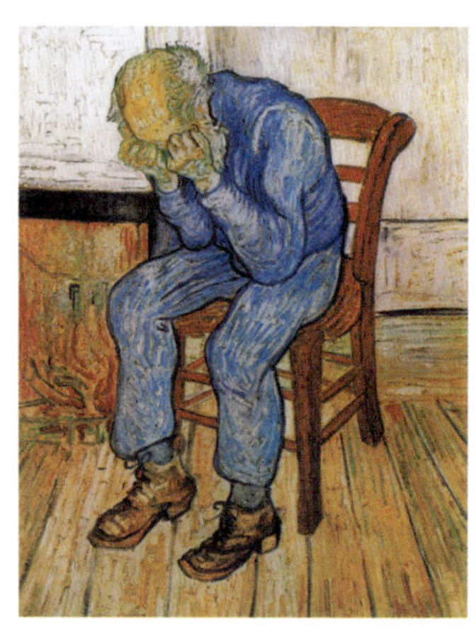

Oil on canvas
80 cm × 64 cm
(31½ in × 21¼ in)

March-April 1890
Saint-Rémy-de-Provence

As Van Gogh was working on *Almond Blossom* (page 176) in February 1890 he was beset by an attack. He later described this to Theo: 'Work was going well, the last canvas of the branches in blossom ... painted with calm and a greater sureness of touch. And the next day done for like a brute. Difficult to understand things like that, but alas, that's how it is.' (857)

March and April were a despairing time of crisis for Van Gogh. He was, however, still able to create some paintings and drawings, mainly recreations of images from early in his career. Among these was the *Sorrowing Old Man*, a subject that he first depicted in The Hague in a drawing and a lithograph called *At Eternity's Gate* (1882).

The crushing sadness of this image is mirrored in a description of Vincent that Theo included in a letter to his sister-in-law Mien Bonger: 'The doctor recently wrote that for weeks now he's been sitting with his head in his hands and if one speaks to him, he makes signs that he wants to be alone.' (n.1, 863)

Sorrowing Old Man (At Eternity's Gate)

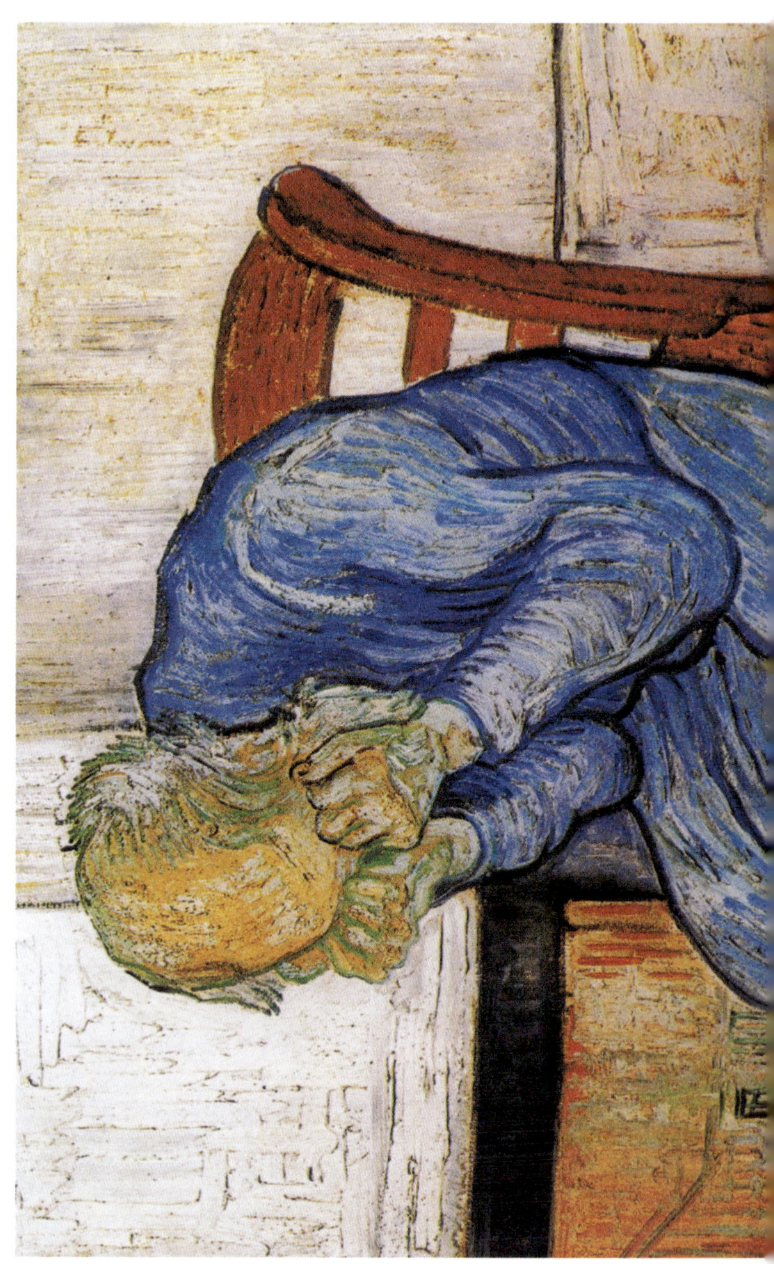

March-April 1890
Saint-Rémy-de-Provence

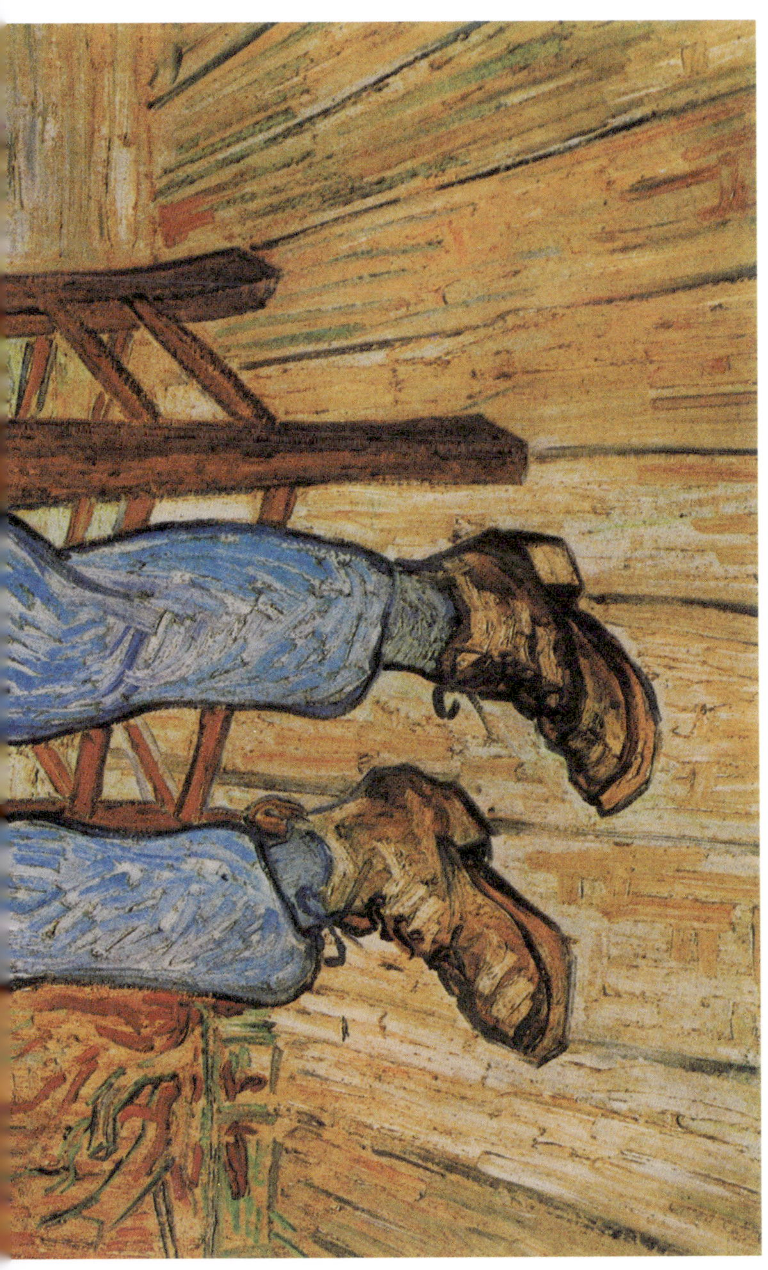

Road with Cypress and Star

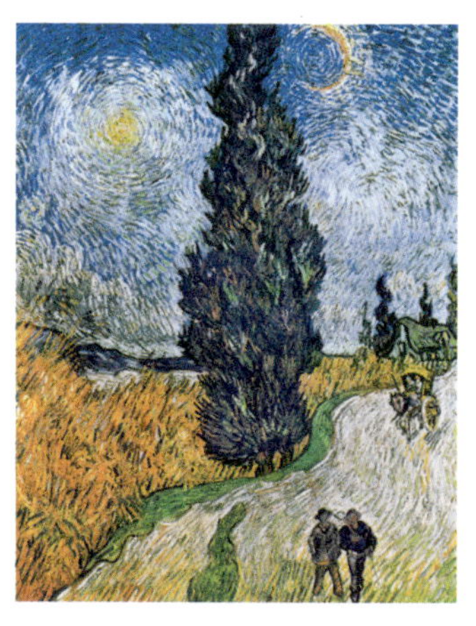

Oil on canvas
90.6 cm × 72 cm
(35⅝ in × 28⅜ in)

May 1890
Saint-Rémy-
de-Provence

During Van Gogh's last few days in Saint-Rémy he still 'worked in a frenzy. Big bouquets of flowers, violet irises, big bouquets of roses. Landscapes.' (RM19) One of the latter was the present canvas, likely the last painting he made at the asylum. In an unsent letter to Gauguin, Van Gogh described the work:

'A last try – a night sky with a moon without brightness, the slender crescent barely emerging from the opaque projected shadow of the earth – a star with exaggerated brightness, if you like, a soft brightness of pink and green in the ultramarine sky where clouds run. Below, a road bordered by tall yellow canes behind which are the blue low Alpilles, an old inn with orange lighted windows and a very tall cypress, very straight, very dark. On the road a yellow carriage harnessed to a white horse, and two late walkers. Very romantic if you like, but also "Provençal" I think.' (RM23)

Reminiscent of the renowned *Starry Night* (page 156), which Van Gogh had painted at the beginning of his stay in Saint-Rémy, this vital, 'Provençal' canvas seems to close out this particular period in his life. The peripatetic artist was to be on the road again.

Road with Cypress and Star

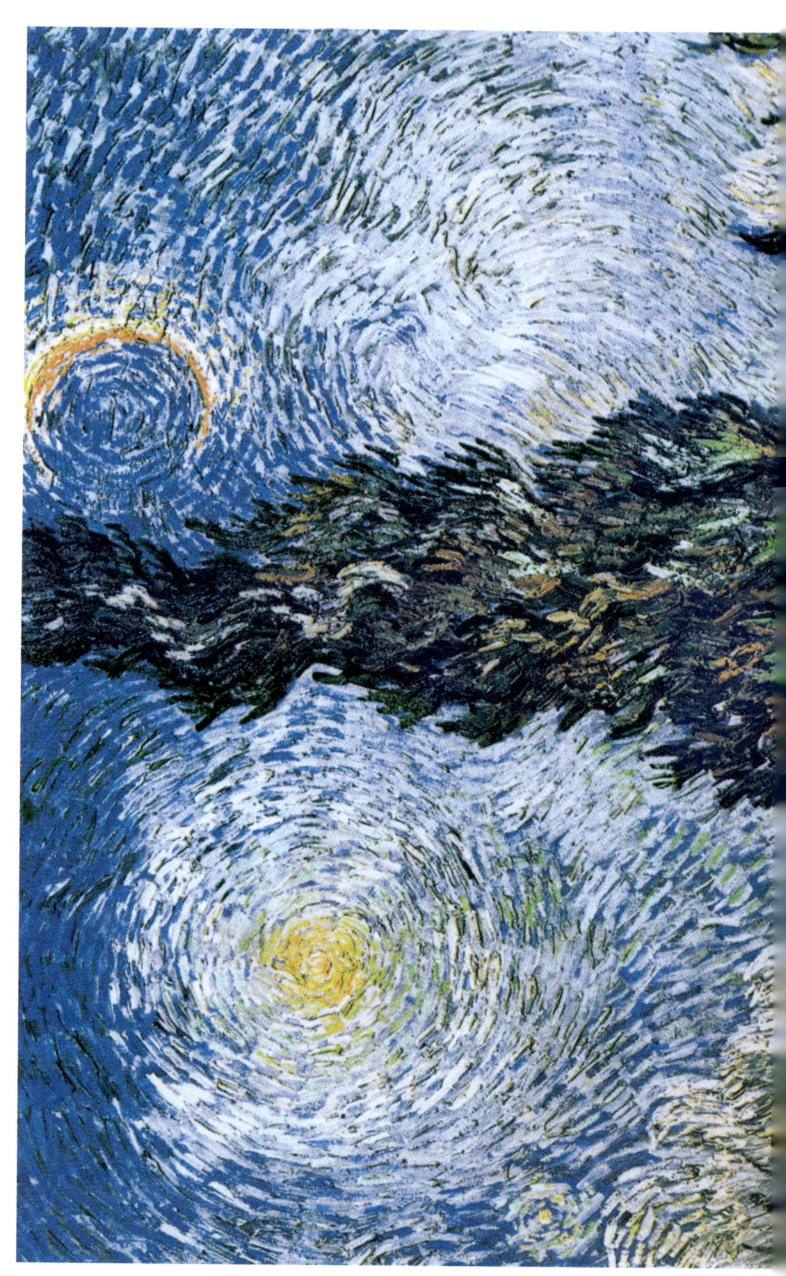

May 1890
Saint-Rémy-de-Provence

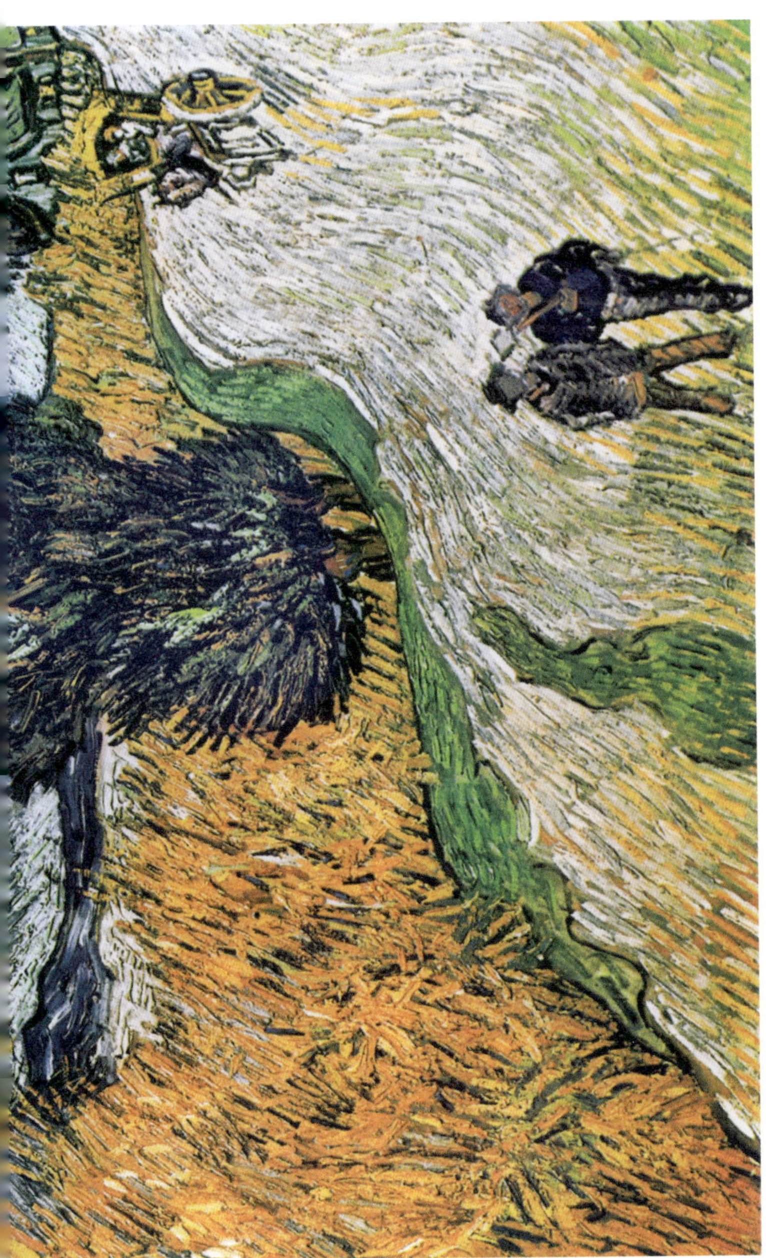

Street in Auvers-sur-Oise

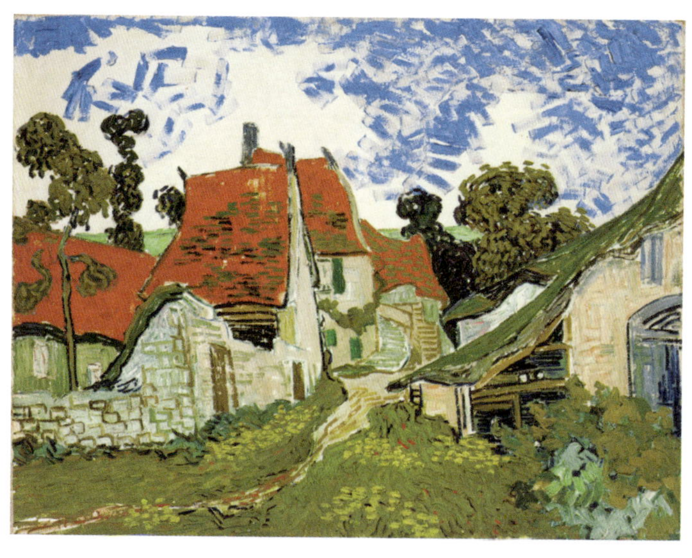

Oil on canvas
73.5 cm × 92.5 cm
(28⅞ in × 36⅜ in)

May 1890
Auvers-sur-Oise

On 16 May 1890 Van Gogh left Saint-Rémy. He had for a while expressed his wish to leave the asylum and to move back to northern France. Therefore, through a recommendation of the painter Camille Pissarro, Theo arranged that Vincent be placed in the care of a doctor, Paul Gachet, in Auvers-sur-Oise, a village around thirty kilometres northwest of Paris.

After visiting Theo, Jo and his nephew Vincent in Paris, Van Gogh arrived in Auvers on 20 May. He wrote to them the same day, saying how beautiful it was, with 'among other things many old thatched roofs'. He added that he would paint a few canvases of the village, 'for really it's gravely beautiful, it's the heart of the countryside, distinctive and picturesque.' (873)

In this brightly coloured composition with its storybook houses, we clearly see Van Gogh's unbridled enthusiasm for his new environment. We can sense the joy with which he applied the rapid brushstrokes, thick and dense in the foreground and more summary in the creation of the unfinished sky. It was one of the earliest of more than thirty paintings that Van Gogh would make in the last two months of his life.

Street in Auvers-sur-Oise

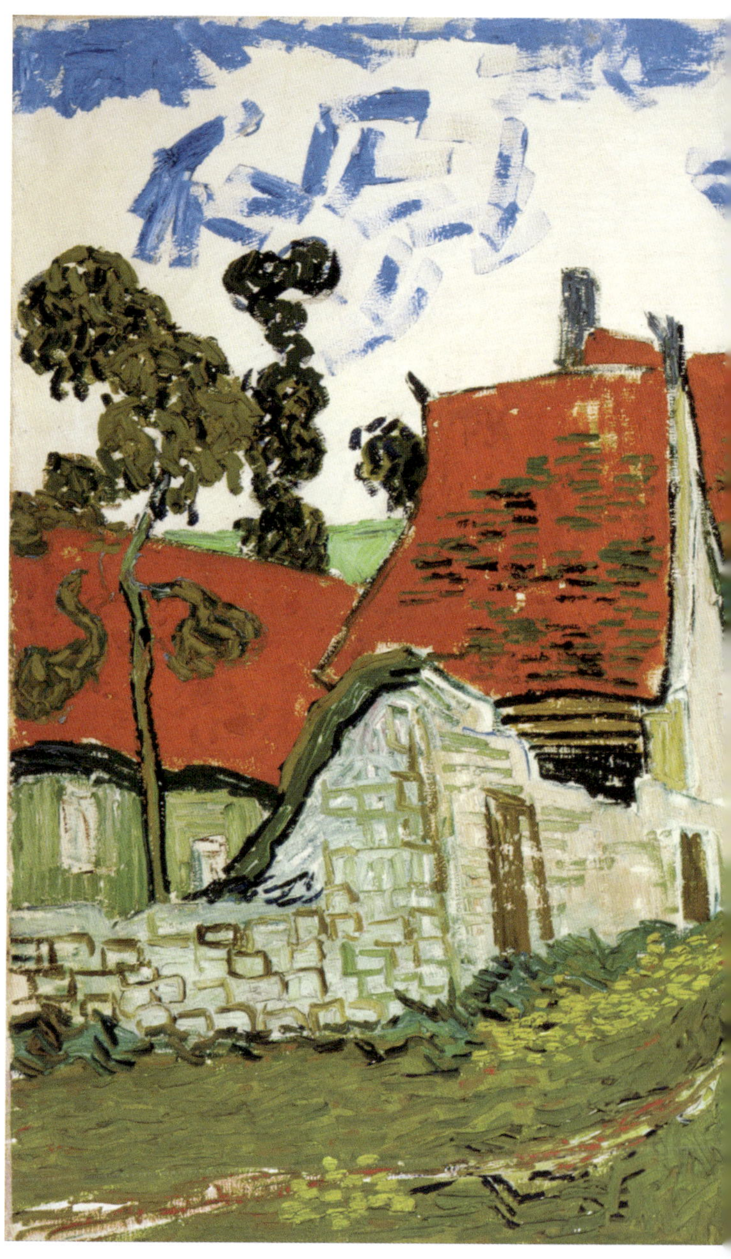

May 1890
Auvers-sur-Oise

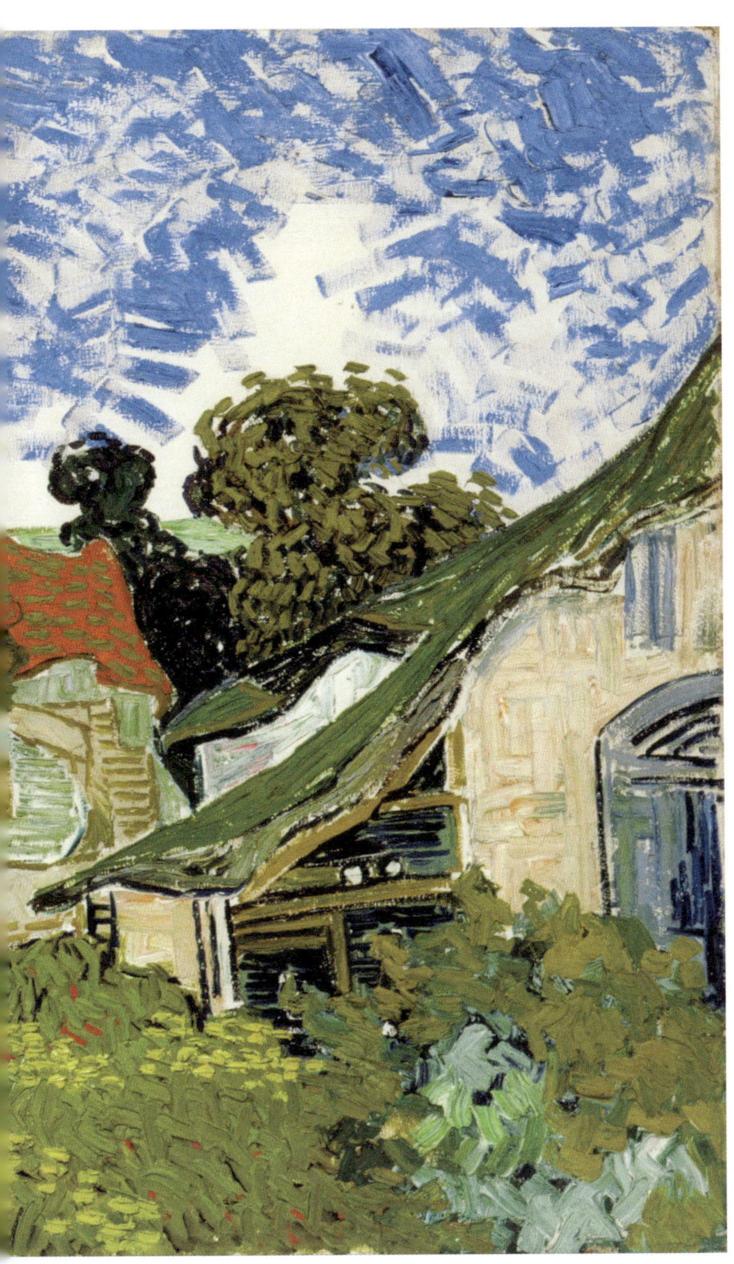

The Church at Auvers

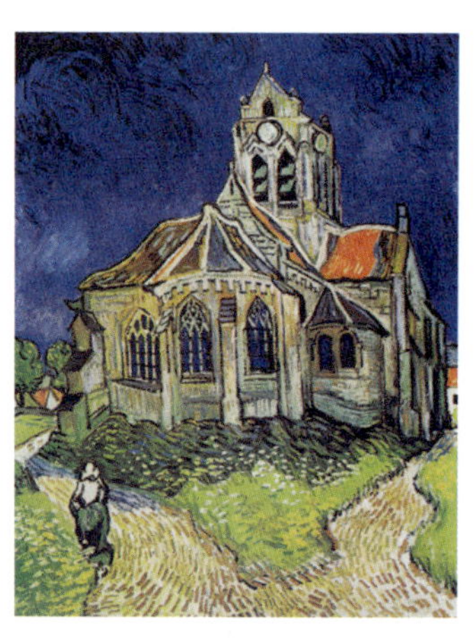

Oil on canvas
93.5 cm × 74.5 cm
(36¾ in × 29⅜ in)

June 1890
Auvers-sur-Oise

When Van Gogh arrived in Auvers he rented a room at the Auberge Ravoux. Inspired by his new surroundings, he then embarked on another hugely productive period of work, as already indicated by *Street in Auvers-sur-Oise* (page 188). This included a large painting of the village church. He told Wil that this reminded him of studies he'd made of the old tower in Nuenen, but 'only now the colour is probably more expressive, more sumptuous.' (879)

If we compare the present work with *The Parsonage Garden at Nuenen* (page 16), where the old church tower is visible in the background, we can see just how much Van Gogh's approach to colour changed over the course of six years. As the Van Gogh expert Jan Hulsker has observed, his qualifying 'probably' is redundant.

In *The Church at Auvers* the deep cobalt blue sky, which is reflected in the 'ultramarine blue patches' (879) of the stained-glass windows, is particularly stirring, though each of the colours magnifies the effect of the others. The picture's vitality is furthered by the wavy forms of the path and the church's roofline, as though even these inanimate objects are infused with life and emotion.

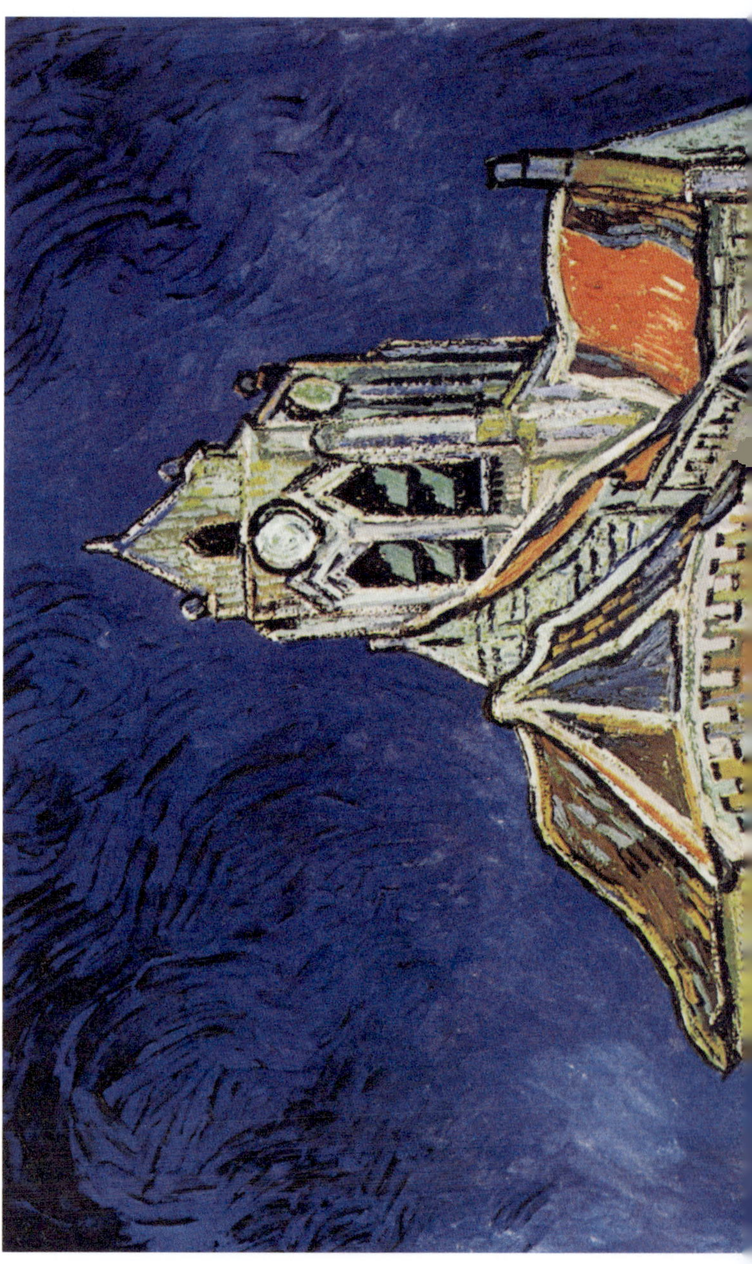

June 1890
Auvers-sur-Oise

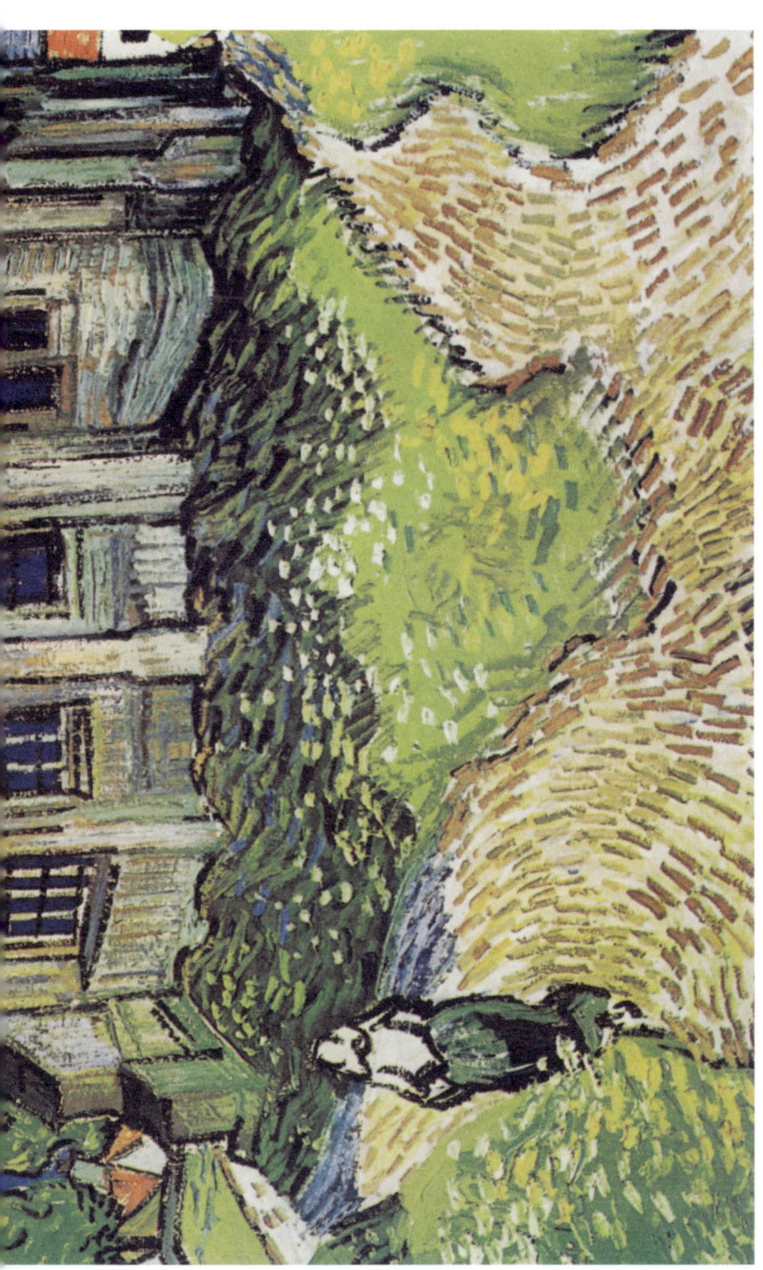

Portrait of Dr Gachet

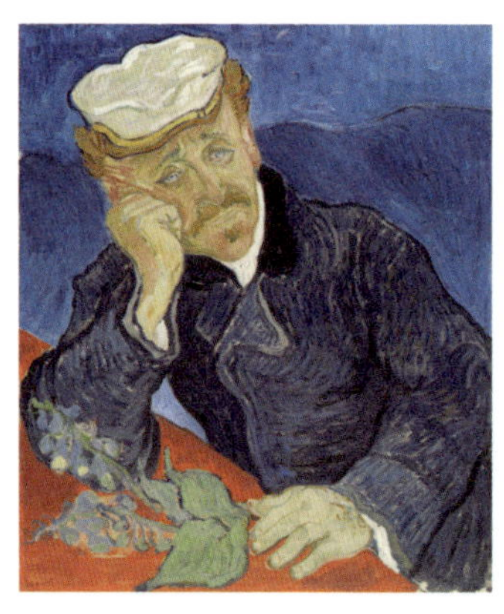

Oil on canvas
67 cm × 56 cm
(23⅖ in × 22 in)

June 1890
Auvers-sur-Oise

After meeting the doctor who was to assume his care in Auvers, Van Gogh gave a rather wry account of his character: 'I've seen Dr Gachet, who gave me the impression of being rather eccentric, but his doctor's experience must keep him balanced himself while combating the nervous ailment from which it seems to me he's certainly suffering at least as seriously as I am.' (873)

Dr Gachet was also an amateur artist who knew several of the French art avant-garde, and he and Van Gogh became good friends. Van Gogh depicted him in an etching (Van Gogh's first) and in two paintings. Particularly illuminating is how Van Gogh described his portraits of Dr Gachet as being 'in the same sentiment' as his penetrating *Self-Portrait* (page 164) of September 1889, which he said the doctor was 'absolutely *fanatical* about' (877).

In the present work, superb in its colouring, composition and depth of feeling, the doctor, who practised in homoeopathy, holds a healing foxglove. But his melancholy is clear, for Van Gogh portrays him 'with the deeply sad expression of our time.' (RM23)

Portrait of Dr Gachet

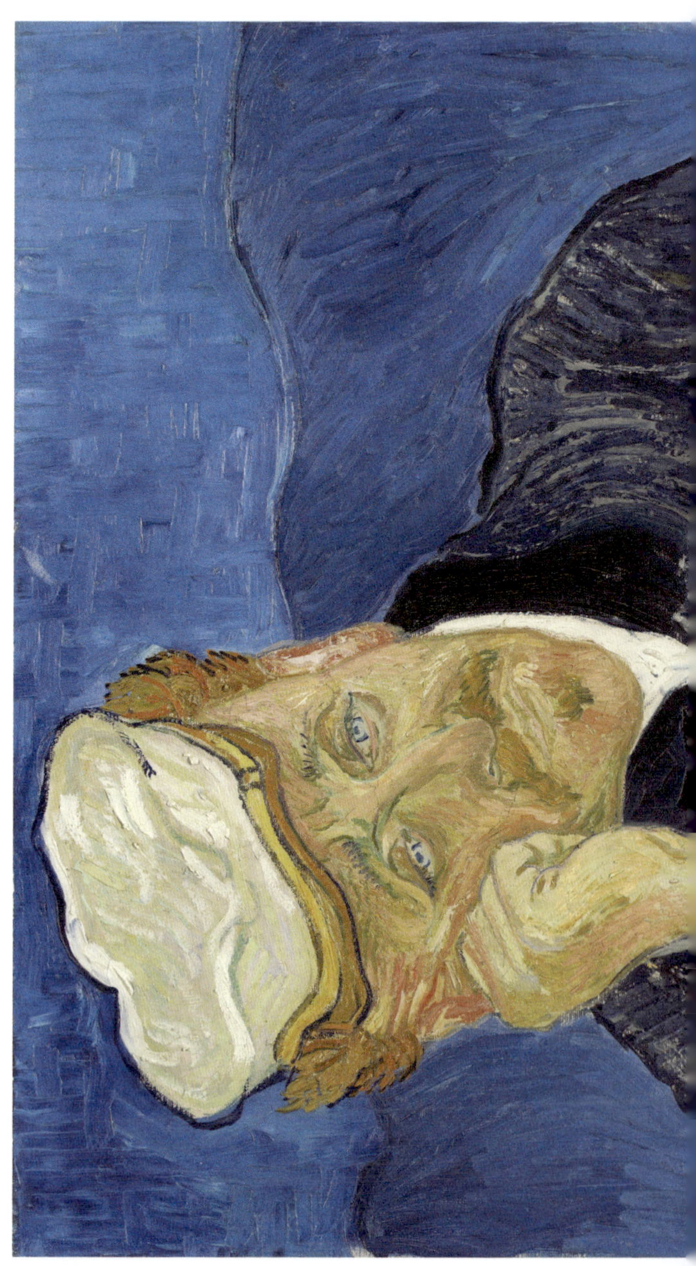

June 1890
Auvers-sur-Oise

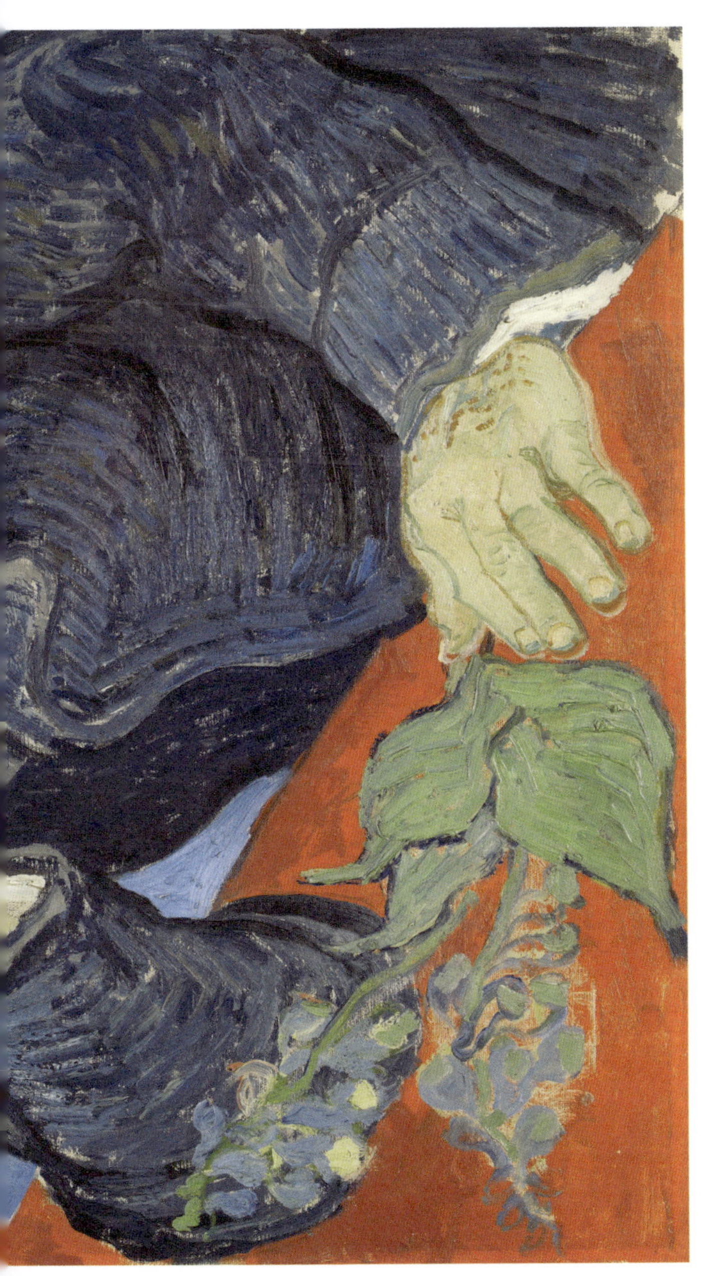

Wheatfield with Crows

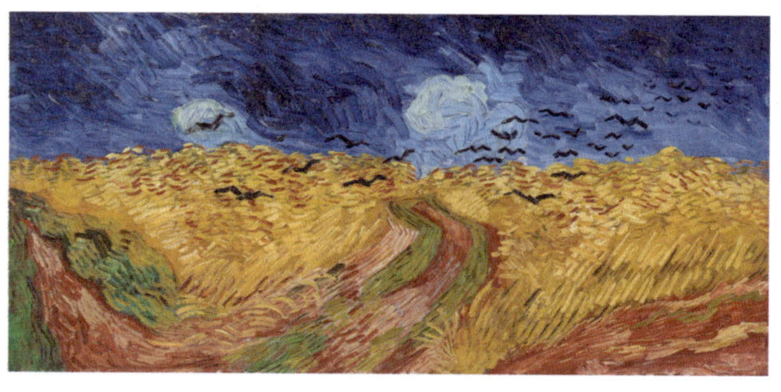

Oil on canvas
50.5 cm × 103 cm
(19⅞ in × 40½ in)

July 1890
Auvers-sur-Oise

In the final month of Van Gogh's life he painted several landscapes, including *Wheatfield with Crows*. This famous painting is often viewed as a harbinger of Van Gogh's suicide, but there is no proof this was his last work as is sometimes claimed. It does, however, encapsulate the painter's brilliant expressionism and the illness that threatened him.

The horizontally elongated canvas is painted with thick, rapid brushstrokes in bold, complementary colours. Yet any notion of a rural idyll is undermined by the dark sky and the black crows, which are masterly rendered with mere dashes of paint. A sense of unease is furthered by the inclusion of three paths, the destinations of which are unknowable.

In one of his last letters to Theo, Van Gogh wrote that in creating his recent wheatfield paintings he 'made a point of trying to express sadness, extreme loneliness', but he added that they also represented 'what I consider healthy and fortifying about the countryside.' (898) Nature gave Van Gogh strength and hope, but ultimately he could no longer fight off the sadness. He died in Auvers of a self-inflicted gunshot wound on 29 July 1890.

Wheatfield with Crows

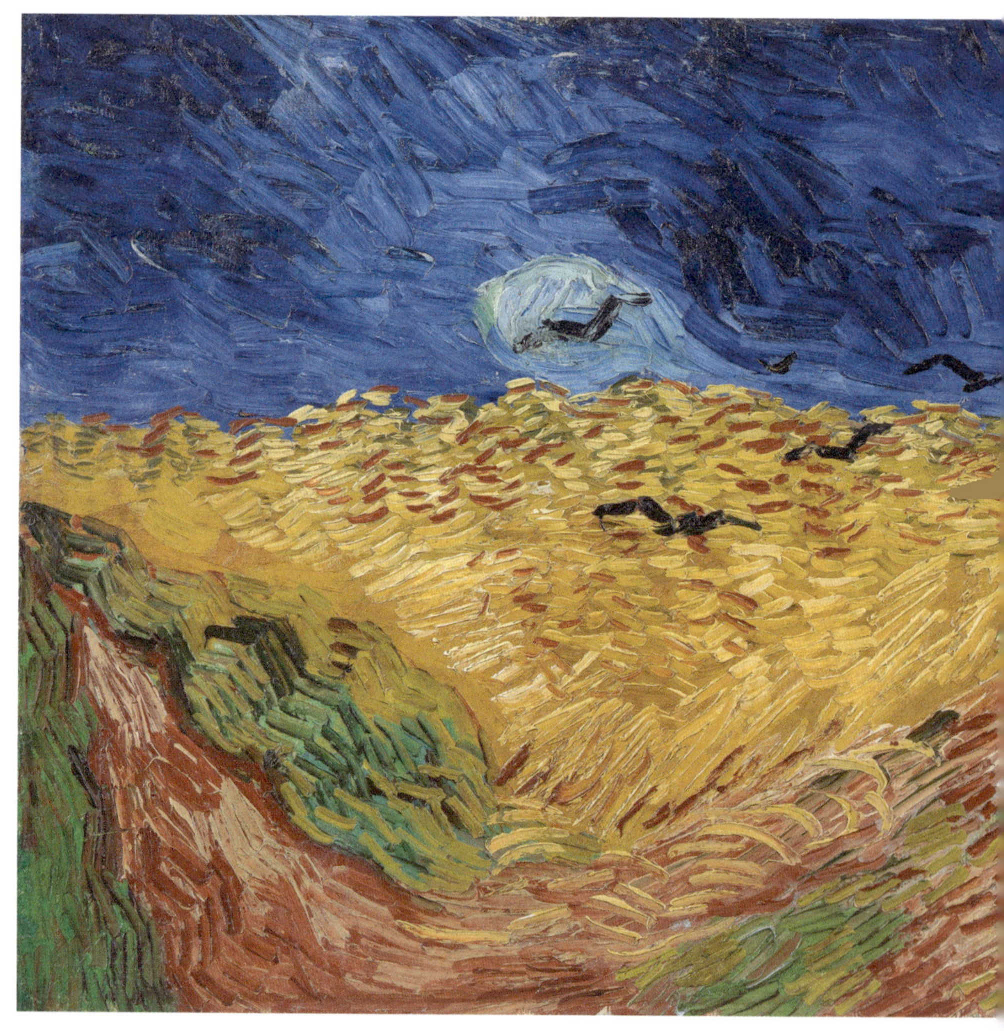

July 1890
Auvers-sur-Oise

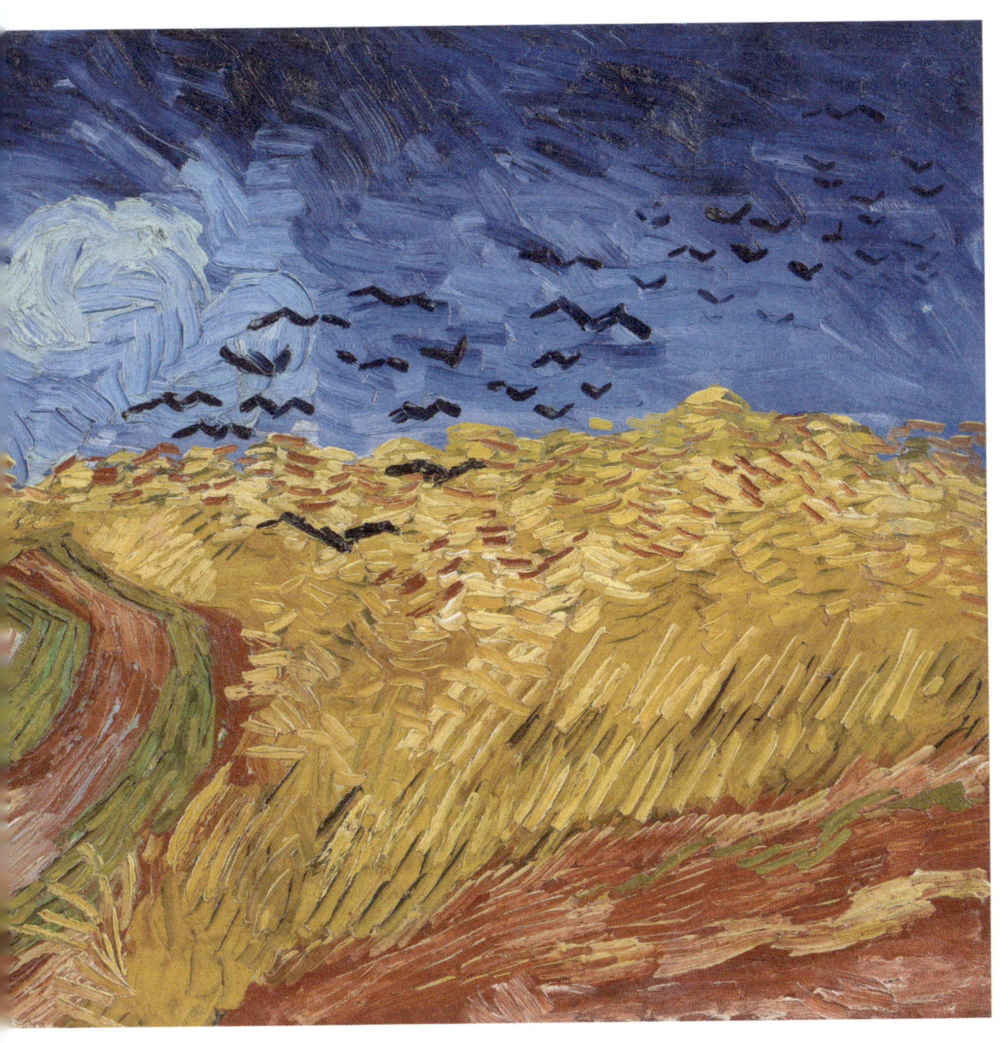

About the author

Sally Grant is an art historian, curator, and critic with a passion for the intersection of art, culture, and travel. She holds a PhD in Art History and Italian Studies from the University of Sydney, and her writing has appeared in *Artforum*, *Australian Book Review*, *Ms. Magazine*, *Hamptons Art Hub*, *Gourmet Traveller*, *BBC Culture* and *Guggenheim Articles*, among other publications. She has also contributed catalogue entries for Christie's Post-War and Contemporary Art Department in New York.

Sally's scholarly research focuses on early-modern Europe, with a particular emphasis on Venice and the Veneto. She has been a Summer Fellow at Harvard University's Dumbarton Oaks, an Honorary Research Associate of the Australasian Centre for Italian Studies, and her work has been recognised with awards and research funding, including from the Gladys Krieble Delmas Foundation.

Originally from north-east Scotland, Sally's lifelong wanderlust began at age eighteen when she travelled to Venice to work as a nanny. She has since lived and worked in Greece, Germany, Hong Kong (China), and Australia, where she earned her degrees, before eventually settling in New York with her husband.

Index of works

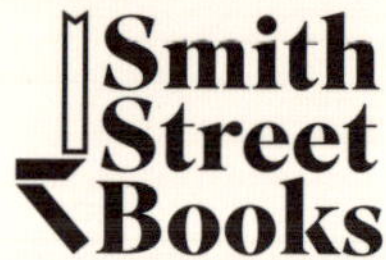

Published in 2026 by Smith Street Books
Naarm (Melbourne) | Australia
smithstreetbooks.com

Distributed outside of ANZ, North & Latin America by
Thames & Hudson Ltd., 6–24 Britannia Street, London, WC1X 9JD
thamesandhudson.com

EU Authorised Representative: Interart S.A.R.L.
19 rue Charles Auray, 93500 Pantin, Paris, France
productsafety@thameshudson.co.uk; www.interart.fr

ISBN: 978-1-9232-3973-9

Smith Street Books respectfully acknowledges the Wurundjeri People of the Kulin Nation, who are the Traditional Owners of the land on which we work, and we pay our respects to their Elders past and present.

Publisher: Hannah Koelmeyer
Project editor: Elena Callcott
Design concept: A Friend of Mine
Design layout: Nikola Roberts
Proofreader: Ana Jacobsen
Production manager: Aisling Coughlan

Printed & bound in China by C&C Offset Printing Co., Ltd.

Book 430
10 9 8 7 6 5 4 3 2 1

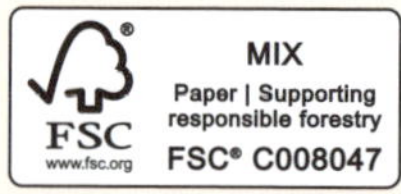

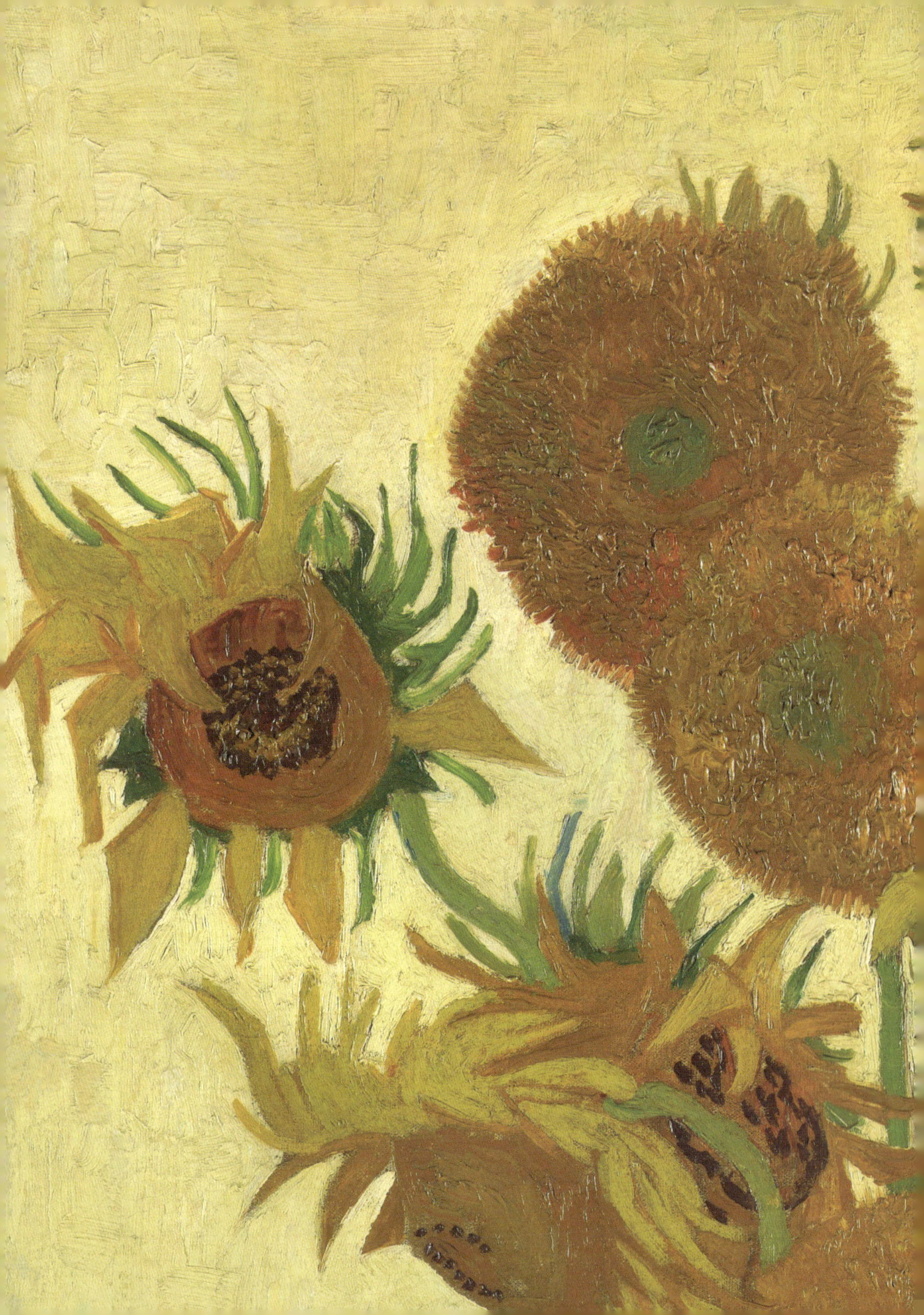